" . . . the foundation of every human relationship involves caring about oneself and others,
and the art of good leadership is to understand—and practice—this fundamental truth. "

—*Clara Adams-Ender*

Clara L. Adams-Ender

with Blair S. Walker

CAPE Associates, Inc.
Lake Ridge, VA

MY RISE

TO THE STARS

How A Sharecropper's
Daughter Became An
Army General

To Nancy,

I am so proud of you and your contributions through entertainment. I do wish you all the best always.

Clara L. Adams-Ender
Brigadier General
US Army, Retired

LIBRARY OF CONGRESS CONTROL NUMBER
2001116704

ISBN: 0-9709401-0-6

Caring About People with Enthusiam (CAPE)
Associates, Inc.
3088 Woods Cove Lane
Lake Ridge, VA 22192

Cover and book design by Wil Payton

To Mother, Caretha Leach, who taught me to love and appreciate myself as a woman, to Daddy, Otha Leach, who somehow knew I'd be a general and to my husband, Heinz, who always believed in me.

Contents

Acknowledgments

The countless numbers of people who have encouraged and helped me bring this book to fruition are too numerous to mention by name, and I thank them all. However, there are some that I must single out because of the uniqueness and significance of their contributions.

A special thank you goes to my literary agent, Carol Randolph, for her honesty and candid opinions about my ability to write and the appropriate focus for this book. She has been a constant source of advice and support throughout this entire process. I am also grateful to her close friend and associate, Barbara Vance, who introduced me to Carol. Barbara is also my publicist. The association, working relationship and friendship among us have made a powerful threesome in guiding this project to a successful end.

The search for a co-writer began with Carol and Barbara. After several false starts, I was introduced to Blair S. Walker. I thank him for his expertise and gift of making ideas and stories come alive, adding color and fanfare to give the reader a reason to turn the page. Without him, the manuscript would still be in disjointed parts in my office. He truly has a way with words that has helped him write a bestseller already. I also thank his wife, Felicia, and daughters Blair and Bria for their constant and unwavering support.

The ominous task of copyediting went primarily to Dr. Sandra Ford Johnson, a dear friend of many years. Sandra was especially suited as an editor, because she was a military spouse when we met over 25 years ago, and she knew firsthand about many of my military experiences. As an administrator in the public school system, Sandra and I had spent countless hours discussing issues of women in the workplace and successful accomplishment of career goals. Thank you, Sandy, for your painstaking efforts, critical eye and your kind and firm advice.

Other persons who read, edited and reviewed the whole or part of the manuscript were Dr. Horace G. Danner, Professor of English, University of Maryland at College Park, Honorable Ruby B. DeMesme, former Assistant Secretary of the Air Force and Dr. Margaret Schefflin, former DACOWITS member. Special thanks go to Dr. Joyce G. Bowles, Professor of Nursing, Bowie State University and my best friend, who read every edition of the manuscript. Her skills as a psychiatric nurse were also useful in keeping me grounded in reality.

A military trade association, the Association of the United States Army (AUSA), also reviewed the manuscript. My special thanks and debt of gratitude to Lt. Gen. Ted Stroup, a close friend and comrade-in-arms, who is Vice President for Education at AUSA. He and his colleagues made helpful suggestions from a military perspective.

My immediate family members and friends have been close to this project and have provided helpful input. My husband, Heinz, has been a great source of strength and support, and only nagged about my early risings and late hours occasionally. Our son Ingo, physician and cardiologist, reviewed materials with the mind of a critical thinker and the needs of younger people. My siblings, Bettie, Aaron, Ray, Rosa, Doretha, Mary, James, Shirley and Charles, agreed to and gave interviews about our growing up and laughed with me about "the good ole days." Their helpful suggestions and memories of our past added perspective and credibility to the work. Lt.Col. (Ret.) Cynthia Houston-Brickey, longtime friend and colleague, offered words of encouragement to keep moving forward. Lt. Gen. Edward Honor and his lovely wife, Phyllis, were always there to help me remember the lessons learned. Special thanks to Jack and Magee Spencer, Harry and JoAnn Junk, Jim and Merrill Dick and Frosty and Betty Hutton, our mentors and friends in network marketing, who encouraged Heinz and me to continue our lives of service to others.

Many people were involved in the research and advice for this project. I particularly thank Colonel (Ret.) John Hudock, Judge Evelyn Palfrey, Attorneys Marquita Brooks, Andrew Ridley and Kathleen Braga, Penny Shaw, Pete Crear, Michael Hale, Phyllis Casseler, Claudette Best, Lt. Col. Jeannie Tibbetts, Mary E.V. Frank and Ulrike Stoops.

And to all the countless others, the people who were not mentioned by name, who have influenced and impacted my life in ways that helped to make me a better person. You know who you are and what we have shared in the past. I stood on many of your shoulders to reach my goals and to excel. Thank you very much. I shall always remember and be grateful to you.

Foreword

Exciting! Exhilarating! Revealing! Inspirational! These are but a few of the emotions I felt while reading this book. While it is written in a simple, conversational style, it is anything but simple. All of the complex issues portrayed in a "rags to riches" scenario are depicted in Clara's book. You'll laugh with her, cry with her, cheer her on and ultimately be very proud of her and what she managed to achieve despite the odds against her. You'll appreciate her strength of character, work ethic, values and can-do attitude.

Clearly, the story of Clara Adams-Ender is exactly what young, black women should read for inspiration and as a road map to find an exit from their circumscribed lives. But this is also a story with dimensions of universal appeal. Women and men of all races and creeds will find this book compelling reading.

Clara's story is a social history of the poor rural south of the 1940s and 1950s. It is a military history of Army nurses covering nearly four decades when Clara was affiliated with the Army Nurse Corps. It is an account of her spiritual journey–the story of a woman balancing parental expectations, personal aspirations, work, play and love. It is also the story of a soldier and warrior, who was persistent in overcoming obstacles and was determined to live the Army's motto to be all that she could be.

Clara's journey can be seen in all of the stated dimensions. However, as much as it adds to our social, military and political histories, it is also a vivid portrayal of how Americans use and share power. There are at least two views of power evident in this story. One view is that power is in scarce supply; that if I gain power, you lose power; that power is either given, taken or withheld, and is a finite commodity. The other view of power is that power is abundant; that we create power and, in fact, the only way we acquire power is to create it from within ourselves. That is to say, if I gain power, it is not at your expense; rather it is good for you when I am more powerful. In the latter view of power, everyone wins and benefits.

One might think that the story of a sharecropper's daughter

becoming an Army general is a personal story, and it is. This book chronicles a journey from the tobacco fields of North Carolina to the heights of the Army's elite leadership team. Through astute storytelling, Clara reveals a woman who never forgot where she came from and always kept the dreams and goals in mind of where she was going. Her spirituality and determination reflect a woman who perceived and received her mission of excellence early in life and followed a path less traveled with the help of mentors and friends.

Beyond the personal realm, this book chronicles a story of power in America, how it is shared or not shared, and how power is created. The link between power and such attributes as hard work, serving people, intelligence, persistence, integrity, generosity, family loyalty and love of God and country is documented in this motivational tale. Clara Adams-Ender has proven that she is a creator of power. It was inevitable that Clara would "rise to the stars."

Claudia J. Kennedy
Lieutenant General
US Army, Retired

Preface

As I reflect upon growing up on a tobacco farm in North Carolina in the 1940s and1950s, I note that the contributions of women to the making of America was mostly undervalued, ignored and not respected. I, too, was guilty of not valuing women's contributions, preferring to work and play outside with my brothers rather than do the cooking and housework inside with my sister. It was my mother who planted the first seeds of reality in my head–I would grow up to be a woman and in order to be valued and appreciated for what I did, I must first value and appreciate what I must do myself. That little lesson did not resonate very well with me as a teenager, but it began to make good sense by the time I left college. It was about the same time that I decided that one day I would write a story of my life's journey, because I would have a story to tell.

I wrote this memoir to share my journey in life to this point, because there is still much more living to do. I call it a memoir because it is my memories of places, events, circumstances and situations, and mostly my recollection of my relationships with the people I encountered.

My story is mainly one of being persistent in overcoming obstacles. Overcoming obstacles is a process, which begins with how one views obstacles. I tend to see obstacles not as something to stop my progress, but as something to be overcome by going over, under, around or through to reach my goal. That idea propelled me to great heights throughout my life and I wanted to share it with others. I wanted to convey the message that life is real, and it's not what happens to you that is important, it's how you react to what happens to you. Whether you take a positive or negative view of the obstacles you face will determine how you react and respond to them. It is a matter of choice and attitude for anyone and everyone.

I wrote this story for women, whom I know will be able to relate to some of my stories and experiences. While they may not have been in the military, they will still be able to identify with similar situations in their work world. It is my hope that my story will provide other ways of reacting and behaving which will reflect the respect and appreciation they feel for themselves. I have sought to provide examples of ways to create power. I sincerely believe that the way in which women create power is useful and necessary in maintaining peace and harmony in our world.

I wrote this story for leaders, aspiring and established, to help convey a message that there is no one path to leadership. It is necessary to establish some basic values like commitment, integrity, love of God and country, pride in performance and a sense of caring and serving, willingness to be mentored and to mentor, keep a good sense of humor and often seek the roads less traveled. In my story, one may note that no matter what obstacles must be faced, staying focused on the goal of the journey becomes paramount.

This book is not a definitive account of history, policy or events in which I was involved in my thirty-four years of association with the United States Army. Rather, these are my memories of the people with whom I associated, some of my significant encounters with them and the triumphs, sorrows, joys and pains that occurred as a result. For these are the things that happen continuously along the road of life's journey.

Chapter I

Ambushed!

Before I rose to the rank of Army general, long before I directed the activities of more than 22,000 Army nurses worldwide or served as a base commander, I was one of those soldiers who avoided generals like the plague. Just the sight of those little silver stars used to set my heart aquiver!

That was back in the days when I was a lieutenant and later a captain. Back then, if I saw a general approaching, I'd do an about-face and move out smartly in the opposite direction. Nothing good could come from hobnobbing or even exchanging niceties, with an officer holding so much authority over my little universe. There were about eight million ways I could potentially screw up or say something stupid in a general's presence, a line of reasoning that also held true for colonels.

So I was not thrilled to be standing at attention in my green combat fatigues in front of the desk of Col. Dick Bentley, the executive officer of the medical training staff at Ft. Sam Houston, in San Antonio, Texas.

The year was 1967 and I had just been promoted from first lieutenant to captain a few years earlier. I had been a military nurse for six years and my career was really starting to take off. Not only had I just attended a training course for nurses with a lot more seniority than me, but I also was teaching at Ft. Sam Houston's medical training center, another posting reserved for officers and medics with far more experience.

It was an incredibly hectic time to be at Ft. Sam, because the base was frantically pumping out Army medics to deal with the escalating carnage taking place in Vietnam.

I wanted to go to Vietnam myself in the worst way, but until those orders came I was pleased to be steadily rising through the officer ranks without apple polishing or stepping on anyone's corns.

So even though I wasn't tickled to be standing ramrod straight in front of the `Ex-Oh,' I had no reason to suspect I might be in any sort of trouble, which only heightened the impact of the ambush I was stepping into. Not everyone was delighted to see that 28-year-old Capt. Clara Mae Leach appeared to be on a military fast track.

I could feel beads of sweat rolling down my neck as I waited for Col. Bentley on a typically scorching summer afternoon in San Antonio. I had been busily training medics when a sergeant told me to report to Col. Bentley as soon as possible.

"Stand at ease, Captain Leach," Col. Bentley ordered, glancing up from some papers on his desk. I intuitively knew that whatever he was studying had to do with me. I also sensed that whatever it was wouldn't be a boon to my budding career. "How are you doing, Captain?"

Dreaded small talk with top Army brass. "I'm doing fine, Sir."

Col. Bentley's high-octane secretary popped into his office for a moment. "Do you think I need to close the door, Colonel?"

"No, I think Clara and I can handle this without any trouble."

Turning back to me, he waved at a plain-looking couch in a corner of his air-conditioned office. "Have a seat, Captain." His demeanor was easy, almost informal, but I dared not relax my guard.

"I've got this paper over here and I'm going to give you a copy of it," Col. Bentley said. "I want you to go home and read it. And after you do, remember this: You may be working hard here at Ft. Sam and thinking everybody is pleased with what you're doing. But you need to remember that some people may not be pleased. You're doing a fine job, but keep what I said in mind, okay?"

"Yes sir." What the hell was he talking about? I knew there was a good reason I made a habit of avoiding generals and colonels.

Col. Bentley casually placed the mystery papers inside a white envelope. We made some more small talk for about a minute, and then mercifully it was time for me to leave.

"One other thing, Capt. Leach–I want you to know that I've taken care of this situation, so you don't have to worry about it at all," Col. Bentley said as I was about to depart his office.

I've never cloaked my emotions terribly well and probably appeared somewhat rattled as I snapped off a crisp salute and marched out of Col. Bentley's office.

What was in that envelope? I stared at it hard, simultaneously curious and repulsed. I don't run from unpleasant situations, but I don't go out of my way to embrace drama, either. I would deal with whatever was in the envelope when I got to my home, which was just off-post, close to the installation's rear gate.

So I dropped the envelope into my briefcase and didn't open it until I arrived at my little two-bedroom home at the end of the workday.

I kicked off my shoes after walking through the front door, hung up my hat and plopped down on the couch. My hands were trembling as I popped open my briefcase and slowly opened the envelope from Col Bentley. I pulled out a sheet of paper with military letterhead on it, began reading and soon had tears rolling down my cheeks and onto my uniform.

And they weren't tears of joy.

Basically, that letter represented the biggest load of horse manure ever leveled at me over the course of a military career that has now spanned thirty-four years.

A particularly hateful supervisor holding the rank of major had falsely accused me of stealing two-bit medical supplies—bandages, paper towels and the like—from a supply area on base. She also accused a really nice sergeant I worked with of being my partner in crime.

But make no mistake about it—Captain Clara Leach was the prize trophy that major was gunning for. And toward that end, she was willing to besmirch the reputations of two innocent soldiers and scuttle their careers if necessary.

Befitting someone with her foul personality, my antagonist was no beauty. She was about five-foot-three, on the chubby side, bespectacled and had straight black hair, which hung unceremoniously just below her earlobes.

I had been working at Ft. Sam Houston for just under a year when she was transferred there as my supervisor. Immediately, our relationship crackled with the kind of warmth and mutual admiration that Ken Starr and Bill Clinton typically displayed for each other. This major had a dictatorial leadership style and only a passing familiarity with the word 'impartial.'

Instead, she blatantly played favorites and routinely eased officers she liked into coveted assignments at Ft. Sam Houston. I happened to work in one regarded as a plum—the ward training center, which is a high visibility area dignitaries are generally trotted through when visiting Ft. Sam Houston.

The major had tried to have a crony take over my job and had been rebuffed by the commandant of the medical training center. So she handily concocted a tale about me and the sergeant stealing two-bit medical supplies.

Not content to let the matter rest there, she then had her work of fiction placed in my personnel file, which Col. Bentley had also placed in the envelope.

After digesting all this in stunned silence, I got mad and had myself an angry cry in the privacy of my home. Then I very carefully refolded that letter and placed it back in the envelope. For about the next fifteen years I held on to it, to remind the naïve country girl from Willow Springs, North Carolina, that everybody didn't behave in the same honest, above-board manner she did.

But during that dismal evening in San Antonio, my immediate concern was to clear my name of the outrageous claims that had been leveled against me. I needed desperately to expunge that letter from my record; otherwise, it would short-circuit my career.

My supervisor had shown herself to be an unscrupulous person who would stop at nothing, including lying, to derail me. Still, I would have to look into her deceitful face every day and remain respectful while fighting somehow to exonerate myself.

For that alone, I prayed to the Lord for strength.

That didn't mean, however, that I couldn't fantasize about pummeling her into a bloody, semi-conscious pulp. So I sat on the couch doling out the first of many imaginary whippings that major would receive for putting my career as an Army officer and nurse in serious jeopardy.

Chapter II

Life at Chez Leach

Growing up poor on a farm and working shoulder-to-shoulder with a big, loving family is a tremendous way to build character. That kind of upbringing taught me early on about handling responsibility and getting along with people.

And when your parents happen to be Otha and Caretha Leach, you get rock-solid values drilled into you that square you away for a lifetime.

That's how I got started on this planet, in a one-stoplight hamlet called Willow Springs, North Carolina. I had a tremendous childhood, in a rural crucible that prepared me well for the great things that later unfolded in my life.

I worked my fingers to the bone, got my hide tanned occasionally and received the kind of unwavering guidance and affection that some of today's kids seem desperately to need.

'Tough love' they like to call it these days. Well, I got plenty of tough love and tender love, too.

I even got a pretty decent public school education, provided by no-nonsense black teachers who were determined to churn out productive citizens in defiance of Jim Crow laws.

There are an awful lot of fine memories associated with my childhood, but let's be crystal clear about one thing—I never did care much for Willow Springs. And I'm not referring to its black and white residents, who were God-fearing, decent people. What drove me crazy was rural life in North Carolina during the 1940s and 1950s. The word provincial doesn't even begin to describe how limiting it was.

Even as a young girl, I knew there was a mesmerizing world out there that offered a lot more stimulation than my hometown ever could. It didn't matter that I'd never seen that world or set foot outside North Carolina. I couldn't wait to leave Willow Springs.

I entered this world the fourth of 10 children on July 11, 1939, in a bedroom of my parents' small wood-frame house. Me and my nine brothers and sisters were all born at home, not in some fancy hospital surrounded by cutting-edge medical technology.

One of my grandmothers served as my mother's midwife. That may sound strange today, but when I was a child, being born at home wasn't a big deal in the sticks of North Carolina.

My nine siblings and I were each born healthy, although I caught pneumonia when I was three weeks old and am told that my health situation got to be pretty precarious.

Thankfully, Grandma was a medical jack of all trades—in addition to being a midwife, she could also nurse you back to health if the croup or some other malady got a hold of you. She draped poultices filled with mustard and other ingredients on my tiny body and helped me overcome my bout with pneumonia.

When I was older, every time Grandma saw me she'd say: "You better watch how you live, because you owe me your life!"

My Daddy worked as a sharecropper on about 30 acres of land owned by a tall, thin white man named Bud Lipscomb, or `Mr. Bud,' as all the sharecropping families called him.

Daddy, who never made it past third grade, grew tobacco. My mother had gone as far as sixth grade and spent the majority of her life working as a homemaker—which is probably the equivalent of five or six full-time jobs when you have a family of 12.

Mother was of average height and build, while Daddy was known around town as 'Mr. Five-by-Five.' The moniker reflected a popular jazz ditty of the times whose opening lines were, 'Mister Five-by-Five, five feet tall and five feet wide.'

One of the hardest-working men I've ever encountered, my father never shortchanged himself when it came to food. Ever. He was a short, rotund man, so the nickname Five-by-Five was probably appropriate.

However, it was only bandied about by people outside the Leach family; Mother, my brothers and sisters and I, never dared to utter 'Five-By-Five,' even though Daddy laughed good-naturedly whenever he heard it.

I have never known where my parents got their motivation or their work ethic, but they passed it on to me and my siblings. My parents were also sticklers for all of their children getting an education.

Mother and Daddy may not have had much formal education, but they imparted two of the most important lessons I've ever learned. The first had to do with my being somebody, and that I shouldn't hang around anyone who tried to convince me otherwise. That's where my strong self-esteem and self-respect stems from.

Lesson No. 2 was that I was capable of becoming whatever I chose, as long as I was willing to work hard and never give up. From that I learned the significance of persistence and setting goals.

When it came to conveying those messages, my parents had a tag-team delivery system. One or the other would utter those bromides without fail.

They didn't agree on everything though, like Daddy's love of cigars. Blue Ribbon cigars, to be exact. He'd fire those thick, stinky things up in the house after dinner, take two long, leisurely drags, then stub the cigars out.

"You really shouldn't smoke in this house with all these children," Mother would scold him disgustedly. "It's not a good example. You ought to give those things up."

Daddy's reaction would be to act as if he was suddenly struck deaf. He definitely mastered the art of selective hearing. He'd calmly suck in his two drags, extinguish the Blue Ribbon and light up again the very next night.

I still detest the stench of cigars to this day.

Not to put too fine a point on it, the wood frame house my family and I lived in was probably one step above a shack. It had a living room that doubled as a family room, a kitchen with a wood-burning stove and three small bedrooms. Dull white paint adorned the outside of our home, before Daddy nailed white asbestos shingles to it in a bid to insulate against cold weather.

The Leach clan grew in bunches, starting with The First Four, to which I belonged. The Last Six followed us. The latter group prompted Daddy to add another room to our diminutive abode.

The Last Six lived a much different life from the First Four, because when I returned from my first year of college during Christmas break, The Last Six already had their own television set!

The Leach family got its first TV in 1952, a used, brown number that Daddy monopolized until he fell asleep in his favorite chair. Only then would one of The First Four quietly dare to switch the TV to something we wanted to see.

The inside of Chez Leach featured a few plain, unvarnished wooden chairs, a kitchen table I think Daddy or one of my uncles made, a well-worn sofa that showed where peoples' heinies had worn down the fabric, and pale green paint on the walls. The only wall hangings were a calendar from a company from which Mother used to buy vanilla flavoring, a picture of a contemplative white Christ with his hands folded in prayer and a reproduction of the Last Supper. I'll bet 99.9 percent of black Southern homes had copies of those two pictures when I was coming up.

Later, as the Leach kids grew up and moved on, pictures of us in our high school and college graduation garb began to appear throughout the house, along with pictures of earnest-looking young folk decked out in military uniforms.

Fortunately, what makes a home environment extraordinary isn't whether it appears in Better Homes & Gardens, but the degree of love and respect within. The mutual affection in the Leach household was bountiful and always on display. There weren't a lot of creature comforts, and I wore a steady succession of clothes handed down from my sister Bettie, who's five years older than I am.

Daddy was taciturn with us kids and wasn't real big on physical displays of affection, like touching and hugging. But there was no mistaking his deep and abiding feelings for his offspring.

Mother, on the other hand, was quick to lavish hugs and kisses upon her children. She fed us emotionally, spiritually and physically and her sound counsel continued to support me into adulthood.

A road filled with rocks and tan-colored dirt led to our house. Less than 100 feet away was a sylvan patch of forest where deer, rabbits and squirrels could often be seen cavorting. A little creek, which frequently overran its banks after a hard rain, was nearby and my brothers loved to dive into it, wearing frayed, cut-off jeans.

Not me, however. I had little desire to get anywhere near that muddy, nasty-looking body of water, and as a result, never learned to swim as a child.

I became familiar with all kinds of wildlife during my early years, including little red bugs called chiggers. Those damn things always seemed to gravitate to the straw-filled mattress Bettie and I shared. Tiny pests smaller than the head of a pin, chiggers must have teeth and jaws bigger than a mule's, because they could bite like nobody's business.

Mother took special care to ensure that our beds were chigger-free at night, but a few would always slip past her defenses, making you kick your legs, slap at your body and yell out in the dark. The bites were more irritating than anything.

In front of our home existed a massive, luxuriant vegetable garden that flourished during the spring and summer months.

When we needed something that couldn't be plucked from our garden, Willow Springs had a little country store Daddy used to visit in his maroon '46 Ford sedan. A white man named Walter Myatt ran that store, where we bought light groceries and feed for our cows.

Willow Springs also had a minuscule post office.

When Daddy needed to shop at a supermarket, he drove 20 miles to Fuquay-Varina, a town that had several large grocery stores.

I seldom got to go to Fuquay-Varina unless I needed shoes or something like that. But the boys got to go every Saturday. Daddy would get them all dressed up; then, the males would go see a movie, while Mother and my sisters and I stayed home and took care of housework. I didn't feel real good about that arrangement, although I knew better than to say anything.

For me, trips to Mr. Myatt's country store in Willow Springs usually had to suffice. I loved those visits because the store had Baby Ruths, Mars bars, Tootsie Rolls and Pepsi-Cola. The sodas would be in a flat, metal freezer filled with ice. Like most children, I used to be addicted to candy and soda.

For Daddy, I think that what he liked best about Myatt's store was being able to buy stuff on credit.

Mr. Myatt would pull a little green book from behind the counter and write down credit transactions in it. When the time came for Daddy to ante up, out came the green book.

The other thing we had in Willow Springs was a little hardware store that had a lone gasoline pump outside.

My favorite time of the year in Willow Springs was summer. Its arrival was heralded by a beguiling mix of delicate fragrances, not to mention a riot of yellows, reds and whites, thanks to flowers that Mother planted.

On the side of our house opposite the forest lurked the bane of my existence—fields where row after row of green leafy, fragrant tobacco rippled in the warm summer wind. I was exempt from working in the tobacco fields until I was eight, but after that I was a tobacco-field fixture until I left for college.

For the Leach kids, there was no question of us hanging around the house until we were 25, or older, like some children do. There was sort of an unwritten rule that we had to vacate the premises after high school, because space was at a premium.

On second thought, I take that back: You could hang around as long as you liked, with the understanding that Otha Leach would have your butt sweating in those sweltering tobacco fields day in and day out. All of the Leach siblings were keen to get away from our agrarian roots and never return!

Sunday represented a welcome break from the routine and tended to be a big deal in most Southern households. The night before, Mother would heat a massive straightening comb on the wood-burning stove, then attack the girls' kinky hair with it.

Everybody had to take a bath and lay out his or her Sunday best for the following morning. The girls wore dresses made from gingham feed sacks. The feed companies used to put pretty red, orange and purple floral designs on the sacks, for the express purpose of the sack being converted into clothing. Each sack would yield about two yards of cloth that Mother would expertly cut, then sew. I usually went with Daddy to buy his feed to make sure that he got sacks with the designs that Mother needed for the next garment.

Underwear was made from white feed sacks with material almost like muslin. It had to be bleached well, so you wouldn't be walking around with Robinson's Feed emblazoned on your behind!

When the time came for Sunday worship, we'd all ride about five miles to the Saint Anna Free Will Baptist Church.

The Awakening

When I was four years old, something happened that forever transformed my narrow little world. And my big sister, Bettie, provided the catalyst.

She used to come home from elementary school carrying books for homework and would sometimes open one of her books and read to me.

It was the most fascinating thing – how were dynamic, lively stories emanating from static pieces of paper filled with funny-looking black symbols? I couldn't fathom that for the life of me.

So I'd bug and badger Bettie to read to me, as only a four-year-old sister can. Bettie eventually became so weary of Clara Mae's pestering that she made an exasperated promise–she would teach me how to read.

Maybe she thought I wouldn't find reading to be as easy as it looked. But mastering the alphabet proved simple and soon we were covering rudimentary words such as "dog" and "cat". In no time, word was circulating through the Leach household that Clara Mae was reading at the age of four.

It wasn't long before I was breezing through the same books Bettie was reading for her homework. To be perfectly honest, I wasn't stunned or astounded by this–most four-year-olds don't have failure on their list of potential accomplishments. It's only after we get older that we allow self-doubt and pessimism to creep into our thoughts.

My father, who never went beyond third grade because he had to work, was amazed I had mastered reading before entering school. He would put me on his knee and watch me read, as he turned the pages. I later found out that he was learning from me as I read.

Something else I learned early was the importance of work. There's always plenty of it on a farm, believe me. Just because I was four and couldn't yet pick tobacco didn't mean I got a free ride. I started doing chores around the same time I began to read.

One day Daddy grabbed my hand and started walking in the direction of the barn. We trudged through the barn door, past several mules and a tractor that was parked off to one side. As we got closer to a black and white cow with a little calf standing beside it, Daddy stopped.

Stooping so we'd be eye-to-eye, he began speaking in a soft voice. "You're a smart little girl, Clara Mae," Daddy said, smiling. "You know how important it is for us to have milk around the house. Mother uses it for cooking–she even makes butter with it, right?"

I nodded solemnly, not quite sure what butter or barns had to do with me.

"Well, from here on in, I'm putting you in charge of getting milk for us. You're going to have to be a big girl and take care of this every day. Think you can handle that?"

"Sure, Daddy, I can do it."

Now, when you're four, a cow appears to be roughly the

same size as a brontosaurus. But even at that tender age, I had picked up on how important it was to carry your weight within a family. And I wanted to play my part in keeping the household functioning.

Learning how to milk a cow was a trip. For one thing, I had never put my hands on a cow's udder before. It was pinkish, about as big around as my head and filled with glands that made it feel soft and rubbery.

I had seen cows being milked before and the deal didn't strike me as rocket science. Just grab one of the teats, pull on it and milk comes out. So that's what I started to do. Except that no fluid of any kind appeared, not a drop. I began putting more pressure on the teat and squeezing it to get things moving. Still nothing.

By now, Daddy wasn't even trying to hide his mirth. From my udder-level perspective, I failed to see what was so humorous. After Daddy enjoyed a hearty chuckle at my expense, he showed me the proper way to milk a cow. Not surprisingly, I was so tentative that it took us half an hour to complete a job that should have taken only ten minutes. But I succeeded in filling my little aluminum pail with milk.

I was nearly bursting with pride when my beaming Mother accepted that bucket from me. She pulled a Mason jar from the cabinet, placed cheesecloth over its mouth, and then poured the milk through the cheesecloth, straining out any hair, gnats or anything else that may have fallen into the bucket.

Some of the milk was destined for a clay churn used to make butter. The soft, yellow butter would be whipped as much as possible to get all the water out, before it was placed on little butter dishes made of pink and green Depression glass.

I used to put that butter on my molasses and ham in the morning. Let me tell you, that was some good eating.

The milk left in the churn after the butter was skimmed from the top was buttermilk. Mother used that to make biscuits and sometimes it served as an ingredient for her cakes.

So I clearly had a very important duty to take care of for the Leach household. And I took care of my milk-gathering responsibilities like a pro. For about three months, I carried out my new job without a hitch, before getting a startling lesson regarding the bovine mammary system.

When a horsefly or another insect bites a cow on its teat, the teat gets sore. And there's nothing a cow with sore teats hates worse than to have them manhandled, especially by some rough four-year-old kid.

So one day as I was trying to milk the cow, it kept moving around and squirming when I tried to manipulate its udder. I was alarmed to have so much meat on the hoof sashaying around my head and generally acting skittish. But Daddy had told me how important it was to get that milk, and I wasn't about to let the family down on account of some reluctant cow, so I pressed forward.

That black and white beast kept getting more and more agitated and was doing an increasingly fast four-step in its stall, forcing me to grope at a moving target, which just exacerbated things. But I was getting my milk, doggone it! Give me a task and I will see it through to completion. A trait that would eventually pay off handsomely was already firmly in place back then.

By now the cow was doing the jitterbug and even kicking her legs outward in an effort to drive me away. Our test of wills ended suddenly when one of those kicks connected with the aluminum milk pail, Clang! I watched in horror as the pail sailed briefly through the air, then crashed to the ground sideways, sending its white contents splashing against the side of the stall in slow motion.

Lord, have mercy! Nobody had to tell me what that meant, namely that Mother or Daddy would wear out my backside with a switch, because no one would ever believe the cow knocked the bucket over, instead of me. I switched on the waterworks and started bawling my heart out. Loud.

Since I didn't cry often, everybody figured something must have gone terribly wrong and flew to the barn. Daddy gently examined the cow and discovered it had been bitten on its teat by an insect.

The sore teat had to be drained of milk, to avoid further problems. So Daddy showed me how to milk an udder very gingerly when a cow is having problems. One might say this was an early lesson in being flexible and altering one's approach to get a desired result. Sometimes an iron fist is effective, but more often the velvet glove is the ticket.

The other thing that cow episode highlights is how people living in Willow Springs during the 1940s imprinted a strong work ethic on even the youngest family member. In a farm-based community, every able body was needed to make a contribution.

Daddy always used to say that my siblings and I always needed to be working, always needed to be busy, because idle hands gave Satan a chance to get his claws into you. He meant that literally, too. So he made sure that my little brown hands were always a blur.

I was taught early to be a workaholic, something I would have to unlearn much, much later in life. Daddy's opinions and viewpoints had a strong impact on the early part of my life.

I learned to fully appreciate Mother's wise counsel when I was older, much as I learned to appreciate the perspectives of women later in life. I initially saw women's work as tough and repetitive and not as important as what men did. Somehow, that also got translated into whatever they had to say was also not as valuable as what men had to say. I certainly had a lot of learning and living to do.

In addition to being the Leach family's dairymaid, I was also its okra queen. I had to plant the okra, watch over it and harvest it in the summer time. That wouldn't have been so bad except that okra plants have protective spines that give one's fingers a painful workout. I quietly endured that ordeal in the name of helping the family.

I also served as a washerwoman and outhouse cleaner extraordinaire. Needless to say, this responsibility thrilled me to no end. I called for Lysol, a mop and a bucket to clean the floor and the sides of the outhouse, as well as the commode seat. The final task was to sprinkle some lime at the bottom, as if that would make things smell springtime fresh.

Fortunately, I found time to play as hard as I worked during my childhood, but not with silly, frilly dolls, or by holding sappy, imaginary tea parties.

Instead, my thing was to play with the boys. Their in-your-face banter, roughhousing and feats of derring-do were right up my alley.

That pattern of preferring the company of males to that of females stayed with me from childhood right to joining the upper echelons of the male-dominated military.

The reason was simple – in Willow Springs boys got to rip and roar in the fresh air and sunshine. Girls, on the other hand, were herded toward safe, stereotypical activities that forever had them cooped up indoors.

Literally and figuratively, I wanted to have plenty of room to explore and be free. And where better to do fascinating things

such as catch frogs, jump from haylofts and throw rocks at hor-
nets' nests than the outdoors?

There was a period in my childhood where I got to spend
hour after hour outdoors, Monday through Saturday. Not quite
in the way I had envisioned, though.

Chapter III

Ramblin' Man

If you did an in-depth analysis of my DNA, you'd probably find a wanderlust gene passed down from my maternal grandfather, Zedekiah Sapp. A big time dreamer, Grandpa Zed grew up in Florida and later migrated to North Carolina with his wife and family to find work in the tobacco fields.

Like me, Grandpa Zed didn't care much for field work and often talked about returning to the sunny beaches of Florida and fantasized about traveling to exotic locales he'd heard about on the radio or seen in a book.

You might think that would be a mere pipe dream for someone with a wife and nine children. Not for Grandpa, though – one day he just calmly walked out of the tobacco fields and left Willow Springs for parts unknown. Left his big family behind and never looked back.

Not surprisingly, that decision earned him a lifetime of enmity in some quarters.

Grandpa Zed clambered aboard a freight train, hobo-style, and rode the rails 800 miles from North Carolina to Miami!

By and by, he got a job with the railroad and worked his way up to Pullman porter. He generally rode the Miami-Los Angeles train, and met people from all walks of life, including movers and shakers from the film industry.

Grandpa Zed would find his way back to Willow Springs every now and then, usually as a front man for a well-known black evangelist. The holy roller of the moment always set about prying Willow Springs and Raleigh residents from their meager, hard-earned savings. Not only that, but he could usually count on a freshly killed chicken for dinner and a comfortable bed covered by a nice spread to lay his head on.

It wouldn't surprise me if Grandpa Zed had been getting a cut of the evangelists' proceeds, either.

Like Grandpa Zed, I also dreamed of worldwide travel, adventure and discovery. Later in life, I quizzed him about his decision to leave his family. With emotions ranging from great sadness to euphoria, he told his side of the story, of his travels and of his failed efforts to return to Grandma and his children.

It's not my job to pass judgment on what he did, but Grandpa Zed taught me that you've got to chase your really important dreams and be willing to make great sacrifices to realize them. When Grandpa died at the age of ninety, all was well with his soul, and there was no doubt the man had lived his life his unique way.

Like my grandfather, I left Willow Springs and traveled far and wide. I even managed to do so before I was ten, thanks to my love of reading. Rome was a place I wanted desperately to see, and I read book after book about Italy long before I was fortunate enough to actually see it later in life.

Books were my best friends–they provided entertainment and fuel for dreams and aspirations. I could read a book and be anywhere, anytime I wanted to go. One reason I've never been real big on sitting around and watching a lot of television is because your imagination conjures up far more exciting stuff when you read. You exercise sections of gray matter that TV never even touches.

I used to read anywhere from 60 to 100 books each summer. Daddy loved the fact that Betty and I had a hunger for reading. He always emphasized the importance of getting an education, because that's one thing no one can ever take away from you.

One day when I was about five and reading an Ebony magazine, I encountered a picture of a black woman decked out in a regal-looking black robe. She radiated such dignity that I was immediately taken with her.

"What's she do?" I asked my parents.

One of them grabbed the magazine from my grubby hands. "Oh, she's a judge."

"What do you have to do if you want to be a judge?"

"First, you have to become a lawyer."

That cinched it for me–I was going to be a lawyer, because I wanted to be just like that regal black lady in Ebony. Daddy, of course, had other plans that he revealed later.

Some nights after everyone had gone to bed, I would slip a silver flashlight out of my desk drawer and flick it on. Bettie loved to read too, but drew the line when it came to my nocturnal flashlight sessions. The glow kept her from sleeping, and she would threaten to turn me in unless I doused the light.

I had no way of knowing it, but my reading was preparing me to excel academically. Sometimes it got me into hot water; on rare occasions when Mother would assign me a household chore and I'd shirk it to go read a book somewhere.

No Rugrats For Me!

One duty that definitely couldn't be avoided was taking care of my snot-nosed younger brothers and sisters, who seemed to arrive like clockwork every year or two. My parents had 10 children in the span of 21 years, so it was inevitable that some of us would arrive very close in birth ages. By the time I was eight, I had three sisters and a brother younger than I.

So I had to serve as the built-in babysitter because the adults and my older siblings all had to work in the tobacco fields. This started when I was only five years old. While the big Leaches broiled in the sun, I had some pretty heavy responsibilities of my own to contend with.

We always ate a big meal in the middle of the day, and my mother got the food going on the stove before she went out in the mornings. Since she couldn't run in from the fields every few minutes to stir pots of food on the stove, that monumental task fell to me. Why monumental? Well, have you ever had an entire hungry family glaring at you because you let their main meal burn?

Me either–I made sure I had that pot-stirring business covered.

I hadn't mastered the art of telling time by the time I was five. However, Mother worked out a little system that let me stir food at just the right moment. She'd march me into the kitchen where we had a clock hanging on the wall. Then mother would find a piece of paper and draw the face of a clock on it.

"When the big hand gets over here and the little hand is right about here, that's when you stir the cabbage. Okay, Clara Mae?"

Coping with that alone would have been no big deal, but don't forget that I was also trapped in the house with my younger brothers and sisters! Rosa would be yelling that she wanted some bread to snack on; meanwhile, I would be holding another baby whose diaper needed changing, while simultaneously rocking the cradle of another sibling I was trying to help nod off.

I used to wonder, "Where on earth are all these babies coming from?" All the washing of baby bottles and dirty diapers and whimpering and screaming and fighting was sheer drudgery. And the end of the day, I would be absolutely exhausted.

This went on for about three summers, because I didn't start in the fields until I was eight. The experience seared something into my head that stayed with me the rest of my life–I did not want children! Didn't want to bear 'em, didn't want to care for 'em. Period.

I never did have children, either, and I can honestly say that I don't feel like I missed anything. My occasional maternal yearnings have been more than satisfied by playing with nieces and nephews, or with friends' kids. Much later in life, I inherited a teenage son, which is a heck of a lot different from a helpless mass of protoplasm totally dependent on you for its survival.

Daddy's Little Girl

I adored and respected my father, but our relationship was a lot more complex than my showing adoration and respect. I think he liked the fact that I challenged him occasionally. I had a habit of standing up for my point of view and of using logic and facts to support my arguments. Daddy loved it when I did that.

Which is odd, because in some ways he had a very stereotypical view of females and what their role should be.

Yet, he allowed me to go head to head with him in a respectful way, but didn't tolerate that kind of stuff from my brothers. I think Daddy liked that I was always questioning things, always looking at things analytically.

When I was growing up, he'd tell my brothers and sisters something and they'd follow his command to the letter, rather than risk incurring Daddy's wrath. Leave it to little ol' me, on the other hand, to innocently ask: "How come? Why? What's the reason for that?"

From time to time, the Leach kids would gather together and discuss things that were important in our little world. Stuff like getting more time off from chores and working in the tobacco fields.

Since Bettie was the oldest, she usually took the concerns of the Leach children to our father. I recall that when I was about seven or eight, we were trying to get the Fourth of July off. Daddy tended to view holidays with disdain, especially if the request came from one of his kids.

So Bettie went to Daddy with our holiday request and was immediately rejected. She returned looking crestfallen and down at the mouth. After she relayed her story, I said, "Bettie, what can I do to help with this? Because instead of just having one thing to ask for, you should have had another plan. Like maybe half a day off or something. That's better than nothing, right?"

Bettie was in no mood for my guff.

"Well, if you think you can do a better job, go ahead and do it," she said, rolling her eyes evilly.

"Okay, I will."

That started my role as the official mouthpiece for the Leach siblings. I didn't win that particular discussion, because Daddy wasn't about to reverse an edict he'd already issued to his oldest child.

Whenever I went to Daddy with a request, I always felt like an impassioned lawyer arguing a case before a judge. Judge Daddy tended to sit there listening to my heart-felt arguments, never saying that I did a good job or my points were well made.

But I'd usually detect a sparkle in his eye and a hint of a smile whenever I'd won my case. I think he really liked to be challenged every now and then, and I was certainly up for that. Later on, Mother would come over to me and say, "Listen, Otha said you all can have this amount of time to do this, and then later on you can work."

When the other kids noticed I had a knack for getting what we wanted, they started helping me prepare speeches to present to Daddy.

Those head-to-head encounters with my father are still helpful today. They taught me to think through what I'm going to say beforehand, and to buttress my arguments with facts, not emotion.

Daddy tended to apply a common sense test to arguments brought before his court. If I couldn't demonstrate underlying common sense, my position was bound to fail, causing it to be unceremoniously dismissed.

Another thing that sharpened my debating skills was having conversations with Mother, ostensibly to help her with quilting. Those sessions taught me how to talk to adults while expressing myself in a respectful way. You could say whatever you wanted to Mother, as long as you did it respectfully.

Emotion didn't get you far with either Mother or Daddy. If you were crying and hollering, Mother would just let you sit until you got yourself together. Daddy would just flat out ignore you.

Chapter IV

Watch Your Mouth Boy!

When most people find out that I grew up during the 1940s and 1950s, the daughter of a black, southern sharecropper, they automatically assume that bigotry and racism informed and molded my upbringing.

That wasn't quite the case, though.

I grew up and worked beside white sharecropping families, and it wasn't really that big a deal. Everybody went to the same grocery store and worked in the same fields.

What determined who got embraced and who was ostracized was all about one's work ethic, not skin color. There was such an incredible amount of work to do year-round that nobody liked lazy people. So whether you were black or white, if you showed an aversion to work, you got snubbed.

Not only could you get kicked out of the fields for lollygagging, but that would also make you a pariah.

One thing black folks couldn't do that whites could was eat in certain restaurants. But it wasn't as though poor sharecropping families did a lot of eating out, anyway.

I grew up in a world with few disparities or inequities, a world where black and white sharecroppers lived next door to each other and worked shoulder to shoulder. We all co-existed in poverty, and did so peacefully and with respect for one another.

I did not appreciate what a sheltered existence I'd had until I departed Willow Springs. I was a teenager before I discovered whites sipped water from one public fountain, while blacks had to use a different, substandard, fountain.

Thanks to my upbringing, I didn't grow up fearing, or being in awe of, whites.

I can recall only one unpleasant racial incident from my childhood. One time a white boy who was probably about ten had the temerity to call my father "Uncle."

That pissed me off to no end, because white people tended to reserve that moniker for subservient-acting Negroes. A black waiter or shoeshine man might get called "Uncle," but I'd be damned if some white boy was going to call my father that.

"Hey, listen here," I told him heatedly. "My father's name is Otha Leach. And if you ever address him in the future, you would do well to use 'Mr. Leach.' But that 'Uncle' foolishness has to go."

My little lecture didn't go over terribly well, not that I really cared.

Later on, Daddy said he wasn't going to allow his blood pressure to rise over being called "uncle," because it wasn't that big a deal. And he really didn't view it as disrespectful. Daddy happened to add, "This is the way things are."

Based on that last comment, and based on the fact that Daddy never scolded me about upbraiding that white boy, he clearly, but tacitly approved of my actions.

With the exception of that little incident, I was pretty much spared from this country's preoccupation with race, until I entered college and joined the fight for civil rights.

In a way, you could say that I had a white child's upbringing, because I never wasted time drawing mental barriers and telling myself what I could or couldn't pursue based on race. I was raised to believe the field was wide open.

I have my parents to thank for that, because they never let on that Jim Crow laws was killing black folks' dreams day in and day out.

School Days

Clara Mae Leach was one excited little girl when the time finally came to attend public school. I was downright giddy with excitement.

Back in those days, first grade through third grade was classified as primary school by Wake County. Elementary school was fourth through eighth grades, while high school covered grades nine through twelve.

I had a 40-mile roundtrip bus ride to my school, which was located in Fuquay-Varina, North Carolina. The closest primary school was only five miles from my house, but it was for white kids.

My family never dwelled on the fact that schools were segregated, so my brothers, sisters and I never complained about having to ride 20 miles to school while Willow Springs' white pupils only had to travel five. Actually, we were glad to have a longer ride, because that gave us less time for doing chores.

A lot of people think the concept of school busing magically materialized in the aftermath of Brown vs. Board of Education in 1954. It had been around long before that. The main purpose for school busing was, and still is, transportation, not achieving racial integration.

My school was one of three separate, small school buildings on the same parcel of land. The primary school was housed in a worn-down one-story structure made of faded wood. Heat was supplied by a pot-bellied, wood-burning stove, just like at home. Our building was elevated from the ground by brick pilings. It was raised so much that we used to scurry under it for shelter during an unexpected cloudburst.

A few feet away was an equally nondescript building made from planks of weather-beaten wood. That's where the fourth–through eighth-graders attended classes.

The high school was the biggest structure of the three and was made entirely of brick, but still relatively small.

My mother sent my siblings and me off to the school bus lugging metal lunch pails that usually contained huge homemade biscuits filled with slices of ham, in addition to crackers and peanut butter.

I used to be ashamed to eat lunch sometimes, because some kids came to school with sandwiches made from sleek slices of store-bought bread. Meanwhile, I'd be sitting there chomping on biscuit sandwiches that seemed as big around as a man's head. But at least I had food.

Long before the school bus came to my house between 7 a.m. and 7:15am, I had already finishing milking the cow and gathering eggs from the hen house.

I got up every morning at 5:30, which isn't that big of a deal once you get used to it.

I was already excited and animated by then, because I was somebody special at school. That's because I entered first grade with the reading abilities of a fifth-grader, thanks to Bettie. It didn't take my teacher, Mrs. Watts, long to figure out that I was bored to tears in her class.

'See Dick run, see Jane run!' wasn't exactly compelling stuff.

One day, not long after I started attending first grade, Mrs. Watts marched me down to see the principal, Mr. Davis.

"And who might this young lady be?" Mr. Davis asked, looking up with a kindly smile.

"This is Clara Mae Leach," Mrs. Watts said. "Thanks to working at home with her sister, Clara is reading books on the fifth-grade level."

"Is that a fact? Show me what you can do, little bits." Motioning for me to approach him, Mr. Davis rose from his chair and removed a fifth-grade reading book from his bookshelf.

Secretly thrilled they were making such a fuss, I opened the book and read a quick paragraph or two. I looked up expectantly and was delighted to see Mr. Davis and Mrs. Watts beaming.

"Come on, I'm going to take you into the fifth grade," Mr. Davis said. "Because there are kids in there who can't read as well as you and you're only in the first grade." From that point forward, whenever it was time for the first-graders to read, I was taken from my classroom and escorted to the building where third-, fourth- and fifth-grade students were doing reading work.

I would be placed in a chair at the front of the classroom and instructed to read, prompting teachers to say: "If this little first-grader can read your books, I know you can do it." Pronouncements like that didn't necessarily endear me to students in higher grades.

I eventually got skipped from first grade to second grade. And then I got skipped again, into the third grade. This was good, but it also caused me to develop something of a complex. I was always the youngest student in class, so someone was always patting me on the head, saying stupid stuff like: "There, there, Clara, it's going to be all right. Yeah, yeah, Clara, when you're as old as we are, you'll know what we're talking about!"

You have no idea how much I used to loathe it when people did that to me—I couldn't stand condescension directed toward me.

Other than that, I was absolutely in love with school. Probably because my first encounter with education was such a positive one, I have always been a big fan of school.

Once my classes were over, the moment I walked off that orange Wake County school bus at 4:30 p.m., duties awaited. I immediately shed my school clothes, then took care of my second round of milking. And there were other duties, like shucking corn for feed and shelling dried beans and peas.

But I would be in heaven again the next morning, between 7 a.m. and 7:15 a.m., when the same orange school bus whisked me off to a world where teachers placed little Clara Leach on a rather lofty pedestal.

There are two people that I shall always be eternally grateful to when it comes to my early education. One is my older sister, Bettie. The other person is Uncle William, my father's oldest brother.

After Bettie taught me how to read, Uncle William started bringing me little speeches to say in church and other places. And that's how I started public speaking. Uncle William always urged me to stand up straight and talk in a loud, clear voice so I wouldn't be misunderstood.

So I'd speak my lines during Children's Day or some other event, and the congregation would say, `Oh, she speaks so nicely!" In fact, people still tell me that today, and it all goes back to Uncle William.

Even at a young age, I knew public speaking was a skill I needed if I wanted to be a lawyer. That was my career path and nothing was going to deter me. That lady wearing the black robe in Ebony was going to have some company.

Chapter V

Loving The Skin I'm In

Black people come in all hues, from milky white to a black so dark it has a bluish tint. My complexion falls on the darker side of the register, approximating the shade of dark chocolate.

I'm totally comfortable with the way I look today, but that wasn't always the case. Back in the '40s and '50s, well before the slogan 'Black is beautiful,' dark skin tones weren't exactly coveted by most African Americans.

Instead, fine wavy hair that escaped the attentions of a hot comb and buttery brown skin were what drove black males and females to distraction. Not to put too fine a point on it, but many members of the African-American community considered dark skin ugly. Unattractive. Undesirable.

That message came across loud and clear in terms of which students were favored by teachers, and by other students, when I started going to public school. I challenge you to find a black person who grew up in the 1950s who can recall a dark-skinned prom queen!

This nonsense first came to my attention when I was about six or seven years old, but it really got pronounced by the time I got to sixth grade.

The amazing thing about this was the teachers picking all these red-bone and high-yellow kids had dark skin like mine. It was all part of a warped value system that some black people still embrace today–the closer you are to being white, the better off and more beautiful you are.

It had gotten to the point that one day, when I was moping around the house that Mother took notice. Clara Mae was usually chirping around the house like a perky little bird, so any deviation from that behavior was quite noticeable

My mother pulled me aside and gave her fourth-born a loving once-over. "Clara Mae, what is the matter with you?" she asked. Her voice was filled with concern, which automatically made me feel a little better.

I told Mother that regardless of what I did in class, when I raised my hand, the teacher would never call on me.

Instead, a kid with straight hair and fair skin always got picked. Some of them were really smart, but so was I. Since I had already skipped two grades, there was no question of my intelligence or of my ability to perform. While I related this to Mother, I started crying because the arbitrariness of the situation was getting me down.

"Let me tell you something," Mother said, wiping my tears, "The thing you have to understand is that beauty is only skin deep. You are my child and you are beautiful to me. And if no one ever says that about you, it's what you think about yourself that counts."

Everything Mother said made perfect sense and her words were a soothing balm for my bruised feelings. Still, being rejected over something as senseless as the amount of melanin in my skin stung. This really got my competitive juices going at school.

Throughout my life I have tried to turn anger and other negative emotions into something constructive. So that was the path I chose following my eye-opening encounter with black-on-black bigotry. I spent a lot of time getting even smarter, because I knew knowledge could never be snatched from me, regardless of whether I was high yellow or black as midnight.

I'm not the most self-analytical person in the world, but it's clear those early snubs and slights I experienced due to skin color further motivated me to excel. They lit a fire under me that drove me to succeed not just at academics, but at whatever endeavor I tackled.

That whole deal taught me that you couldn't afford to let yourself get bogged down by trivial garbage. A person's outer covering is clearly trivial and not terribly important in the grand scheme of things.

Dealing with those color-struck teachers also taught me something about myself namely, that I could face what I thought were serious obstacles, like rejection, and get over it.

Instead of fixating on my outward appearance, I just spent more time figuring out how to get noticed for being the best student.

Years later, when dark skin and huge Afros became a badge of honor and James Brown was shouting "Say it loud, I'm black and I'm proud!" on AM stations around the country, I couldn't help but notice some of my café au lait brothers and sisters looking uncomfortable and forlorn.

My heart went out to them, because I knew exactly how they felt. Something as uncontrollable as the color of one's skin, and how people can sometimes react to that, can be a baffling, demeaning thing.

Goodbye Paratrooper Wings!

When I observe today's kids and how they get their parents to buy them the latest pair of jeans or tennis shoes, I have to laugh.

For one thing, Mother was never big on young ladies wearing pants, so most of the time I had to wear a dress. And far from being hip or fashionable, jeans were something to be worn when we were about to go into the tobacco fields. As for shoes, my favorites were a pair of brown numbers that looked remarkably like my bare feet.

I hated wearing shoes and still do today. When I enter my house, the first thing I do is take off my shoes and let my feet breathe.

Because I was really tough on shoes and wore them out every six months, my parents invariably bought sturdy brogans that were tough on my poor dogs.

If I had ever flounced into the Leach household demanding that my parents purchase me the trendiest fashions, the result would have been predictable and quite painful.

Besides, if I had nice clothes, I would have destroyed them in no time. Because I loved hanging out with the boys, doing stuff like playing baseball. My gender wasn't important as long as I could hit as far and run as fast and as hard as they could. And since that was the case, they accepted me unconditionally, which meant a lot to me.

When baseball games ended, usually with me on the winning side, we'd all go to a hayloft and become Army paratroopers heroically swooping down on unsuspecting German and Japanese soldiers.

Meanwhile, in school I was consistently the top or the second-best student in my class. So all was right with the world, that is, until I got to be 12 years old and went into the eighth grade.

That was when Mother pulled me aside for a little talk. She'd made up her mind it was time for the Leach family tomboy to disappear.

"Clara Mae, you are becoming a young woman," she intoned solemnly. "So we've got to make a couple of little changes. First of all, the roughhousing that you do with boys–flying out of haylofts, sliding all over the fields when you play baseball–has got to stop! It just ain't ladylike."

"Another thing–you've got to start wearing shoes all the time! You don't see me going around barefoot, do you? Or your sister Bettie? Ladies wear shoes, Clara Mae."

The shoe thing hurt, but the directive to stop playing with the boys was a killer. When I walked outside, stunned, the trees, grass and even the sky somehow seemed different. I knew I could no longer fly through the fields, kicking up puffs of tawny dust in the brilliant North Carolina sunshine with my bare feet.

The outdoors had always been my personal playpen, but now it had been turned into an extension of school, church and the inside of our house.

It never occurred to me to keep cavorting secretly with the guys. When my parents told me to do something, they usually needed to say it just once.

I followed Mother's moratorium to the letter, but I certainly didn't like it. Aside from reading everything I could get my hands on, carousing with my brothers and their friends was the other thing I enjoyed most in life.

It didn't take long for the wisdom underlying Mother's caveat to assert itself though. A few weeks after our little conversation, my menstrual period came, prompting another mother/daughter summit, this time about the mysterious things that were happening to my body. Mother segued from that into a discussion about babies and where they came from.

In about a month, I had gone from rough and tumble, slugging outfielder to a potential mama! Bettie helped me with this transition, having experienced her first period some years earlier.

I was ready to concede that starting in center field for the New York Yankees probably wasn't in the cards. Still, nothing had happened that would prevent me from becoming a cracker-jack lawyer, so I was still in good shape.

Another major development that occurred when I was 12 was my housework load finally started to lighten. Hallelujah!

That's because there were now four girls to help Mother out with the female duties around the house, instead of just

Bettie and me.

All of the Leach women remained handy in the kitchen, though. I was the cake maker, Mother made pies, Bettie cooked the meat, Rosa cooked vegetables and my youngest sister, Doretha, was the official vegetable picker. Combined, the five of us could whip up a mean dinner.

On the caregiver front, I was no longer the Leach babysitter because the youngest Leaches were getting older and more self-sufficient. Bawling siblings and stinking diapers were finally a thing of the past. My parents had stopped having children and that was all right with me!

When it came time for me to graduate from eighth grade, I was the No. 2 pupil in our class. That feat was accomplished despite missing 30 days out of a 180-day school year because of critically important farm work.

Mother used to fret about that, while Daddy merely said, "This is what we have to do. This is reality."

I had an infinitely more exciting reality to look forward to–I was about to enter high school. And once those four years were over, I was going to leave Willow Springs and its farming lifestyle in the dust.

Chapter VI

Defying Daddy

One thing in life that I positively love is making money. Being able to line my pockets has been a major motivational factor in my life and my career.

Before anyone gets the wrong impression, I don't worship currency, nor am I a craven moneygrubber. Rather, my love of cash stems from the independence that it brings.

The song says, "God bless the child that's got its own," and life has repeatedly shown me there's an awful lot of truth to that ditty!

That wasn't the case when I was a child and was working in the broiling tobacco fields of Willow Springs. When payday came, the money that was due to my brothers and sisters and me always seemed to wind up in Daddy's hands. And there it always seemed to stay.

It seemed to me then, and still does today, that if income is being generated by the sweat of my brow, the earnings should touch my hands before anyone else's.

So I came up with a scheme to make up for some of the income I lost to Daddy. To understand how my enterprise worked, you have to appreciate that Aaron and Raymond did not care for school or schoolwork. Their apathy worked to my advantage.

Even though my brothers were a grade ahead of me, they tended to seek me out for help with homework. Initially, I assisted them free of charge, but not for long.

One day after I'd helped Aaron with his homework, he made the mistake of saying he'd gladly pay me in the future.

Once that precedent was established, there was no way I was going to have one brother pay while the other got a free ride. It was time for Raymond to ante up, too!

I put the screws to my brothers when it came to a fee. They had to pay the princely sum of fifty cents a pop. Per brother. The fee was non-negotiable–they could take the deal or leave it.

They moaned and groaned about blackmail, extortion, etc., and I nodded sympathetically. But I didn't budge.

That arrangement not only provided me a steady source of income, but it allowed me to do school work a grade level ahead of my peers.

By the time I entered high school, I had already done high school math, English, science, civics and history; and gotten paid for it.

I also sewed clothes to make money. Mother taught me the basics, and I perfected my technique in home economics class in high school. I charged four dollars to make a dress that wasn't too complicated. The going price for a Clara Mae shirt was five dollars.

My homework profits were used to buy cookies, candy bars and sodas, which I wolfed down on the sly. With nine brothers and sisters constantly on the prowl, goodies had a way of disappearing quickly. My sewing profits were used to buy fabric to make school clothes for my sisters and me. I learned how to share with others very early in my life.

Mademoiselle Leach

There was no graduation ceremony when I left eighth grade for high school. My classmates and I simply moved into the high school building, a transition we were thrilled to be making. High schoolers had a mystique about them, a certain savoir-faire that was quite desirable.

I enjoyed my four years in high school tremendously, because I was constantly introduced to new things that engaged me and held my interest. Reading my brothers' books and doing their homework was one thing, but there's no substitute for actually being in a chemistry lab, for example, and participating in lab experiments.

I have always been a curious soul and love everything about the process of funneling knowledge into my head. Whereas some folks live to eat, I live to devour intellectual stimuli. Fuquay Springs Consolidated High School afforded me plenty of opportunities for that.

The school was consolidated because it served every black community within a 20-mile radius. The teachers at Fuquay Springs gave special attention to kids who were college-bound. Today, it's no big thing for black children to attend college, even

Ivy League universities. But in the 40s, it was definitely a big deal. It's only a slight exaggeration to say that college-bound black kids carried the hopes and dreams of a race on their slender shoulders.

My civics and history teacher, J. Simona Lee, made doubly sure that the pupils under her tutelage were prepared to succeed in a college environment. A single woman who detested her first name–which was James, because her father wanted a boy–Miss Lee used only her first initial.

She was thin, prowled her classroom with a flat-footed gait, wore glasses and had a sizable gap in her teeth. Not your classic beauty by a long shot, but not a homely woman, either. Miss Lee was dark-skinned, favored spinster's clothing and reminded me a great deal of abolitionist Mary McCloud Bethune.

Two things about Miss Lee's teaching technique stand out in my mind: the fact that she rode my young behind and her unwillingness to give praise.

That latter point took some getting used to, because I had grown accustomed to lavish compliments from instructors. Don't get me wrong, because Miss Lee definitely encouraged me, but she never, ever told me I was doing a good job.

Instead, she used to gaze at my classmates and me and remark in a vaguely condescending tone: "You all are sitting over here looking quite satisfied with your performance in my class. Let me tell you something, young people–being satisfied and getting complacent will never get you what you want out of life."

Miss Lee fired me up, because she seemed to have it in her head that we weren't trying, and consequently would never make much of ourselves. I was determined to prove her wrong. She must have picked up on this, because something of a rivalry developed between Miss Lee and me.

One day in her class, a fierce debate erupted about the merits of a jury trial, compared with a trial tried by a judge and no jury. Three students–including yours truly–argued passionately for jury trials, and three other pupils came down in favor of non-jury trials. I was in my glory, fancied myself a legal eagle, was very opinionated and never ducked spirited debates.

Up to that point, Miss Lee had never taken sides during a classroom debate. But that day, she sided with the bench-trial contingent and helped them argue against me. I say against me, because I was pretty much carrying the argument on the jury trial side of the equation. I was flabbergasted!

Miss Lee, who also taught French and called the girls 'Mademoiselle,' and the boys 'Monsieur,' stood at one point and rapped her bony fingers on the blackboard, a signal for us to pipe down.

"Mademoiselle Leach," she droned, peering at me, ostrich-like, through her spectacles. "That was a good try by you and your colleagues, but I'm afraid the three of you have fallen short of the burden of proof!"

Her demeanor was somewhat stern and she was unsmiling, as always. Wounded, I turned to my colleagues, Elijah Booker and Lenora Thomas. I knew I'd done more research than anyone else and had articulated my point of view convincingly and with verve. What did it take to satisfy this woman?

In retrospect, Miss Lee was one of the most motivational teachers I have ever had. In her opinion, being satisfied and complacent were two luxuries African Americans could ill afford in the 1950s.

To stave off that mindset, Miss Lee constantly told us that to succeed, we would have to be twice as good as white people.

My classmates and I all loved Miss Lee, and I feel incredibly fortunate to have been one of her students. She made us appreciate that an average, or slightly above average, effort just doesn't cut it.

By the way, regarding the question of whether jury or non-jury trials are preferable, I still think I won!

Another class that floated my boat was drama. It was taught by Miss High, a very young woman who was also the instructor for English and composition.

A part of me enjoys being the center of attention. I relish it when every eye and ear in the audience is awaiting my next move. Miss High's drama class definitely appealed to the Smithfield ham side of my personality.

I was never cast as a romantic lead in plays, because that wasn't my style. Rather, I tended to get roles where I played a cut-up who had funny lines and was always getting into mischief.

Miss High often praised my loud, clear speaking voice, which easily projected into the audience. Again, dear Uncle William gets the credit for that.

We did two major plays a year in high school, plus a Christmas pageant. Miss High always gave me a part.

Because I lived on a farm, I couldn't practice after school because I had to leave immediately after class to handle my chores. However, when the time came for dress rehearsals, Daddy always made the 40-mile roundtrip from our house to school and back so I could attend. Miss High never worried about my preparation, because she was confident I'd have my lines memorized cold by the time dress rehearsals rolled around.

One course I didn't particularly like was math. On more than one occasion, I prayed: 'Dear Lord, please let me get past this next test and I promise I'll be able to take it from there!'

I never earned higher than a 'B' in geometry or algebra. The mathematical side of my brain has just never fired on all cylinders. I wish that weren't the case, given that I wound up working in a science-based profession. Instead, I learned enough math to get by and had to work like the dickens to get a decent grade.

Most people's recollections of high school usually include those first dabbles at romance, and I'm no different.

What would high school be without a puppy love crush? Mine was on a teacher named Edmund Haywood, who taught general history, U.S. government, choir club and music.

I don't think he ever knew he was the object of my affections. On second thought, maybe he did, since high school girls tend to make googoo eyes around males they have crushes on.

Mr. Haywood was a six-foot, big-boned man with an ebony complexion and the beginnings of a bald spot on his pate. And, my goodness, he was loud! He used to cut loose a laugh that rattled our tiny high school building.

Mr. Haywood was such a nice individual. He was single and whenever I saw him, my heart used to beat faster. But I was cool about my infatuation.

One time I got involved in an essay-writing contest, and Mr. Haywood decided he would coach me. I had to read my essay out loud, and Mr. Haywood showed me how to achieve the right frame of mind before speaking. I still refer to his advice.

"Clara, it's very important for your mind to be at ease whenever you have to speak before people," he said in his deep, melodious voice. "You need to walk in front of your audience and take about 10 seconds to get yourself together. Here's a little trick—look out at the people you're about to address and say to yourself, 'Listen here, all of you, if you could do this speech better than I can, then you'd be up here doing it and I'd be sitting in the audience listening!'"

I giggled, in part due to that mental image and in part because girls always giggle when in the throes of amore.

"Then take a deep breath and let it out slowly," Mr. Haywood said, looking at me with those heavenly eyes. "Then you can start your speech feeling relaxed."

The man was absolutely right.

After I graduated from high school, I ran into Mr. Haywood again many years later, while I was a colonel at Walter Reed Army Medical Center. Mr. Haywood was living in Philadelphia at the time and had seen my name in a newspaper, so I drove from Washington, D.C., to see him. He must have been around 65 and still had the same great James Earl Jones voice.

In addition to Mr. Haywood, several boys also caught my eye in high school. Two were Kelso Adams and Robert Thomas. I had no inkling Kelso would wind up becoming my first husband. It was never a case of my saying, "This is the boy I'm going to marry!"

At that stage in my life, boys were people I could have a good conversation with about some book I was reading or about something taking place in class. Best of all, I could talk sports with them.

Remember, most of my socialization took place in the company of boys. Even though I could no longer run and play with them, I could at least talk their language. And they liked me because I gave them an opportunity to discuss things they knew something about.

Kelso loved baseball, so that's what dominated our conversations. My father followed the Brooklyn Dodgers, so that was the team I followed, too.

Robert, on the other hand, was a tall fellow who played basketball and knew that game well. So, basketball was what we generally chewed the fat about.

If this all sounds incredibly innocent, you have to remember that back in those days, black high school students weren't anywhere near as forward as they are today. There wasn't a lot of kissing and petting and suggestive dancing going on, because the mores and morals of those days were considerably different.

It goes without saying that Daddy wouldn't have allowed me to date even if I had wanted to. So, Kelso and I didn't become an item until the junior prom.

He was a worldly sixteen-year-old, while I was fifteen.

Naturally, Daddy said I was too young to go to the junior prom, but I wore him down. He agreed to drop me off personally, but warned that I had better be ready and waiting when he returned at 11 o'clock. That point was non-negotiable.

I got all dolled up and rode 20 miles into Fuquay-Varina alongside my doting father. When we arrived at the prom, Kelso was there waiting for me, looking quite spiffy.

"Have a good time, Clara Mae," Daddy said, as he opened the car door for me. "Remember what I said, now."

"Okay, Daddy," I replied, eager for my father to leave. "Thanks for the ride."

Daddy continued to linger, oblivious to my desperate desire for him to vanish. Instead of hopping into his car, he stood directly in front of Kelso.

"Son, I'll be back to pick up Clara Mae at eleven, understand?"

The music was jumping and kids were twirling around and having a good old time when Kelso and I made our way into the gymnasium. Word spread that somebody had some alcohol, but I knew better than to get involved with any drinking–the odds of surviving the ensuing beating would be slim indeed.

Besides, I was more than happy to chatter excitedly with Kelso and my friends as I watched people dance. I had never spent so much time with a boy in a date-like setting and was having great fun. In fact, I felt sad when the clock started to edge toward eleven o'clock. I didn't want the magical evening to end.

So, I did something I had never done before–I defied my father.

"Kelso, can you please drive me back to Willow Springs?" I asked sweetly, glancing at my watch. It was 10:45. I knew my father was making the 20-mile trip from Willow Springs even as I spoke. He would be livid when he couldn't find me, but at the moment I didn't care.

Kelso clearly understood that my father was coming, too, but he eagerly complied with my request. He had his reasons.

So we left the school and walked over to Kelso's car, a four-door sedan with a loud muffler and a stick shift lever on the steering wheel. I felt giddy as we set out for Willow Springs, because I was having the time of my young life just being in his presence.

We weren't that far from my house when Kelso surprised me

by turning off the highway and driving down a side road that was out of view of traffic. He turned his headlights off and turned toward me. Uh oh.

"I just need a little kiss, Clara," he said, grinning.

His lips were surprisingly soft and felt good against mine. He was very sure of himself and not at all nervous, as if he'd done this before. And goodness, somebody must have turned on the heater in Kelso's car! As I felt his tongue probing for mine, I knew I had reached a critical crossroads.

I knew what Kelso wanted, because I wanted it, too. Do I keep moving forward and let these good feelings grow, or do I slam on the brakes?

A vision flashed through my head of how I used to stand over the stove and cook while my younger siblings screamed and fought around me. I did not want kids–this had to stop. Right now!

"Come on now, Kelso," I said, scooting away from him. Daddy was already going to kill me, so what sense was there in getting pregnant to boot?

"What's wrong, Clara? Is something wrong?" Kelso's voice had a pleading quality. I was floating in that gray area where "no" could easily become "yes," so I needed to get out of that car and away from Kelso as quickly as possible.

"I just need to go home, that's all. I'm already in big trouble!"

The porch light came on the second Kelso's tires hit our gravel driveway. Daddy's car was parked beside the house. All I could think was, "Oh my God! Lord, please deliver me, please help me."

The front door opened with agonizing slowness and it was Mother, not Daddy, who emerged. Worry lines creased her forehead and her lips were clamped into an annoyed grimace.

"How are you doing, Mrs. Leach," Kelso asked with a calmness I found astounding.

"Fine. And you?" Her eyes ignored Kelso and were boring into mine.

"Clara Mae, your father went down to the school and said he couldn't find you."

"I looked for him, Mother, but I didn't see him." The lie rolled off my lips with surprising ease. Kelso wisely bid my mother and me adieu at that juncture, and drove off, leaving me to deal with Mother alone.

"Your father is not pleased," Mother observed icily, not exactly delivering a news flash. "He is sleeping and will deal with you in the morning."

I went to bed and had the best and the worst night of my young life. On the one hand, my thoughts were suffused with the dreamy time I'd just spent with Kelso, including his seduction attempt. It felt good to be viewed as desirable, and I was proud that I'd stopped things before they'd spiraled out of control.

On the other hand, I was terrified about what might happen the following morning. I had defied and lied to my father, forcing him to make an unnecessary 40-mile trip. Then I'd lied to Mother. What wrath would Daddy unleash when he laid eyes on me?

Any way you cut it, I forayed into virgin territory the night of my junior prom!

My heart was pumping so hard I thought a couple of ribs might break when Daddy and I finally came face to face. I had difficulty maintaining eye contact with him longer than the time it takes to blink.

I knew, and I'm real sure Daddy knew, what the real story of the previous night had been. I was totally at his mercy.

"I went to the school last night and did not see you, Clara Mae," Daddy said, taking care to accentuate every syllable of my name. "I guess you came home with Kelso, then?"

"Yes sir, Kelso brought me home."

"So who is this Kelso person, Clara Mae?"

I took a deep breath. "He's just a friend, Daddy. I introduced you to him when you drove me to choir practice one time."

"I see. Well, I don't appreciate having my time wasted. Or my gas either, for that matter. You just make sure that doesn't ever happen again, do you understand?"

"Yes sir."

And that was it. I managed to escape with my dignity pretty much intact, not to mention my rear end. I was grateful to Daddy for not having brought down the hammer. I suspect Mother must have gotten his ear before our little talk, although she never said anything to me.

When the time came for my senior prom, Daddy was reluctant to let me go. But my brothers were both dating seniors at my high school and were going to the prom also, so I was allowed to go.

Afterward, Kelso didn't detour down any dark roads. To my relief.

Chapter VII

A Dream Deferred

I worked my butt off to be valedictorian of my high school class. I would have snagged it, too, were it not for a roadblock named Cecilia Richardson.

We both had pretty good grades, which was easy for me since I was a school junkie. But I think what tipped the scales in Cecilia's favor was that I always had to miss school during those crucial days when the tobacco crop had to be harvested.

So I was relegated to No. 2, meaning I was the class salutatorian.

I have no regrets about how that played out, because I gave 110 percent, as usual. As for my absenteeism, that's just the way it was for kids who lived on farms. I couldn't alter that fact, so there was no sense fretting over it.

Anyway, being salutatorian was a pretty decent achievement, considering that I was the only sixteen-year-old in our graduating class. I still had a speech to give during the graduation ceremony. I still had a chance to shine.

The Country Store Gang

Between my junior and senior years of high school, my dream of becoming a lawyer was dealt a severe blow. And it was Daddy who burst my bubble. More accurately, it was he and the boys at Walter Myatt's country store.

This highly opinionated clique of black and white farmers gathered daily outside Mr. Myatt's business to chew over what was happening with their families, their farms, and whatever.

When I first got wind of this fraternity, my initial impression was—wow, men gossip a lot more than women!

At the end of the workday, the gang would drift over to Myatt's place, parking their cars on the sandy dirt in front of his store. Milk bottle crates served as chairs, a plug of chewing tobacco got passed around and bottles of pop were bought—old man Myatt didn't sell liquor and didn't allow any tasting on his property. Then the country store crew would commence to holding court and spitting tobacco juice.

Those boys clung to some rather narrow views about females and their place in society. When Daddy forbade me to become a lawyer, I have no doubt the invisible hand of the Country Store Gang was behind that edict.

In 1952, the year Bettie went off to college, Daddy sauntered in one day after a session at Myatt's store and solemnly announced that it was a waste of time for women to go to college. "Because all they're going to do is grow up and get married," Daddy sagely intoned.

Do you know that to this day, there are some people who still subscribe to that ridiculous point of view!

Anyway, Mother wasn't having any of it. I didn't see her put her foot down often with Daddy, but she prevailed every time she did. She was determined to have all of her children–not just the boys–get a shot at a quality education.

As a matter of fact, in some regards Mother believed girls needed more opportunities than boys.

"I don't care who says what," Mother said quietly to Daddy, alluding to the Country Store Gang. "My child is going to graduate from high school, and she's going to college in the fall."

And that was that. We didn't hear much of the wit and wisdom of the Country Store Gang around the house after that . . . until the summer after my junior year in high school.

It seems the store boys had cast their two cents worth against my desire to become a lawyer.

I had planned to apply to several colleges when high school resumed and was talking to Daddy about that.

"Well, Clara Mae," Daddy said, leaning against our cow barn, "I'm the one who's gonna shell out the dough for this college thing. As long as that's the case, I think you need to go to nursing school. That's a solid, stable profession for you to be in. Did you know North Carolina Agricultural & Technical College has a new nursing school?"

What the–nursing school! Up till that moment I had never given a second's thought to becoming a nurse. For what??

I looked at Daddy hard to see if he was joking. He wasn't. His expression was neutral and he looked comfortable with his decision. One that would affect the rest of my life.

Frankly, I didn't know what to think. Daddy seemed genuinely to have my best interests at heart. I think he felt he needed to direct me in some kind of way. But I was still very angry and resentful over what he had done, although I never communicated that to him.

I probably didn't have to, because I don't mask emotions terribly well. You can look at my face and tell when I'm out of sorts about something. Nursing of all things!

Daddy never gave Bettie any guidelines when she went off to college. She told my father she wanted to major in English and he said, "Here's the money, Honey. Have fun!"

Like I said, Daddy and I had a complicated, enigmatic relationship at times. I still don't have the slightest idea what that nursing brainstorm was about, or how he found out about A&T's new nursing program.

But after I cooled off, I figured I would give this nursing thing a shot, while all the while looking for ways to get into law school later.

If Daddy was willing to subsidize a nursing school education, so be it. If that's where his money was going, that's where I was going. So I let him know I'd be attending North Carolina A&T as a nursing student.

As I sat at the kitchen table filling out the nursing school application, Daddy stood behind me, peering over my shoulder to make sure everything was in order. He even gave me the fee to send in with my application, and drove me to the post office to mail it.

I was accepted into A&T's nursing program before I graduated from high school.

All I can tell you is that life is chock-full of mysteries. However, I managed to turn that situation into a magnificent positive, if I do say so myself.

Ending School With a Bang

Two weeks before graduation, my father and I were enjoying a leisurely chat as he drove me to choir practice at our church in Willow Springs.

I had been singing in the choir since I was about six or seven, and was part of a young people's gospel quartet whose other members included my sister Bettie and my brothers Aaron and Raymond. Everybody around Willow Springs was familiar with

The Leach Quartet, whose smallest member—me—sang in a beautiful, controlled contralto.

When work in the tobacco fields got to be too monotonous, which was always the case, the four of us would liven things up by breaking into song. Since Daddy was a deacon in our church, our gospel singing definitely had his seal of approval.

So he was a willing, enthusiastic chauffeur as we headed to church that particular afternoon in May 1956.

My sister Rosa was also in the car, but being uncharacteristically quiet. That allowed me to happily bask in Daddy's undivided attention before following in the footsteps of my older sister Bettie, who by then was a student at North Carolina A&T. So I wouldn't be around the house too much longer.

Daddy and I were enjoying our reverie as we approached a group of young black men pushing a disabled car near the side of the road. In less time than it takes to say it, the vehicle veered unexpectedly into our path as Daddy came up on it.

With a horrible cacophony of grinding metal and shattering glass, our car smashed into the disabled vehicle, propelling me from the back seat, where I had been sitting with Rosa. I flew face-forward into the back of the front seat.

One second I was sitting comfortably, the next I was lying on the floor of our car, seeing stars. I had split my bottom lip and my blouse was quickly turning crimson.

Rosa had managed to brace herself somewhat and came through the ordeal with minor cuts and bruises.

When our car finally ground to a halt, there was a moment of stunned silence where nobody said a word. The only sound was the ominous hissing of our sedan, as eddies of white steam whirled from beneath its crumpled hood.

"You okay back there, Clara Mae? Rosa?" my father finally uttered in a strained voice.

"I'm all right, Daddy," I mumbled through a mouth that had suddenly had three lips, instead of usual two. "Are you hurt?"

My father moaned in a way that scared Rosa and me. "I can't move my leg up here—my leg is caught!" he said through gritted teeth.

Daddy had sustained a deep, vicious-looking laceration on his right knee. The guys who had been pushing their vehicle immediately surrounded our car and tried without success to free my father. Dazed, bloody and in need of medical attention, Daddy, Rosa and I remained in our vehicle.

Fortunately the young men had scampered away from their car just prior to the crash, so none of them were injured. They hovered about anxiously, expressing concern for us one moment, dismay over the damage to their vehicle the next.

We hadn't been going terribly fast, because Daddy was definitely no speed demon. But in the days when cars had metal dashboards and lacked seat belts and airbags, even a minor collision could be devastating.

At one point I hoisted myself up to look in the rearview mirror. The bloodstained face staring back at me shocked me so badly that I quickly sank back down. I gingerly pressed my hand up against my mouth, partially to staunch the flow of blood and partially to shield my lip from view.

An ambulance glided onto the scene with surprising swiftness, siren blaring. Two attendants hopped out and helped Daddy free himself, then they gently placed him on a stretcher. They took a quick look at Rosa and me and decided that Daddy needed their help the most.

I overheard Daddy moan that his chest was hurting as the doors to the ambulance swung shut, before transporting him to a hospital in Raleigh.

Rosa and I were driven to a local doctor's office. In all the confusion, I really can't say who deposited us there, but one thing I'll never forget is the doctor who treated me. He was one mean, ill-mannered son of a gun with the bedside manner of a pit viper.

After I became a nurse, whenever I felt an urge to be short with a patient, I would always think back to that doctor and quickly get myself in check.

For some reason, this white physician had it burned into his brain that the car accident was somehow my fault and that I had been out fooling around with boys pushing the disabled car! The entire time he was stitching my lip and shooting it full of Novocain, he lectured me in a totally condescending tone saying, "This is what happens when you're out drinking and driving at all times of the night."

I was absolutely livid. Here, I've just been in an accident through no fault of my own, I'm bleeding and hurting, I don't know where my father is or what condition he's in and some fool physician is sitting here admonishing me.

Because I couldn't even feel my numb lip, which Dr.

Omniscient was busily running sutures through, there was no way I could respond to his nonsense!

It was one of the strangest, most humiliating experiences I have ever endured.

In the midst of this madness, this doctor somehow found out that I was one of Otha Leach's children.

"Oh my goodness, I'm sorry!" he cried out. "Otha is a good, decent man, and there's no way one of his children would be involved in any tomfoolery!" With that, he changed his tune.

Uncle William eventually took Rosa and me home that night, rescuing us from the Twilight Zone. Daddy had some bruised ribs and some huge, painful-looking stitches in his knee, but was otherwise okay; just out of commission for a while. He finally had a legitimate excuse to disappear while my siblings and I toiled in the tobacco fields.

As for me, I still had a salutatorian speech to make and in a very few days.

I made it, too, standing tall and enunciating every word to perfection, fat lip and all. And loving every second of it. As I did so, I was able to gaze out at a proud family that included Daddy, who had hobbled to the graduation ceremony on crutches.

After the ceremony ended and I was saying goodbye to my closest friends, Kelso wandered over for a few words. It was a rather awkward moment for both of us.

We didn't have any great burning romance or anything, but we still liked each other quite a bit and realized we were going to be separated shortly. So we tried to figure out a way to stay in contact.

Kelso wasn't going off to college. Instead, he planned to attend a technical school to study masonry. Our parting was definitely sad for me.

However, my joy over the prospect of making it to North Carolina A&T vastly outweighed any sense of loss. When my letter of acceptance came, I was ecstatic to be selected to go to college.I could go to school every day and spend hours in the library just reading books and dreaming.

There would always be time for men, I reasoned, whereas college represented a once-in-a-lifetime opportunity.

Chapter VIII

Escape From Willow Springs

About 120 miles northwest of Willow Springs as the crow flies, lay the beautiful, tree-lined campus of my alma mater, North Carolina Agricultural & Technical State University. When I went there in the fall of 1956, A&T hadn't attained university status yet and was still a college.

A historically black college, or HBCU, A&T has been around since 1891 and is on the outskirts of Greensboro, a city that makes up part of an urban triangle along with the cities of High Point and Winston-Salem. To reach Market Street, Greensboro's main downtown drag, all I had to do was walk a mere ten blocks.

You have no idea what a relief it was to be trading the bucolic ambiance of Willow Springs for a more urban environment.

I had been to A&T's campus a number of times to visit my sister Bettie, who was now in her senior year. Yet, as I rolled onto the campus in a car holding Daddy, Mother, Uncle William and some of my brothers and sisters, a familiar sight at the front gate still impressed me.

Hanging from a white post was a huge sign painted blue and gold, the school's colors. It simply read, North Carolina A&T College. Affirmation that I had reached the big time.

I started beaming the second I laid eyes on that sign and grinned even wider at the memory of how Bettie had sobbed and carried on during her first day here. Far from feeling homesick, I was ecstatic to be at A&T. In keeping with my effervescent, happy mood, the weather was clear and beautiful that first day of school.

For the first time ever, all I had to do was be a student. I didn't have to milk cows, clean pigs' intestines to make chitterlings, wash clothes for a family of twelve or miss classes because I had to harvest tobacco.

Daddy was quieter during the three-hour drive from Willow Springs than he'd been when we drove Bettie to campus for the first time. He never told me I was the apple of his eye, but I always felt I was his favorite child. I think that's why he was always trying to direct my life, something he didn't do with my siblings.

Daddy regularly said something that has always stuck with me: "Clara Mae, you have to make sure that you get done what you're capable of doing. Because you're going to have to assume a lot of responsibility in this life."

I was never sure exactly what he meant by that. But I was thinking about those words as the two of us, Mother, a few of my brothers and sisters and Uncle William headed toward North Carolina A&T to begin my college career.

Jesse Jackson was an A&T Aggie as was Dr. Ronald McNair, the black astronaut killed when the space shuttle Challenger exploded. I'm sure that during their first day on A&T's campus, they probably saw a tableau that mirrored what I was seeing: Acre after lovely acre of green grass almost too pretty to walk on, stately oak trees and large brick buildings fronted by massive white Georgian columns.

Other scenes tend to play out year after year, too, like the disdainful silence with which juniors and seniors greet discombobulated incoming students.

The first day of school always dawns with scared-looking freshmen and their loved ones dragging trunks and suitcases hither and yon across A&T's campus. Thanks to my visits with Bettie, I knew exactly where I was going, and made a beeline for my dormitory with self-assured steps.

Once my belongings had been stowed in my second-floor room, I walked back outside to see my family off. Mother gave me a long, loving hug in the parking lot, kissed me and held me a little bit more for good measure.

"Just say yes, ma'am and no ma'am," were Mother's parting words. "Don't disrespect your elders."

As was Daddy's custom, he stubbornly avoided any display of physical affection. Instead, he reached into his jacket pocket and grandly handed me an envelope stuffed with twenty- and fifty-dollar bills.

"This is your tuition for the first quarter," he said almost gruffly. "I can pay your tuition, room and board, but all the extra money you need, you'll have to make that on your own."

That substituted for "I love you, Clara Mae, and I'm going to miss you."

It didn't matter what Daddy chose to do—I gave him a big hug anyway, which probably embarrassed him. Like I cared.

"Well, I wish you good luck," Daddy told me. "I know you're going to do all right."

But the person who seemed proudest was my beloved Uncle William, who had driven to A&T behind Daddy's car. Uncle William was the first member of the Leach family to graduate from high school. He had considered going to college, but marriage and children had derailed his plans.

So he attended college vicariously, through Bettie and me.

I bade him farewell, along with my brothers and sisters. I was eager to break the umbilical cord, return to my room and finally start living life on my own. But I'll tell you what—on my own didn't feel like I thought it would. To be honest, after my family left, I felt a little lost, not being around the people I'd grown up with.

Bettie wasted little time showing me the ropes around campus. In fact, she came by my room so often, I sometimes wondered why she was being so solicitous.

Much later I learned there was an element of skullduggery to this, because Mother had secretly asked her to make sure I didn't have clothes and other personal effects strewn about my room, heaping shame to the family name.

Bettie was also instructed to make sure that my bed was made at all times and that there were no roaches in my room! In fairness, I was definitely something of a slob prior to joining the military. My laissez faire attitude toward housekeeping grew even more lax at college, away from Mother's vigilant gaze, but I didn't get so outrageous that I sullied the Leach reputation.

A cousin of mine, Margarine Sapp, was a sophomore at A&T during my freshman year. So, in addition to Bettie, I had another relative on campus to help ease my transition.

From Day One, it was funny to observe the lines of demarcation black students were erecting between themselves at A&T. Naturally you had the usual dark skin/light skin, rich/poor nonsense. But you also had country versus city.

What set city kids apart was the tendency of many of them to strut around campus trying to act all sophisticated and superior compared with their country cousins.

We country kids, on the other hand, stood out because of our dowdy clothes and our naivete. Plus, if you looked close enough, you'd often see specks of red clay on brogans from the boonies. I didn't have any red clay on mine, because most of the dirt in Willow Springs had a dusty consistency. But apparently, my origins were easy enough for folks to ascertain.

I'd be walking through the campus and overhear, "Look at that country girl over there. Still has red mud on her shoes! Heh, heh."

That kind of silly stuff didn't bother me, because I was concentrating on standing out when it was time to get grades and diplomas. I was a country gal from the word "go" and I had no problem with that.

My first week at A&T was filled with orientation activities, as well as registering for classes.

One day the new nursing students were asked to assemble inside a nursing school classroom. Swinging open the door to the assigned room, I was astounded to spy row after row of seats–there had to be room for at least two hundred students in there! This was mind-boggling to someone whose graduating class contained twenty-seven pupils.

While I gawked at my surroundings, a black woman wearing a pristine-looking, white nurse uniform slowly approached a podium in the front of the classroom. She wore a white cap as naturally as if it were her hair. Her highly starched uniform looked stiffer than a knight's armor. Immaculate white stockings disappeared into comfortable-looking, gleaming white shoes.

Willetta Jones radiated the kind of poise usually associated with fashion models. Without uttering a word, this classy New Yorker made one of the most dramatic entrances I'd ever seen. You don't have to bellow at nursing students, or Army troops, to command their attention.

I was in absolute awe of Dean Jones, because she looked like a nurse one would expect to see on General Hospital or something. She instilled a fear in me that all nurses were supposed to exude a grace like hers, which I didn't think I was capable of developing.

"Good morning, and welcome to the A&T School of Nursing. I am Dean Willetta Jones, and I would like to welcome you freshmen nursing students," Dean Jones said in a soft, soothing voice. "Some of you will do well, because you have the desire and ability to be nurses. Some of you will not do well and, unfortunately, we'll say goodbye to you before you graduate."

Scanning her rapt audience, Jones paused and looked into the front row, directly at me. "But there's another group of you who have the ability, but not the desire. We'll find out who you are! All of this will be revealed in the coming weeks."

No desire? We'll find you!

Lady, you don't know me! I was already determined to set A&T on fire, and now I had what appeared to be a direct challenge from the nursing school's dean.

One thing was definitely clear—Dean Jones' demure demeanor concealed an iron fist. I made a mental note to stay on her good side.

"Wow, did you hear her? That woman sounds serious as a heart attack, huh?"

Walking back to my dorm, I turned to see the anxious-looking face of fellow nursing student Lily Pendarvis. A big-busted gal who was also from small-town North Carolina, Lily would become one of my tightest buddies at A&T.

"She sure does," I said, forcing a chuckle. "And I think she was looking in your direction the entire time."

Laughing gaily, Lily tossed back her head, flipping her straight, shoulder-length black hair. "No honey, I'm pretty sure she looked right at you. Plus I thought I saw your name on that clipboard she was holding . . . what is your name, anyway?"

Good ol' Lily watched my back at A&T. And before the year was out, she would literally become my eyes, if not my ears.

The Intimidator

Nursing school curriculum is heavily weighted in favor of the natural sciences, meaning my first college courses were in zoology, biology and those types of subjects.

Zoology was taught by an instructor named Mr. Williams, whose first name I can't recall to save my life. Back in those days, black college students addressed professors by 'doctor' so and so or 'miss' thus and such. First-name familiarity was seen as impudent and disrespectful.

I may not remember Mr. Williams first name, but I vividly recall that he was tall and rangy, somewhat pale, wore horn-rimmed glasses and seemed to be angry perpetually.

He preened about his classroom like an ostentatious rooster, inundating students with minutiae about plant and animal species. Like gold prospectors, we were expected to sift through his informational avalanche to find the nuggets Mr. Williams wanted us to retain.

I had done basic biology in high school, but Mr. Williams' teaching style was a bit overwhelming for me. Presumably he thought he was being helpful by occasionally citing reference books, which I dutifully tracked down in the library. But making heads or tails of his class was a becoming an increasingly futile endeavor.

A couple of times I made an appointment to see Mr. Williams after class. But whenever I asked him to clarify something, he would scrunch up his angular face as though he smelled something that smelled awful.

After making it clear how incredibly stupid my query was, he'd proceed to answer in a manner that indicated he was too insulted to even respond. Clearly, instructing A&T freshmen was beneath his towering intellect.

His obnoxious and arrogant style irritated me to the nth degree. Just what is a professor's job, if not to teach? It's certainly not to lord over anxious young students, as Mr. Williams did.

You can interact with people on a number of levels, with the intellectual plane being just one. However, someone with a second-grade education can easily tell when they're being disrespected. I wanted badly to confront Mr. Williams about his boorish behavior, but Mother's words about respecting my elders kept ringing in my ears.

Plus I felt a little intimidated by him, to tell the truth, because he was the teacher and held all the power.

I couldn't say anything, but I had other ways of showing my displeasure. Whenever I entered Mr. Williams' class, I wore a scowl that remained on my face until I left. When I asked questions in class, which was very seldom, I looked at Mr. Williams in a way that clearly conveyed my low regard.

Definitely, it was behavior that was rude and out of character for Clara Mae Leach, but I had had it with this guy.

He loved to write things on the board, which also irritated me. Materials written on the board never seemed to connect in a way that made sense to me. I definitely didn't want to have another conference with Mr. Williams, but I still wasn't grasping zoology. So with great reluctance, I scheduled another meeting.

Before entering his office, I vowed not to leave until I understood exactly what he was talking about. It was a difficult task, given the big words he was so terribly fond of bandying about.

When we met, he was condescending as usual, but this time I didn't take the bait. I just blotted out his behavior and concentrated on the information I was trying to get. I think I must have worn him out, because I stayed in his office for over an hour, being stubborn and going after him in a passive/aggressive manner.

Whenever the light came on, and I could repeat what he had said to me, seemed to please him tremendously.

"Oh, Miss Leach, you're really doing quite well," he crowed. "I'm really very proud of the way you've grasped this information."

I remained stern and unsmiling, because I was still pissed.

"I don't know what you're so concerned about," Mr. Williams offered, "because you're doing very well in my class."

This shocked me. But having heard it, I was eager to get as far away from that pompous young man as my legs would carry me.

"I think I've taken up enough of your time," I said, gathering my books. "I'll head on back to my dormitory and study. Thank you for your time, Sir." With that, I picked up my belongings and started to leave his office.

As my hand hovered over the doorknob, Mr. Williams spoke. "You're going to make it in this class; you're going to pass zoology. But you don't have to hate me in the process."

I paused for a split second, bade Mr. Williams good night, and left.

That was my first encounter with a teacher who caused me to feel anger to a great degree. I didn't have many teachers like that, thank God. But he was one that really got my goat. I didn't really hate him as a person, I just didn't like his behavior at all.

However, I passed his course, as he said I would. In fact, I almost made the dean's list during my first quarter at A&T. It was gratifying to be taking college-level courses and still getting decent grades.

Still, I cringed whenever professors wrote anything on the blackboard. For some reason, stuff written on the board just didn't compute.

Lily Pendarvis took good notes, bless her heart, and she shared them with me. And whenever the teacher asked me about something on the blackboard, Lily would whisper the question and I would give the answer.

I knew that I probably needed glasses. It's just that my vanity couldn't handle the thought of walking around campus like some little four-eyed nerd. It got to the point where I memorized the eye chart at the school doctor's office, so they wouldn't prescribe spectacles. Heck, as long as I could get Lily to be my Seeing Eye dog in class, what was the problem?

She kept admonishing me, talking about "Clara, you're going to have to fix this problem one day."

I told Lily that as long as we continued to do well with our grades, it wasn't a big deal. But my reliance on Lily was becoming an increasingly burdensome arrangement. So during my freshman year at A&T, I finally broke down and got my first pair of glasses.

To my relief, nobody treated me like a bespectacled freak. And to be honest, when I finally saw the blackboard clearly, along with all the info I'd been missing, I felt rather sheepish.

Something else had come into sharp focus for me, namely, A&T's nursing curriculum was very difficult and rather satisfying. It was beginning to dawn on me that my desire to attend law school was really about the need to feel challenged. And nursing studies were more than meeting that need.

I hadn't forgotten about the law profession, but was starting to realize that I could be perfectly happy doing something else. That epiphany brought massive relief to someone who had been steered into a profession of someone else's choosing.

The Fixer-Upper

In addition to Lily, I was tight buddies with another freshman nursing student named Pauline Brown, from Bluffton, South Carolina. Pauline's right leg was about eight inches shorter than her left, so she had to wear an elevated shoe on her right foot. A young lady who possessed a bubbly personality and could dance up a storm, Pauline had bright brown eyes with long, glossy eyelashes like a fashion model. She talked in a low, seductive voice and absolutely loved flirting with boys. In fact, I admired the way she easily wrapped them around her little finger, relegating her disability to a non-issue.

Pauline was the person who taught me how to dance, after I came to her in a panic one day. A young man I admired had invited me to a spring dance, which was great, except that I didn't know the first thing about dancing.

Daddy forbade dancing in our house, because he was convinced rock-and-roll music was "of the devil" and that juke joints were sinful places. So Pauline calmly took me to her room, turned on the record player and gave me a crash course in cutting the rug.

Lily and Pauline were my aces, because I rarely saw my roommates, who studied secretarial science and accounting. While Lily and Pauline were my partners in crime, they never quite warmed to each other. They weren't adversaries or anything; they just never quite clicked.

So it was a thing where I would hang out with one or the other, but rarely both at the same time.

Unfortunately, during my first year at A&T I gradually came to see less and less of Lily and Pauline. First, Pauline got all tied up with some boy named Alfred, who she thought was the greatest thing since sliced bread. Then Lily became a regular item with some fellow named Napoleon.

The upshot of this was that I lost my best buddies to Cupid's dumb old arrows. To fill the resulting void, I followed a lifelong pattern of seeking out the comradeship of men.

Every day, a gaggle of football players congregated outside A&T's dining hall, where they would stand and loiter like hulking oaks. I was curious as to why, so one day I boldly sauntered into the oak forest and introduced myself. We quickly became fast friends, I guess because they were thrilled to encounter a woman who could talks sports and not be intimidated by all the testosterone in the air.

It turned out most of those guys were rather backward socially. Big burly he-men on the outside, they turned out to be big teddy bears with tons of girl problems. Believe it or not, one of the main difficulties they had was talking to women, so I became Miss Fix-It, I guess you could say.

The football players would decide which matches they wanted to make, then I'd be the person who'd carry the news to the lucky gal. I must have been a humorous sight, being all of five-foot-six and ninety-five pounds and surrounded by football players weighing two hundred fifty pounds and more. This tomboy was in her glory.

Every now and then a female student would cattily confront me, believing I had designs on a football player she had goo-goo eyes for. Wrong, wrong, wrong!

Although I was seventeen, romance still wasn't something I attached great significance to. The only thing I wanted from my oversized male companions was friendship.

One night I was up late studying in the library, when who should appear like a vision but another student named Willie. When you're not looking for amore–Pow! You get ambushed. The two of us quickly had a hot and heavy thing going on and were an item around campus. On one date, we went to this off-campus soda fountain run by a black man named Boss Webster. If you and a member of the opposite sex were seen at Boss's, that officially made you an item.

One day, Willie and I had an off-campus rendezvous at a dwelling rented by one of Willie's friends. I was surprised to find the place unoccupied when we got there. I tell you, it's amazing how coincidences spring up when guys have designs on women.

I was a virgin when I entered that dwelling, but not when I left. Despite my oft-stated aversion to having children, I had absolutely no regrets about the way that situation played out.

Willie and I eventually drifted apart, though. Which was just as well, because in addition to taking care of school work, I was holding down a job. Daddy wasn't joking when he said expenses beyond tuition and room and board were my responsibility.

So I took a job in Greensboro doing housecleaning and sewing for a widow named Mama Alexander, who was the mother of a prominent black female lawyer. A stout, fair-skinned, energetic woman, Mama Alexander owned a huge three-story house that stood on a corner lot. She paid me fifty cents an hour and all the food I could eat, to come in and clean and dust twice a week.

The food part of that arrangement was a godsend for a hyperactive college student whose stomach seemed to growl twenty-four hours a day.

But as much as anything, I think Mama Alexander wanted some companionship in that big house, someone she could talk to besides the flowers and plants she loved to cultivate.

Mama Alexander was very inventive about coming up with excuses why I needed to take a work break. That was fine with me, because I wasn't real crazy about house cleaning anyway. During my breaks, she would bring me cold soda pop and homemade cakes, then we'd sit and chat as I devoured my little treats.

Mama Alexander was an educated woman who was well versed in the arts and music. In addition, she was a proficient pianist who often zipped off an expertly played concerto as I straightened up and washed her expensive china.

Sometimes her daughter would come by, to Mama Alexander's delight. The two of them obviously had a loving relationship and enjoyed being around each other. I felt pangs of homesickness whenever I watched them interact, because I would invariably think of Mother.

Toward the end of my first year at A&T, an ominous development was starting to brew back home. Everyone was in good health, so that wasn't an issue. However, the same couldn't be said of Daddy's tobacco-growing business.

The previous year's harvest was nowhere near what he'd hoped it would be due to drought and disease, meaning the family's income had been severely curtailed. It also meant he could no longer afford to send me to North Carolina A&T.

As my freshman year wound down, I prayed to God for a miracle that would let me stay at A&T. But none came. So, in the spring of 1957 I dropped out of school, uncertain when, or if, I might return.

Chapter IX

Uncle Sam To The Rescue

If you want to see fireworks, put two know-it-alls in the same room and introduce a topic of conversation. Any topic will do.

That's the kind of vibe I had with Moses Martin, who was my sister Bettie's boyfriend in the summer of 1957. I had dropped out of North Carolina A&T and moved to Newark, New Jersey, to live with Bettie, who was doing some substitute teaching and working full time in a mental health hospital.

I certainly wasn't going to go back to Willow Springs, where the last thing my financially strapped family needed was another greedy mouth to feed. Plus, I wasn't keen on returning to those godforsaken tobacco fields.

So I moved up North with my big sister, marking the first time this bumpkin had crossed the North Carolina border.

As my train pulled into the station in Newark, I had no clue Bettie was about to spring the mighty Moses on me. Gawd, he was one rough, gruff, talking know-it-all! He did know quite a bit, actually, but not as much as he thought. I'd put his success rate at about seventy-five percent.

I, on the other hand, did know everything at the omniscient age of eighteen. So we set about educating each other daily on everything from A to Z, while Bettie sat on the sidelines, laughing her tail off.

After initially living with an aunt of ours who resided in Newark, Bettie had moved into a one-bedroom apartment in a modest working-class neighborhood. She gladly brought her little sister into her somewhat-cramped abode. Her place had an unusual set-up in that we shared a kitchen with a tenant living in another apartment.

I don't recall his name, but I remember he was a black dude in his thirties who was one strange cat. I say this because he tried to drive a wedge between my sister and me by lying on us! When Bettie wasn't there, he'd concoct a lie about something Bettie had allegedly done or said. When she was there without me, he'd relate a divisive tale about me.

I'd never experienced such deceit from anyone before, but Bettie and I eventually wised up and got him straight.

During most of my first week in Newark I didn't venture out a lot. I stayed inside watching TV and reading, because my culture shock was so great that I needed to get my bearings. Before long, however, I was going out quite a bit, including trips to New York City with Bettie and Moses.

Goodness, what a spectacular place Manhattan was, especially Harlem! The city's dizzying array of strange sights and sounds left me slack-jawed on many occasions. Moses would walk down the street with Bettie on one arm and me on the other, and we'd take in places like the Apollo and the Baby Grand Club, where the crème de la crème of black entertainment appeared regularly.

After taking in a show and having a bite to eat, we'd hop on a bus and head back to New Jersey.

Within a month of moving in with Bettie, I managed to nail down an assembly-line job with a company that made aircraft parts. They paid me something like six or seven bucks an hour, which was big money in the late 1950s.

But I couldn't hold a candle to what Moses was knocking down. He was doing masonry work at construction sites and pulling in an unheard-of fifteen dollars an hour. I think that's part of the reason he was so cocky.

Before I came to Newark, Daddy had made it clear I was to send whatever money I could back to North Carolina to help the family, which I did gladly. As if to underscore the sense of urgency back home, Mother sent a letter explaining that my money orders were much appreciated, because the last two tobacco crops hadn't been up to snuff.

Making a financial contribution wasn't any skin off my back because I was single and had more money than I knew what to do with. Plus, if you can't help your own family, whom can you help?

Bettie, who was also sending money home, had a little warning for me: "Clara, any time you're dealing with Daddy and money, he sees it as a gift, not a loan. So make sure you look out for yourself and save enough to get back into school, okay?"

In time Daddy did get his financial house in order. And by the summer of 1958, I had squirreled away sufficient cash to attend North Carolina A&T in the fall.

I will always look back with fondness on the year I spent in Newark between my freshman and sophomore years at A&T. I certainly wouldn't have chosen for things to develop the way they did, but it turned out to be a broadening experience.

Those forays into Manhattan were an invaluable part of my education. So was punching a time clock and doing nine-to-five work on a factory assembly line.

As for that doggone Moses, don't you know that Bettie went and married him a few years later? I think she did it just to get under my skin!

They stayed hitched for more than thirty years, too, until Moses—my favorite debate partner of all time—passed on. May God bless his all-knowing soul.

Gimme the Forms!

I was one grateful sister when I returned to A&T. I had gotten a reprieve and was fully savoring the experience of being back in college. My dear friends Pauline Brown and Lily Pendarvis were immersed in third-year nursing studies when I returned and were hanging with a different crowd, so I didn't see as much of them as I had before.

Willie was still around, too, but our relationship was different. We were strictly friends, and platonic ones at that.

I was glad to see all three of them and was appreciating the college experience in a way I never had, before my studies were interrupted. I guess I sort of took being at A&T for granted before the money ran out.

During the second quarter of my sophomore year, my classmates and I started doing something called nursing fundamentals. To fulfill the course work, I had to go to hospitals two days a week, four hours each day. We started tackling basic nursing skills like bathing patients, emptying bedpans, taking vital signs—all those mundane little tasks that are critical to providing good patient care.

We second-year students prepared by practicing on each other in something called a nursing skills laboratory. We'd take each other's blood pressure and temperature, give each other baths and practice techniques for moving patients around without injuring them or ourselves.

Then we moved on to dealing with honest-to-God sick people in a hospital environment. We started at Greensboro's hospital for black citizens, L. Richardson Memorial Hospital.

Once we'd perfected our routine there, we also began to operate out of one of Greensboro's white hospitals, Moses Cone Hospital. Before entering the clinical phase of my education, I had to buy eight light gray nurse uniforms to wear in the hospitals.

My initial visit to L. Richardson marked the first time I'd ever entered a hospital. Remember, my mother bore me and my nine siblings at home, and we never went to the hospital for the usual childhood illnesses.

My most vivid first-day memory of L. Richardson was the smell inside that place. The air reeked of a disinfectant whose odor couldn't be avoided regardless of where you went.

As students, we had to be at L. Richardson at seven in the morning and were driven there with one of A&T's nursing instructors, who talked to us about what to expect.

I was assigned to a surgery ward and given two patients to look after. The first sick person put under my care was a middle-aged black woman who'd had abdominal surgery a few days earlier. Thank goodness, she was a pleasant, talkative woman. One of the first duties I performed as a nurse was to give this woman a bath, and it took me an hour to give a bath that should have lasted fifteen minutes.

Like most nursing students, I think the first thing I had to master was time management. At first it seems as though you don't have enough time to handle your allotted tasks. But you get faster and more efficient. Or else you find a new line of work.

I didn't find dealing with the sick and infirm too difficult, except that I didn't like being around patients who were vomiting or coughing up phlegm. Those two activities bothered me throughout my nursing career. It wasn't the sight or the smell—it was the sound that people made to get rid of that stuff.

The other things I had to do—including dealing with bloody wounds, emptying bedpans, dispensing medications, changing sheets—turned out to be a snap. Equally important, I found that I could walk out the door of L. Richardson and not be an emotional wreck afterward. Some nursing students discovered they weren't cut out to deal with the emotional side of nursing and switched majors during their sophomore year.

The first time one of my patients died took place at L. Richardson. He was a poor man in his forties, he had liver cancer, a malady that had turned the whites of his eyes yellow. As his immortal soul was departing his body, doctors and nurses were scurrying around his hospital room, doing CPR, administering oxygen, basically everything in their power to keep this gentleman around a bit longer.

Well, none of it worked and he was lying in bed after they finished and a doctor had pronounced him dead. I recall the stillness in the room, as well as a pervasive sense of finality. I stood there staring at this man, appreciating that he would never take another breath, realizing that everyone who loved him would never see him alive again.

His body had to be prepared for the mortuary, meaning that all orifices—mouth, anus and penis—had to be covered with bandages, so that body fluids wouldn't drain prematurely.

I was with another nursing student named Myra who was supposed to be helping me get the corpse ready for the mortuary. Myra was a stitch who usually had some hilarious nonsense to relate or a joke to tell, but not that day. Everyone had left the hospital room except for us and the deceased cancer patient, who had a sheet covering his body.

Myra stood in the doorway, halfway in the room and halfway in the hallway. Her gaze traveled to the dead man, then quickly back to me.

"Do not even ask me to help, okay?" Myra said in a teeny, tiny little voice.

"But you're assigned to help me get him prepared!"

Myra blanched visibly and she started shaking her head. "Girl, I am afraid of dead bodies, do you hear me?"

I couldn't believe what I was hearing. A future nurse who's afraid of dead bodies! We had a lot of work to do and I was not in the mood for silly shenanigans. "What is this man going to do to you? This man is *dead*—he is not going to get up. It's not even late at night, Myra, it's early in the morning."

This only made Myra dig in harder. "Hey, I don't care what time it is, Clara. I just don't like dead bodies. I am *afraid* of dead bodies."

In case I didn't fully understand, Myra turned on her heel and quickly disappeared down the hall. And that was the last I saw of her that morning.

I was tempted to tell our nursing instructor about Myra's aversion to the dearly departed, but I didn't. Her cowardly exit left me with a long list of tasks to accomplish by myself, including getting an ID tag on the deceased man's big toe. How was I going to do everything?

I managed and was later able to chuckle with Myra about the incident. But at the time, I wanted to send her into the great beyond right along with that deceased cancer patient.

The same day he died, I have to admit that I had some difficulty coming to grips with his demise. I tossed and turned in my dormitory bed that night, wondering if there was something else I could have done. Was his death my fault? Was there life after death?

I had a nightmare that night, too, and a couple of sleepless nights afterward, but soon returned to normal.

Before I graduated from A&T, I worked as a nursing student at a Veterans Administration hospital in North Carolina one summer, and a mental hospital in New York State another summer.

It took only a few visits to L. Richardson for me to note that nurses and physicians had an unhealthy, lopsided relationship I didn't care for one iota, primarily because a good number of doctors viewed themselves as little deities and expected nurses to be loyal worshipers.

It was so ridiculous that nursing students were taught to jump to their feet the minute a doctor walked into a room. It didn't matter what you happened to be doing–measuring body fluids, writing notes, whatever–you were expected to spring to your feet.

I did it at first, but I stopped after a while and nobody called me on it. I mean, it just broke my train of thought to have to hop to my feet whenever a physician materialized.

More often than not, the black doctors at L. Richardson and the white ones at Moses Cone acted as though they were omnipotent. One at Moses Cone, an obstetrician, was particularly obnoxious. He asked me a question about a patient one day and I answered it, but apparently his lordship didn't care for my tone of voice.

He related the incident to one of my nursing instructors, a meek woman who was terrified of physicians in general, but especially this obstetrician. Well, she gave me a 'C' in an eleven-credit course, obstetrical nursing, after accusing me of being insubordinate to the obstetrician! I had been doing a bang-up job in this instructor's class, too.

It probably didn't help that the instructor and I had exchanged words about that physician before she gave me my grade. But I had an overall 3.5 grade point average, so she didn't hurt me too badly.

* * * * * * *

During the second quarter of my sophomore year at A&T, I was walking across the campus one day when I noticed a sign hanging from the student union building. Thanks to the hideous horn-rimmed glasses I was wearing, I could actually see what was on the sign.

It featured a white gal wearing very red lipstick and an immaculate-looking, brown U.S. Army uniform. Beneath this woman's welcoming smile were the words, `The Army Nurse Corps Needs You!'

I studied that recruiting poster hard, thinking: 'I'll bet they have money in there. I'm a nursing student, and I'll bet they have money!'

I wish I could tell you my first encounter with the military was accompanied by strains of Stars and Stripes Forever and patriotic thoughts.

But that would be a lie. The fact was, I needed money and I needed it in the worst possible way.

Inside the student union building, I encountered two pleasant Army recruiters who were delighted that this North Carolina A&T nursing student had taken the time to speak with them. One of the recruiters was a singularly unattractive woman who wore the gold oak leaves of an Army major, a dark brown uniform like the woman in the recruiting poster, a khaki-colored shirt and a brown tie.

Every branch of the military, she earnestly informed me, was experiencing a nursing shortage.

So if I would be willing to enter the Army as a nurse, the Army would cover my tuition, room and board in my junior and senior years, plus give me a $250 monthly stipend!

I remember this conversation vividly, because I can say without exaggeration it dramatically changed my life. And it took me about fifteen seconds to decide I wanted a piece of the action.

"Don't you want to know about the obligation you'd incur?" the major asked, gazing at me maternally. "The Army does want something in return for supporting your education, you know."

What the Army wanted was a promise that I'd serve on active duty for three years after I graduated. What's a three-year commitment to someone eighteen years old? Particularly when the commitment comes after my tuition has been paid for my last two years of college? That deal had no-brainer written all over it.

My response to that major was: "May I have the forms, please?"

I was given a bunch of forms necessary to kick off my military career and was told to bring them back signed by my mother and father.

When I came home on Thanksgiving break, I was all prepared to lobby my parents about the Army Student Nurse program. Past experience had already given me a sense of how Daddy would react.

So I presented my case to Mother first. I explained there would be no more A&T money worries if I entered the student nurse program. Plus, I would receive $250 a month above and beyond the costs of my education.

Mother instantly grasped where I was coming from and thought it was a fabulous idea.

One down, one to go.

When Daddy's turn came, he predictably offered up a gender-based objection.

"Clara Mae, I don't know about this," he said. "I don't know if it's such a good idea for women to go into the Army." Daddy didn't elaborate about why it might not be such a good idea.

His stance had hardened even more the next day, after chewing the fat with the Country Store Gang. "You know, I was talking to the fellas down at the store, and they figure Clara Mae wants to go into the Army because she's looking for a man."

Daddy offered this aside to Mother while I was in earshot.

"Well, Otha, there ain't nothing that Clara Mae can do in the Army that she can't do right out here!" Mother shot back. "Furthermore, I don't care what those folks got to say down at the store."

Clearly irritated, Mother got up from the kitchen table, retrieved my Army paperwork and laid it down directly in front of my father. "You sign your name right here on this paper, because we're getting this here scholarship. At least Clara don't have to worry where her school money is coming from."

With Mother standing over him, hands on hips, Daddy signed my Army paperwork on the spot. End of conversation.

Let me tell you, that set me free. Because all I had to worry about from that point forward was paying for the spring quarter of my sophomore year, and for a summer session afterward. Daddy covered both of those and after that, our days of scrambling to generate school money were over.

On September 4, 1959, an Army recruiter picked me up on A&T's campus and drove me to a recruiting station in Charlotte, where I solemnly swore to support and defend the Constitution of the United States. With that ceremony, a military career that coursed through five decades officially took off.

The primary emotion I felt after taking my oath was relief. Relief that I wouldn't have to scratch for every penny and dime and wouldn't be forced to take another forced hiatus from school.

Although I didn't feel any different coming back from Charlotte than I did on the ride down, I was formally a member of the United States Army. Specifically, I was a private in the Women's Army Corps Reserve.

Instead of going off to a military installation, my duty station was the campus of North Carolina A&T. And my mission was to make sure I maintained a 2.5 grade point average, which came out to a 'C.' I figured I could pull that off without too much problem.

I was not a part of A&T's Reserve Officer Training Corps contingent because ROTC didn't accept women back in those days. However, they were very helpful to me in interpreting my orders and getting military uniforms.

A few months before I got out of A&T, I was commissioned a second lieutenant in the Army. Although I wasn't an ROTC member, my gold second lieutenant bars were pinned on my nursing uniform by Army Col. Lawrence Spencer, A&T's professor of military science and tactics.

About 100 people came to the auditorium where my commissioning ceremony took place, most of them ROTC students. There's an old Army tradition that calls for newly commissioned Army officers to pay a dollar bill to the first enlisted person that salutes them.

When I stepped out of that A&T auditorium, about four sergeants working with the ROTC program were lined up near the front door. I returned each of their enthusiastic salutes and handed each a crisp dollar bill.

Those sergeants thought they'd enjoy a good laugh on a green lieutenant who didn't know how to salute properly, but I fooled 'em. I went through the trouble of having some ROTC guys show me the proper way to salute before I got commissioned.

That night, I was so hyped about becoming a lieutenant that it took a long time for my eyes to close. For one thing, I was closer to realizing my long-held dream of seeing other countries.

Plus, I would be receiving additional money from Uncle Sam every month. And one thing I always liked about the Army was that they sent my check directly to me and not to my father first. My name was on the check, and I was the one who decided what to do with it.

That arrangement worked beautifully, as far as I was concerned.

As I tossed in my dorm bed, my thoughts drifted to the sergeants who had saluted me. It occurred to me that they might eventually serve in a unit where I'd have to lead them.

My usual confidence and optimism wavered briefly as I wondered if I could effectively lead men and women, because at twenty years old, I barely had what it took to lead myself.

Domestic War

Learning to be inferior—no, feeling inferior, is a learned behavior. Eleanor Roosevelt once said that no one can make you feel inferior without your consent.

In the late 1950s and early 1960s, young African-American college students were tired of feeling inferior and was in no consenting mood. A&T students were no different, especially this little guy named Ezell Blair, Jr. He was a mouthy little freshman who couldn't have been more than five-feet-three, but he was an in-your-face activist, no question about that.

Ezell and three other freshmen attending A&T—Franklin McCain, Joseph McNeil and David Richmond—were fed up with Jim Crow as it was practiced in Greensboro. They were particularly incensed about a Woolworth's in downtown Greensboro. The department store was all too happy to let blacks shop there and spend money, but only let white folks eat at its lunch counter.

Well, Ezell—who later changed his name to Jibreel Khazan—and his buddies weren't having any of it, and they started holding protests meetings on campus during January 1960. These boys had a deceptively simple, potentially dangerous plan for bringing integration to Woolworth's and to Greensboro—they were going to defy Jim Crow by sitting at Woolworth's lunch counter.

And they wanted to know if anyone wanted to join them?

I was outraged too by the absurdity of segregation in Greensboro, having seen the separate water fountains and the Woolworth lunch counter myself. But to me, and the majority of A&T's students, the foursome's scheme sounded like a surefire ticket to a severe beating, then a night in the city jail, if not worse.

Even so, we did a dry run of a Woolworth integration protest. It took place on campus, with students playing the roles of enraged whites that cursed and spit at the black students who'd crashed their sacred lunch counter.

We did several dry runs, and each time Joseph McNeil gave a powerful, positive talk about how we were to behave and how we must never lose sight of our objective of killing segregation.

On Feb. 1, 1960, Ezell and his three young comrades traveled ten blocks from A&T's campus to downtown Greensboro, where they entered the Woolworth's store and plunked down at the lunch counter.

That was one tense day at A&T, because no one knew if we had seen those brave boys for the last time. They didn't get served any food, but they didn't get their heads caved in, either. They remained in the store, seated at the lunch counter, until Woolworth's closed for business that day.

In the next couple of days, increasing numbers of A&T students, (including me) went down to Woolworth's. We went down in bunches of four and five and I made several trips. During the first one, my stomach felt like a mass of braided steel as I sat down at the lunch counter and ordered a hamburger and a Coke.

The manager, a burly white man with salt and pepper hair, a red face and a red neck, had a rather nasty air about him as he ambled over to us.

"We don't serve nigras in this place,' he said curtly. Instead of saying Negroes or niggers, it was always nigras.

One of the male students I was with said, "Well, we don't eat them." Meaning nigras. "And we don't drink them, either, so could you just serve us a Coke?"

Mr. Red Face just walked away. I was worried that he might call the police, but fortunately he didn't. So we just sat at the counter and were treated like invisible people until our protest shift was over. Then some more A&T students came in and replaced us.

There were several white customers at the counter, none of whom looked thrilled to have us around, but they didn't say anything. White employees and customers glared at us, but fortunately did nothing more.

This standoff business went on for about three weeks—our coming in and ordering, getting called nigras, then getting ignored. But by the third week—lo and behold, we actually got served! It was done grudgingly and with an air of tremendous unspoken hostility, but we were actually eating at Woolworth's lunch counter, same as white folks.

I sat there and drank my Coke and ate my hamburger—which was dry and very bland, by the way. The white girls who made our food stood in front of us as they cooked it, so there was no way anyone could slip us a secret ingredient.

The whole time we sat at the counter, my classmates and I kept our heads swiveling, monitoring the situation inside and outside the store. You could feel the tension, so we didn't dare become complacent or relaxed. We all knew that some of the possible consequences of our actions were that we could be beaten, get arrested, get thrown out of college or maybe get killed. We tried not to think much about the possible consequences.

The A&T lunch-counter protest spread to S.H. Kress, another five-and-dime store in Greensboro, and then black students in Raleigh and Winston-Salem and Charlotte started holding similar demonstrations. Reporters from NBC and the New York Times started appearing on A&T's campus all the time to do stories.

There were a lot of NAACP officials around, too.

At one point during the protest, Woolworth's had to shut down because someone called and said a bomb was in the basement. They never found one, though.

Woolworth's decided to ditch its segregationist policies as a result of the Greensboro protest and a lot of other businesses followed suit. And not just in Greensboro, but in other states, too.

The small role I played in helping bring that about is one of my proudest accomplishments. It was another opportunity to teach about treatment of others with dignity and respect. By the way, the Smithsonian Institution now has part of the lunch counter on display where we A&T protesters did our thing in Greensboro.

* * * * * * *

From my sophomore year until the end of my junior year at A&T, I had an ongoing romance with a gorgeous six-foot-two hunk who had a neatly trimmed, cool-looking mustache, a voice like you wouldn't believe, a mischievous smile and close-cropped hair parted on the right side. I was standing outside the dining hall one day with my football-player buddies, saw this guy and nearly swooned to my knees, do you understand? Love at first sight. He was fine–oh, so fine!

He was from Rocky Mount, North Carolina, and was majoring in agriculture. While we were dating, I found out that he had another girlfriend who worked in a Greensboro hospital. I was initially irritated when I found out about this woman, who's now his wife. However, I was so busy with my studies and nursing duties, it was hardly as though I could spend every waking moment with him.

I never went to bed with that fellow, but I definitely wanted to on a number of occasions. He made me feel things no man ever had.

All of my college friends will tell you I was weak for this fellow, and they wouldn't be lying.

A&T had this huge boulder on campus that we used to perch on and have heavy conversations. I had just completed the winter academic quarter, had received straight 'A's and was talking about fulfilling my commitment to the military after school.

"We could get married, you know, Clara, then you wouldn't have to go," he said in that sexy voice of his. How I kept myself from somersaulting off that rock, I still don't know to this day. Out of a sense of loyalty to the Army, how could I not fulfill my commitment? Yet, I had just received a proposal of marriage!

However, there was no way I was going to answer him until I spoke to Mother first. "Sounds like he's serious," she said of his proposal. "Clara Mae, ever since you were a little girl you've been talking about traveling and seeing a little bit of the world. When you joined the Army, you thought this might be a good way to get that done, along with getting some good experience in nursing."

Yes, that was true.

"I would just ask you, if you're not going to do that now,

Clara Mae, when are you going to do it?" Mother said in a neutral voice.

God, there were so many times I totally appreciated and treasured that woman's counsel. My decision was to stay the course and keep moving forward with my plans to enter the Army. I think this stunned my friend, who threw down a me-or-the-Army ultimatum.

I stuck with the Army. Was that the right decision? It was the one I made, so I guess it was. He was a quarter ahead of me, so his graduation brought the curtain down on our relationship. We cried a bit the day he graduated from A&T in 1960.

During my senior year, I began to casually date another young man named William who worked as an orderly in the operating room at Moses Cone Hospital. We happened to leave the hospital at the same time one day, and he asked for my phone number.

He was kind of a cute guy who kept his hair cut real low all the time. Well, I started seeing him for a bit, and it turned out that he absolutely adored me. I liked him, but I was never in love with him to any great degree. So, please tell me why I got engaged to him a year later?

Darned if I know. To this day, I don't quite understand that deal. I even accepted an engagement ring from him.

I had always made it clear that I was going into the Army after I left A&T. William swore that it didn't matter and said he would wait for me and would always write until I left the military. And he did just that, until I had been in the service for about a year.

He sent me a Dear Jane letter while I was in Korea, saying he couldn't wait any longer. When it came, I understood. In fact, I was relieved.

Not long after graduating cum laude from A&T with a Bachelor of Science degree in nursing, I passed the nursing board exam for the State of North Carolina, meaning I was cleared to practice nursing.

I left A&T with a 3.3 grade point average and was the top nursing student in my class. But GPAs would have little bearing on whether I succeeded or floundered in the alien environment awaiting me after college. I felt like I had a pretty good grasp of nursing in general, but I didn't know squat about Army nursing.

And it goes without saying I didn't know squat about the Army.

Chapter X

Lieutenant, Where Is Your Hat?

One thing the Army excels at is taking care of its own. So when I arrived in San Antonio, Texas, to report to my first duty station, Ft. Sam Houston, there was an Army liaison to help me out, as well as someone from the USO to look out for me.

The assistance was certainly welcome, because I was dog-tired from having ridden on a train for 36 hours from Raleigh, North Carolina, to San Antonio. I could easily have flown, but Mother was very nervous about my flying to Texas, for some reason.

So to appease her, I decided to forego flying and caught the train. I was accompanied by an ugly wooden trunk the Army had issued me for transporting my belongings, some reading materials, a copy of my orders and a certificate showing I was in good standing with the North Carolina Board of Nursing.

To pass the time,I gawked out the train window, watching Southern folks work fields filled with tobacco and corn and feeling totally empathetic. In Biloxi, Mississippi, the train made a stop that lasted about an hour and a half. I sat in my seat the entire time, because Mississippi in 1961 was not a place I had any intention of setting foot in.

After we pulled into San Antonio shortly before noon, an Army sergeant at the train station directed me to a military shuttle bus headed for Ft. Sam Houston. All the passengers on that bus had on civilian clothes and wore anxious expressions.

San Antonio is the nerve center for the Army's medical system. The base conducts basic training for Army medical department officers, as well as medical training for enlisted personnel. Every Army medic gets his or her start at Ft. Sam.

I noticed that the streets of San Antonio were teeming with Latinos, which was an unusual sight for me. There weren't a lot of black folks to be seen, but there were an awful lot of brown folks.

When my shuttle bus reached Ft. Sam's front gate, a stiff, helmeted MP wearing white gloves saluted smartly as the bus eased past. I immediately starting seeing soldiers dressed in khaki uniforms that included khaki shorts!

In case you've never been to San Antonio, it tends to be hot as Hades there, especially during August, which is when I arrived. So the shorts I was seeing were more about practicality than fashion.

I was driven to an area of the base that had four very large buildings and looked for the world like a college campus. It prompted me to think: "Oh, this is just like where I came from. This must be like college."

The bus slowed down and the driver made a leisurely right turn, stopping directly in front of the largest of the four buildings. The other greenhorn officers on that bus and I looked at each other numbly.

We hadn't the slightest clue where to go or what might await us on Ft. Sam Houston. A first lieutenant poked his head through the front door of our bus, the single silver bar on his collar glinting in the sun as he did so.

Totally oblivious to military decorum, my comrades and I disembarked in ragtag fashion, following that lieutenant like obedient ducklings. After we entered the building the bus had stopped in front of, the first thing we had to do was go into the office and sign in.

Then we had to present three copies of our orders indicating that Ft. Sam Houston was our duty station. There's a saying that an army travels on its stomach—well, the U.S. Army travels on its paperwork. And woe to any soldier trying to process into a new duty station without the proper documents and forms.

Once the paperwork shuffle was completed, we new officers were given a few items of Army-issue clothing—underwear, socks and the like—then given $300 to spend for uniforms. Anything over that had to come out of our pockets and, believe me, the cost of our uniforms went well beyond $300.

No one had bothered to inform us of this, unfortunately. Details, details.

Many of the officers with me were from Alabama and Tennessee, and I found some of their Southern accents exotic and hard to understand. They probably felt the same way about my North Carolina twang, which has worn away considerably over the years.

While all this was going on, I don't recall any strong feelings of trepidation or euphoria or anything else. I just recall being wide-eyed, desperately trying to soak in everything that was taking place around me.

Before the day was over, my colleagues and I were herded to a mess hall to eat, then directed to sleeping quarters that were like dormitories and had nice mahogany furniture. There were two of us to a room.

We had to sign a form stating that all the furniture in our room was in good shape and that we planned to leave it that way.

The moment you join the Army you become government issue, which is where the term 'GI' comes from. And the military likes to account for everything, particularly the whereabouts of its people. This didn't bother me because I was aware I hadn't signed up for an extended Club Med vacation or anything.

My colleagues were either graduates of four-year colleges or three-year nursing schools run by hospitals. Most of them were white and female. The Army had eight weeks to turn us into soldiers, as well as military nurses and therapists.

Some of my comrades made me laugh whenever they ventured into San Antonio's strong sunshine. I didn't find it that big a deal, because there's nothing like working long hours in North Carolina tobacco fields to get you prepared to deal with the sun.

But some of those pampered city boys and girls acted as though they might die from heat stroke before our eight-week basic officer training course even got underway.

Fortunately, the women in my class were allowed to wear light green and white uniforms made of a very cool, lightweight material akin to seersucker. You could wash those jokers and hang them in that harsh Texas sunlight and they'd be dry in about ten minutes. Didn't require a lot of ironing, either, which was great.

Before we were fitted for uniforms, the instructors at Ft. Sam Houston began teaching how to get into formation, how to stand in neatly aligned squads and platoons. We quickly learned that the Army has a thing for daily formations–the more the merrier. Formations are a good way to keep track of personnel and they're an efficient means of passing along information. And there was an awful lot of info to be absorbed during my basic training at Ft. Sam.

Another thing I caught onto was the fact that the military is one giant pecking order, a pecking order where those highest on the food chain had the most brass, ribbons and medals dangling from their uniforms.

On the other hand, little second lieutenants like me with gold 'butter bars' on their collars were the privates of the officer corps. Even many sergeants look down their noses at second lieutenants, who in all honesty can sometimes be more of a hindrance than help due to their rawness and inexperience.

Really, a second lieutenant must be shaped and molded into an officer ready to take on responsibility. The smartest way to accomplish that is to hook onto someone—an experienced officer or a senior sergeant—who's been around for a while and knows what she or he is doing.

I need to make something clear here: Although I needed guidance and tutelage in the worst possible way, I was not looking for a personality overhaul, or seeking to have my thinking reprogrammed. I liked the Clara Mae Leach that entered basic training and intended to have that person emerge pretty much intact.

But a few of my colleagues seemed to view basic training as some kind of high-stakes, life-or-death affair. They adopted regimented, by-the-book attitudes that really struck me as being rather asinine. Fortunately, there weren't many in my basic training class who acted like that. But the ones who did really stuck out.

Obviously, one of the first things I had to learn was the hierarchy among Army officers. I was at the bottom of the totem pole or a second lieutenant. From there the next highest rank was first lieutenant, then captain, major, lieutenant colonel, colonel, then brigadier general and on up to four-star general. I was hardly thinking about earning stars during those first frenetic days at Ft. Sam Houston.

I was more concerned about mastering the fine art of marching in formation, keeping an immaculately made bed, learning about military customs and courtesies and Army health care. To be candid, I wasn't even thinking about getting promoted to first lieutenant, much less general. I hadn't proven to anyone's satisfaction that I was military material yet.

One thing I was having a problem with was the practice of 'leaving cover.' Your cover was the military's term for your hat, and every time I went outside I was supposed to wear my hat, unless I happened to be in a no-cover zone.

I was flitting across the huge, concrete quadrangle area in the middle of my training compound one afternoon when I ran into a black male captain. I slowed to a walk and ripped off a crisp salute, as I had been taught to do.

"Good afternoon, Sir," I said, continuing to move forward.

"Your name is Leach," this captain said unexpectedly, reading the nametag on my uniform. "Do you know a Bettie Leach?"

Shocked by that act of seeming clairvoyance, I came to a halt and stood at attention. "Yes, Sir, that's my sister, Sir!" The captain's eyes never left my head as I spoke.

"Lieutenant, where's your hat?"

Grabbing at my head, I came up empty handed. Oh, shit! "Sir, it's over in the classroom. I forgot it."

Capt. Simpkins apparently found me terribly amusing, judging from the smile on his face. "I'll wait for you here," he said evenly. "But each and every time you come outside, you're supposed to have a hat on your head. Understand?"

"Yes Sir."

Capt. William J. Simpkins was a graduate of North Carolina A&T and was stationed at Ft. Sam Houston while taking a personnel course. That night he took me over to the officer's club on base and introduced me to all of his buddies, which was nice of him and helped ease my transition into Ft. Sam Houston and the military.

After that day, I always tucked my hat in my books when I entered a classroom. That way, there was no way I could forget my headgear when I left.

I was one of about forty officers in my basic training course, and one of our primary instructors was an infantry major. In my opinion, he had one of the toughest jobs at Ft. Sam. Many of the new officers in my class could barely distinguish their left feet from their right. There were about forty nurses present, along with physical therapists, dietitians and occupational therapists.

Even though we were just starting our military careers, we ranged in rank from second lieutenant to captain, based on our prior experience in our respective health care professions.

Physicians automatically entered the Army as captains or above and did their basic training at Fort Sam Houston or had none at all. Again that dichotomy had reasserted itself—you couldn't have doctors learning how to march and salute alongside mere nurses and physical therapists!

A fair amount of my course work was devoted to information

about the various branches of the military, which was taught in a class called military art and science. And, of course, we learned about the Army Medical Department and the various things it did to support the Army during armed conflicts and in peacetime.

We were taught about the medical assets and personnel assigned to divisions, corps, companies and that sort of thing. We also practiced basic nursing procedures and had refresher instruction on things like cardiopulmonary resuscitation.

My first day at Ft. Sam, I ran into a fellow neophyte officer named Bill Biddle, who was also a nurse whom I had met while I was at A&T. We were both attending a convention of the National Student Nurses Association, which was held in Miami. Even though I wasn't homesick, it was still good to encounter a familiar face.

During basic training, we were free to venture into San Antonio in the evenings after training was over, but I generally passed on the opportunity because Jim Crow was alive and doing quite well in downtown San Antonio. Given that I was fresh from fighting the lunch counter wars of Greensboro, North Carolina, my patience for that kind of bigoted nonsense was pretty well exhausted.

Sitting in the balconies of San Antonio movie theaters while white patrons munched popcorn and drank their soda pop downstairs held little appeal for me. I mean, really!

Instead, I spent most of my free time roaming Ft. Sam Houston. Major military installations are like self-contained cities–Ft. Sam had movie theaters, bowling alleys, hospitals, and stores, even a library. And black soldiers and white soldiers could enjoy these facilities shoulder-to-shoulder, as equals.

In that regard, at least, the military was light years ahead of the rest of America.

Why go into San Antonio and pay good money to be treated like a second-class citizen?

＊　＊　＊　＊　＊　＊　＊

On the outskirts of San Antonio is a huge parcel of private land known as the Oppenheimer Ranch. The Oppenheimer family who owns it has made tons of money by annually leasing several thousand acres of the ranch to the U.S. Army, which uses it to conduct field exercises.

I loved the Oppenheimer Ranch, because that's where my basic training classmates and I went to play soldier. We'd throw on our combat fatigues and helmets, join up with a convoy of trucks and rumble on out to the field to rough it.

Once we'd assembled in the proper location, another truck would come by and some GIs would toss out several green canvas tents and some tent poles, then wave bye-bye. It was up to us to put those tents together and coexist with Mother Nature.

I absolutely loved being in the field. For one thing, I came from a farm and all that wandering through the woods and stuff reminded me of my childhood days. Field exercises allowed the tomboy Mother had banished to come out, and there was nothing she could do about it!

But the second thing was, I loved to eat whenever we had to rough it. The air was so pure and clean out there that it always seemed to make my food taste eight times better than in the mess hall.

Sometimes we had to eat C-rations, specially packaged and canned food for field maneuvers, so that we could get a sense of how they tasted. I liked those, too.

Another highlight of my stay in San Antonio was a trip I took to Monterrey, Mexico, my first international trip. Monterrey is several hundred miles south of San Antonio, and a non-medical unit on Ft. Sam Houston sponsored the journey. About eighty of us gringos hopped on a big bus for a ride that seemed to last forever.

A black nurse I had befriended in my basic training class, Joyce Singletary, also went along on the Monterrey jaunt, which took place during a three-day Labor Day weekend. When we crossed the border at Laredo, Texas, an armed border official came on the bus and checked everybody's ID.

And then we were off, riding through the arid countryside, through mountain roads filled with wagons being pulled by bulls.

I saw a lot of poverty from my bus window, a lot of Mexican kids selling Chiclets along the side of the road. I'm not quite sure what that was about—maybe they reached the conclusion that all gringos had bad breath or something.

Monterrey is at a higher elevation than San Antonio, so it was cooler there when we finally arrived. We didn't get into our hotel until evening, but the following day I was up bright and early so that I could see the town market. I also went to a bullfight, a truly novel way to pass an afternoon. Ole!

The whole experience was enchanting, including drinking tequila at dinner.

That little trip reaffirmed my decision to join the Army–I had only been in for a few weeks and I had already done some international travel.

I experienced dramatic transformations on a number of fronts during my basic training days. A lifelong Baptist prior to active duty, I started attending Catholic services while at Ft. Sam Houston.

For some reason, Catholicism had intrigued me ever since I first read about it as a child. Looking back, I think much of it had to do with the rituals involved, particularly the chanting, which had a calming effect upon my rebellious soul.

So at the age of twenty-two, I began taking steps to study Catholicism formally, with the goal of converting. That didn't particularly thrill my parents, but later they were pleased I had, at least, claimed a Christian faith. Had I become a Buddhist or a Muslim, that probably would have been a different story.

Part of my routine at Ft. Sam entailed meeting regularly with a priest, so that I could receive instruction.

My eight weeks in San Antonio went by very quickly. Not only did I start to get a decent grasp of what the Army was about and what my role in it was, but I was actually remembering to put my uniform cap on when I went outdoors.

Although I was part of the Green Killing Machine, I didn't touch a weapon the entire time I was in Texas. Women didn't have to undergo weapons training in the Army until 1964, three years after I left the Officer Basic Course. Can't say I feel like I missed anything by skipping the firing range.

With my time at Ft. Sam Houston winding down, I would have a chance to see what kind of nurse Second Lt. Clara Leach was. That would be revealed at Ft. Dix, New Jersey, my first duty station.

Chapter XI

'You're Going To Be A Good Nurse'

Within the world of nursing, registered nurses are at the top of the prestige totem pole. They receive the most education and often have bachelor's, master's and even doctoral degrees.

Practical nurses come next. They're adept at hands-on procedures such as inserting catheters, irrigating wounds and changing dressings, but haven't received in-depth training in nursing theory.

Nursing assistants, or aides, are at the bottom of the pyramid and usually occupy themselves with duties such as giving baths, emptying bedpans and taking vital signs, e.g., temperature, pulse, respiration and blood pressure.

Being that I was a registered nurse and an officer, one of my responsibilities after I arrived at Ft. Dix was to supervise the work of the enlisted and civilian personnel who helped me with patient care. One of them was a practical nurse named Staff Sgt. Richard Zeitlin.

We both worked at Walson Army Hospital, where I was assigned to the surgical intensive nursing unit.

Just before I arrived at Ft. Dix, Walson had opened up a new six-bed intensive care unit. The concept of intensive care for surgical patients was considered new and cutting-edge back in the winter of 1961.

I oversaw the evening and the night shift for the surgical intensive care unit, as well as the recovery room unit. I had been on the job for just a few weeks and noticed that Sgt. Zeitlin had a habit of quietly observing me.

What he saw was a scared kid who survived by thinking fast on her feet and doing a lot of ad libbing. It didn't take Sgt. Zeitlin long to realize that the green second lieutenant nurse from North Carolina could use a life buoy. Or at the very least, a mentor.

Zeitlin had served as an Army medic during the Korean War. Dealing with surgical intensive care in a stateside military hospi-

95

tal probably seemed like a walk in the park after that hellish experience.

Zeitlin and I were the only nurses on duty in the surgical intensive care and recovery units at night. I quickly figured out that the muscular, fifteen-year Army veteran knew his stuff cold.

So I wisely deferred to his judgment whenever I had a major question about something. There were no experienced registered nurses to query, so I bounced things off Zeitlin, who hailed from Philadelphia, looked to be about forty and had dark hair salted with gray.

The military has rules against officers fraternizing with enlisted soldiers, making some officers feel they have a right to be snooty and condescending toward their enlisted brethren. I found that silly and accorded Zeitlin the same level of respect and consideration I wished to be treated with. However, I did stick to being friendly without being familiar, as the saying goes.

One night toward the end of my shift, Zeitlin approached me and made a bit of small talk before cutting to the chase. "Lieutenant," he said in a low voice, "you look like you're going to be a damn good nurse."

I starting beaming, because that was literally the first feedback I'd received since arriving at Ft. Dix. Up to that point, my stint at Walson had been a sink-or-swim proposition. It was becoming clearer by the minute that the Army really was experiencing the nursing shortage the recruiter at North Carolina A&T warned me about.

"But you need some teaching," Zeitlin continued gently, "and I'm going to take the responsibility for doing that."

I wasn't quite sure what I had done to deserve that honor. There hadn't been a great deal of conversation between Zeitlin and me, because I had been terribly busy getting my bearings and learning military nursing. But it was an offer I gratefully accepted.

Some officers think important lessons and information come only from other officers: I knew that kind of elitist attitude would only hold me back if I paid any attention to it.

"I'm flattered that you'd offer to do that," I said extending my hand. "What did you have in mind, Sarge?"

The veteran nurse appeared to have thought through his response.

"Practical nurses are taught about hands-on procedures, whereas registered nurses like you aren't," he said. "You need to know those procedures, and I'll gladly teach them to you. But when a supervisor comes around, you have to act as if you're in charge."

That last comment was spoken archly and with a trace of Sgt. Zeitlin's trademark cynicism, which camouflaged a heart of gold.

"But one day I'm going to go away and see if you learned anything," he said, laughing.

The success I enjoyed in the Army was as much about having capable mentors as it was about my capabilities. Sgt. Zeitlin was the first of many good souls to take me under his wing.

Over the next month Sgt. Zeitlin taught me the difference between textbook military nursing and real-world military nursing. True to his word, he quietly propped me up and no one was the wiser. However, one night before we started our usual night shift, Sgt. Zeitlin laid a challenge at my feet.

"All right, lieutenant, this is your night," he said. "I'm going over to the recovery unit to get some sleep." Then, with a hint of needling, he said, "By the way, call me if you need me."

What he didn't know was, I would die and go to hell before I called him for anything! I was that stubborn, and had that much blind faith in my ability. Still, I was scared. Until you've had someone's life entrusted to you, you can't appreciate what a heavy responsibility that is.

As advertised, Zeitlin ambled over to the recovery unit, hopped into an empty hospital bed and drifted off to sleep. My crutch was gone. Among the patients I had to deal with was a young man with facial fractures, whose feeding tube had become obstructed. Once I figured out how to clear that out, I moved on to another young man with a ruptured appendix who needed constant reassuring his Maker wasn't coming to claim him that night.

And so on and on. I was a fledgling airplane pilot who had to suck it up and solo for the first time. Well, I didn't crash and burn during my shift, which lasted from midnight until eight in the morning. In fact, around four o'clock I was starting to feel good, even a little cocky.

But by the time Zeitlin returned just before our shift was to end, I was haggard.

"How are you doing?" he asked with genuine concern.

All I could muster was "fine" in a voice that sounded like a soft croak.

But my nursing career began in earnest the night before. I had shown that I could deal with the responsibility by myself and not wilt. I still had an awful lot to learn, but my confidence had been boosted immeasurably by an outstanding teacher and individual.

I was working hard and becoming more accomplished at nursing with each passing day. Not only could I do it–I was good at it! Working hard to master something and succeeding has always given me such a delicious rush.

The fact that I was prospering in a cutting-edge area of nursing–surgical intensive care–made my victory all the sweeter.

*　*　*　*　*　*　*

My growth at Ft. Dix wasn't limited just to professional matters. My fourteen-month tour began with my first-ever plane ride, from San Antonio to Newark.

If you remember, I rode a train for thirty-six interminable hours traveling from North Carolina to San Antonio, because Mother was skittish about my flying.

After my terrifying railway excursion through the heart of Klan country, there was no way on God's green earth I was going to ride a train from Texas to New Jersey. Mother was just going to have to come to grips with 20th century transportation this time around.

My first airplane ride was comfortable, and Mother found out about it after the fact. She laughed and gave me a mild scolding–not a bad tradeoff for chopping more than twenty-four hours off my journey.

Being stationed at Ft. Dix put me close to Newark, where Bettie still lived. Being in close proximity to her was great, but so was having my own place to come home to. Moses was still as much of a know-it-all as ever and so was I, and we pretty much resumed where we had left off. And we still tasted Manhattan's rich night life from time to time.

I welcomed those opportunities to socialize, because there weren't many fellow lieutenants to talk with back at Ft. Dix. Walson Army Hospital had a lot of senior officers working there, and they seldom hobnob with lowly lieutenants.

Everything was starting to come into place for me at Ft. Dix, including the spiritual component of my life. A Catholic chaplain at Ft. Dix to whom I had been referred, Father Michael J.

Rogers, helped me finish the conversion to Catholicism that I'd started at Ft. Sam Houston.

I found my new religion fulfilling and treasured the sense of wholeness and peace it brought to my life.

All was right with my world at Ft. Dix, except that some male enlisted soldiers had a sexist habit of not saluting when they encountered female lieutenants. There was no way I was going to be denied the respect that went with my rank. This was a nettlesome problem that male officers seldom, if ever, encountered.

There was this senior white sergeant who just refused to bring his right arm up when I went past, as though I were invisible. He had the temerity to pull that stunt around a bunch of his enlisted friends one day. I came to a dead stop and ordered him to attention.

"Excuse me Sergeant, did you happen to see these lieutenant bars on my collar?" This was less a question than a statement. We both knew he saw them. That was the prelude to a three-minute tongue-lashing doled out in front of his peers.

That episode brought me no joy, and that sergeant needed to be taken to the woodshed. Discipline and good order are a must in the military. Plus, I knew very well that had I been a white male second lieutenant, he would have fallen all over himself to salute me.

News of his dressing down traveled fast around Ft. Dix. Afterward, there was one female second lieutenant at Ft. Dix who never failed to receive a salute the minute an enlisted man saw her coming.

As it should have been in the first place.

I felt gratified to be able to replace my second lieutenant's butter bar with the silver bar of a first lieutenant in September of 1962. Short of slapping your commanding officer or being a hopeless boob, second lieutenants routinely got promoted to first lieutenants after about a year and a half. I made it right on time.

Although still way down on the officer food chain, first lieutenants are accorded far more respect than second lieutenants.

Land of the Morning Calm

In June of 1963, I had my meager belongings crated and shipped off to my next duty assignment—the Republic of Korea.

Korea was known in military parlance as an unaccompanied tour, meaning that transportation and housing for spouses and kiddies weren't authorized.

Although there had been a lull in the Korean War for at least a decade, our GIs were still skirmishing with North Korean forces from time to time. To this day, the war has never officially been declared over–the war was stopped by a truce that remains in place.

When I was there, our boys were sometimes involved in deadly encounters with North Korean forces that went largely unreported in the U.S. press. Segments of the Korean peninsula were incredibly volatile and presented a less than ideal environment for family members.

However, it was an intriguing proving ground for a single military nurse looking to test her newfound skills.

To get there, I had to catch a cross-country flight from New Jersey to San Francisco; then a long, long military flight that left from Travis Air Force Base in California, with refueling stops in Hawaii, Wake Island, and a stopover at an Air Force installation in Tachikawa, Japan.

Before I left the States, I met another new lieutenant named Mary Wise who was also a nurse and was also going to be stationed in Korea. That gal started getting homesick before we even left California!

In Tachikawa, Mary and I met two more new nursing lieutenants also headed for Korea. Lucy Cunningham was a Southern belle from Little Rock, Arkansas, who was very high-energy and used to flit around like a hummingbird. Herbie Nishikawa, of Japanese descent, was born in Hawaii.

Mary and Herbie were my running buddies once we got to Korea. We began to bond in Tachikawa, where we had a three-day layover because a typhoon had made South Korea its temporary home.

I never set foot off that air base in Tachikawa. The young woman who had always dreamed of traveling to exotic locales didn't feel comfortable listening to the indecipherable native tongue, or reading signs that were written in strange symbols that I didn't understand. So I spent the time frequenting the base bowling alley or going to the officer's club with my new friends. I would start my exploration of a country in Korea.

The typhoon that had been tormenting South Korea finally decided to go elsewhere, allowing us to complete the final leg of our trip.

The moment I stepped off that Air Force plane at Kimpo Airport, the unbelievable heat/humidity mix was waiting at the door to greet me. Along with the most god-awful smell my nose had ever encountered, including those from my farm days back in Willow Springs.

That odor emanated from what were known as 'honey buckets,' a misnomer if there ever was one. Honey buckets were the primary way that the South Koreans removed human waste from their homes and used it on their crops in the fields back in 1963. The stench from those things was so pervasive and so powerful that I had to discard clothes I brought back from Korea, because the smell could not be washed or dry-cleaned out of them.

That hurt me to my heart, too, because I sewed some serious rags during my days in the Republic of Korea.

When I was there, the country definitely wasn't the world economic power it has become today. Instead of exporting cars, heavy machinery and electronic equipment, South Korea was still struggling to overcome the devastation the Korean War had wrought on its economy, landscape and people. Poverty and malnutrition were rampant, and living conditions were rough for most Koreans, who overwhelmingly used honey buckets instead of indoor plumbing.

In addition, all kinds of mines and other unexploded ordnance were lying around, posing a hazard to civilians and soldiers alike.

With apologies to Dorothy in the Wizard of Oz, I surely wasn't in Kansas any more!

A bus took my comrades and me to the 121st Evacuation Hospital, a facility seventeen miles north of Seoul that was located within an Army Support Command base. When I look back on my career, this is one posting I always recall with particular fondness.

As you might guess from its name, the principal objective of the Army Support Command was to support combat units, which is ultimately the name of the game in the Army, whether you're a nurse or a clerk typist or a mechanic.

The Army Support Command was located in a little agricultural town called Sinchon, also known as 'Sin City,' undoubtedly, because of the number of houses of prostitution that sprang up to deal with the needs of U.S. soldiers. The military installation at Sinchon had units for medical personnel, transportation, quartermaster, finance, etc.

My living accommodations at Ft. Dix and Ft. Sam Houston were positively luxurious compared with where 121st Evacuation Hospital nurses had to live–pale green Quonset huts, prefabricated metal structures with semicircular roofs that curved downward to form walls. Those Quonset huts were maybe thirty feet wide and about seventy feet long, and were divided into little living units, hootches we called them, for twelve nurses.

Between every two women was a shared bathroom.

I hadn't been at the 121st a good two hours before I was summoned to the hootch of a black nurse captain named Mary Ellen Anderson. Basically, Capt. Anderson politely read me the riot act.

She started out with small talk about the husband she'd left behind in Omaha, Nebraska, while she completed her tour of Korea. Having lulled me to sleep, Capt. Anderson laid down the law.

"I have something important to say as you begin your tour here in Korea, Lieutenant Leach."

"Yes ma'am?"

"You will not, Lieutenant, do anything in this place to embarrass or discredit your fellow Negro officers. Do you understand me? We've spent a lot of time and effort making sure that we have a good reputation over here and we intend to keep things that way. You may see other officers saying and doing all kinds of things, but always remember that I am personally going to be watching you. We clear on that?"

"Yes ma'am." Thank God for Mother, who taught me to obey my elders.

"I'm not saying that you're prone to behave in a certain way, Lieutenant," Capt. Anderson continued. "But rest assured that Negro officers are watched more closely than white officers. That's just the way it is."

That unvarnished fact of life held true not only in Korea, but basically throughout my military career. It was a bit of advice I was glad to get early in the game, particularly in Korea, where military personnel ate, slept and socialized within a relatively small area. When you're living on top of each other for months on end, unlike in the United States, that tends to accentuate the desirable, and the undesirable, aspects of your colleagues' personalities.

The Army wasn't exactly swarming with officers of color in 1963, so we tended to hold ourselves to a higher standard. That was partly out of necessity, because a serious double standard was in place. Oftentimes, a black officer would be dealt with harshly for committing an infraction that would be overlooked or excused if a white officer committed it.

U.S. military personnel had a curfew that lasted from midnight until five-thirty in the morning. You had to be back on the base or firmly ensconced in a Korean dwelling once curfew hit, but you could not be caught wandering around Sinchon. Military police patrolled outside the gates and in the town of Sinchon, looking for curfew offenders. Breaking curfew was a sure-fire way for military officers in Korea to generate a major blemish against their record. Disobeying curfew scuttled your career. That's how serious it was.

Call me a conformist, but I was never even tempted to bend curfew, much less break it. You could run around inside the gates all night if you felt like it, so I never saw any reason to buck the system. It was a different kettle of fish for some of the fellas, though, due to the lure of the Korean women lurking in and around Sinchon. Many of the women were prostitutes.

Sexual and romantic entanglements led many an officer and enlisted man to be dragged back to the compound in disgrace.

Every month, the officers in my unit were read a letter from the commander of the Eighth Army. It told us explicitly that we were guests of the South Korean government and were expected to conduct ourselves accordingly. The letter forbade arguing with, or fighting, South Koreans.

Every month we had to sign a paper acknowledging that we understood what that letter said.

I'd been in-country about three months when a male nurse anesthetist, a first lieutenant, sauntered into Sinchon with a bunch of his buddies one evening, got drunk, and slapped a Korean woman.

Let me tell you, the military got him out of the country within forty-eight hours. He was gone fast. So was his career.

As had been the case at Ft. Dix, I was again assigned to a surgical intensive care nursing unit. Thanks to my crash course at Fitzsimons Army Medical Center, and my hands-on experience at Ft. Dix, I knew what I was doing by the time I reached Korea.

The chief nurse was Lieutenant Colonel Theresa LaPlante. I didn't have a lot of dealings with her, which was fine with me. When a first lieutenant is encountering a lieutenant colonel a great deal, that usually doesn't bode well for the first lieutenant. I wasn't kidding when I said I believed that the brass were to be avoided like the plague when you're a junior officer.

Fortunately, the base at Sinchon was swarming with little lieutenants like me. I became something of a ringleader for about twenty lieutenants. One of our favorite pastimes was to buy albums at the PX. We loved music and bought ourselves those old-fashioned tape players with tape spools that appeared to be as big around as car hubcaps.

Other things I did for fun in Korea were bowling, participating in plays held on our base, and teaching conversational English to Korean high school students.

Oh yeah – did I mention that I also worked my tail off? Nurse Corps lieutenants typically toiled twelve-hour days. I was working night duty, which I detested and which called for working ten consecutive days, followed by four days off.

I promised myself that when I got back to the States, I was going to get a master's degree, because well-educated nurses were placed in leadership positions, which translated to day work, Monday through Friday. Not to mention weekends off.

To a large extent, my healthcare co-workers and I were on a good-will mission during our stay in Korea, meaning that many of our patients tended to be natives, not Americans. Because of this, we often treated diseases and maladies seldom seen back in the States.

I mentioned that substandard living conditions were the norm when I arrived in South Korea in 1963. That meant that many of my Korean patients had long, thin intestinal worms. The worms weren't too much of a bother as long they remained in the intestinal tract, but sometimes a patient would vomit and aspirate those horrible things.

When they got into the trachea and lungs, then you had a problem. We would have to run a tube down the windpipe and get those suckers out.

Head lice were also a problem. They were so common that it was just standard procedure to delouse all Korean patients admitted to the 121st Evacuation Hospital.

Another problem we encountered with distressing regularity was Korean farmers who'd been maimed and blinded by fooling around with unexploded bombs.

If they were lucky enough to disarm a bomb discovered while plowing their fields, the brass from the weapon was worth more than a farmer could make working an entire year.

The problem was, they'd beat on these munitions with hammers to get the timing mechanisms and high explosives out. Talk about your ultimate Russian roulette! Getting killed wasn't the bad thing about having one of those bombs go off—surviving was.

Some of those poor blast survivors would come into the 121st with their hands and feet blown off, empty sockets where eyes had been, intestines hanging out of abdominal walls. You knew that even if you did save them, a Korean with no hands or feet wasn't going to make a living and was doomed to become a freakish street beggar.

Sometimes those bomb farmers would be in such distress that you would just stand there wanting to put them out of their misery. I never did, though, because I took a pledge never to cause death voluntarily.

Nor, to my knowledge, have I ever worked with anyone who performed euthanasia

But I tell you, I've definitely thought about it. It did run through my mind that hastening death may be one of the better things I could do for a particular patient.

Without question, working in the 121st Evacuation Hospital gave me and everyone else on the staff a new appreciation for what it meant to live in the United States. Our national pride took a severe jolt, however, when President Kennedy was assassinated in November 1963.

A lot of us soldiers in Korea at that time were wondering if our countrymen had gone crazy back home. How could they let the President get assassinated? It was a very unsettling time for those of us serving overseas.

Within thirty-six hours of the shooting, the Army Support Command organized a parade to pay homage to President Kennedy.

Another major event I was sorry to have missed was the March on Washington led by Dr. Martin Luther King, Jr.. My sister Bettie sent me photos of the event from the Newark Star Ledger. I really could not imagine the throng of people on the Mall in our nation's capital, and I still try to visualize it every time I go there.

The sacrifices you sometimes make to serve your country go beyond just being out of touch with relatives and friends.

*   *   *   *   *   *   *   *

I tend to be an adventuresome diner who gladly sample local delicacies when I travel abroad. But there was one time in South Korea where I pushed the culinary envelope a little too far.

Custom, as opposed to gluttony, tripped me up. In the Far East, it's considered an affront to refuse food when you are a guest in someone's home. Well, one day this fairly well-to-do Korean family had me and some other military folk over for dinner.

One of the appetizers was a dried fish delicacy that had been hanging on the wall. I know this because I saw it hanging there, covered with so many flies that it was literally black. I never in a million years thought my hosts would fan away those three hundred flies, cut the fish down and serve it to me, which is precisely what happened.

Lemme tell you, this made my stomach roll because I knew flies have no problem buzzing directly from the outhouse to your plate. Plus they defecate on your food . . . yeecchh!

Unbeknown to my hosts, I began to pray furiously: *Uh, Lord, you are going to have to guide me here, because the last thing I want to do is eat this stinking, fly-infested fish. Heeeeelp me, please!*

I figured it was better to risk dysentery than flirt with an international incident. So I forced myself through that ordeal, with a polite smile, no less. I definitely had a Higher Power on my side that day, because under ordinary circumstances I would have upchucked all over the place.

Dried fish aside, I absolutely loved Korean food. With the exception of winter kimchee, a concoction of Chinese cabbages and radishes that the Koreans immerse in salted water and spicy seasonings, then bury in the ground so that it can ferment.

Not only is winter kimchee incredibly pungent, it gives you breath odor that could disable a mule at fifty paces. Not exactly my cup of tea.

Most Koreans adore kimchee, and the aroma of the stuff seemed to be everywhere. It was always on the breath of the Mamasans, our Korean maids, who kept our hootches spotless on the base. Those women delivered a level of personal service that I would love to enjoy again.

Each of the nurses in my hootch paid each of the Mamasans eight dollars a month each. In return, they kept everything clean, washed our uniforms, polished our shoes, shined our brass – you name it, they did it.

One night I had been out barhopping with my buddies until two in the morning. It was during a time when I was working the morning shift, meaning I had to be there at seven o'clock. That's the kind of dumb stuff you do in your twenties.

Anyway, during my half-hour break for lunch the next day, I went back to my hootch, took my uniform off and laid it across a chair and proceeded to close my eyes for a very short nap. By the time I awoke, Mamasan had washed, dried, pressed and hung up my uniform!

Mamasan, who looked to be roughly forty, knew she would never find a job in the Korean economy paying her what she received on the base. So she took very good care of me. In return, I took very good care of her.

And it wasn't just Mamasan, but Koreans in general tended to be a very hard-working lot. Plus they'd give you the shirts off their backs if you took the time to learn about their culture.

I have so many positive memories of my time in South Korea. Unfortunately, the same can't be said of my relationship with a captain I'll call Bruce Henderson. He was a male nurse in my unit who gave me absolute hell. Capt. Henderson nick-named me Miss Goody Two Shoes, and he kind of hated me. Although he was Roman Catholic, he never managed to find his way to Mass. Yet, he criticized me for attending Mass every day and was of the opinion I thought I was better than every-body else. Capt. Henderson went out of his way to be irritating.

He was married and was engaging in all kinds of extramarital stuff in Korea while his wife was back home. I didn't pass judg-ment on him because, frankly I didn't care what he did. However, he thought I was looking down on him because of his carousing and because of his habit of getting sloshed practically every night.

He may have been on to something on that last point, because it didn't make much sense to me to drink every night, then try to give quality nursing care during the day.

I couldn't stand the ground Capt. Henderson walked on, and the feeling was mutual. If you look up "horse's ass" in the dic-tionary, you'll find his picture.

One night I was at the officer's club sitting at a table and talking with friends, when Capt. Horse's–uh, Capt. Henderson, entered the club in a highly inebriated state. Nothing unusual there, but then he walked directly to my table and sat down.

"Miss Goody Two Shoes," he said, slurring his words, "you think you have all the answers to everything, all the answers to how people are supposed to behave! You also spend all your time trying to influence people and how they feel about other folks. Why don't you get a life?"

Having made a total fool of himself, Capt. Henderson sat there looking at me, waiting for my response.

Well, I learned long ago to never argue with drunks, and I saw no reason to make an exception that night. So after a few very uncomfortable minutes, he went off to continue getting blasted elsewhere.

The following day, Capt. Henderson acted a bit embarrassed, but he never mentioned what had taken place the previous night. Nor did he apologize. That was fine with me, but another nurse who was also a lieutenant threw considerations of rank to the wind and lit into Capt. Henderson.

"You seemed to jump all over Clara for no reason and we didn't understand that," she said disgustedly. "What was that all about?"

Capt. Henderson never really answered her question. I think what really happened was his conscience was kicking his tail, so he lashed out at me in one of his alcoholic hazes. Whatever. Takes all types to make a world go 'round.

Alcohol seemed to be the drug of choice for G.I.s many miles from family members and friends. You really did need some kind of a safety valve in Korea to deal with job-related pressures, as well as the loneliness.

That's why there was so much adultery and drinking and chasing of whores. Me, I took an occasional nip every now and then and channeled my sexual energies into dancing. Some of those nights I danced the night away at the officer's club were in addition to being inordinately fond of cutting the rug.

From time to time, my colleagues decided it was time to "kill all the Russians." Eager to help stem the tide of Communism, I'd join in, knocking back black Russians with the best of 'em. My other vice was smoking cigarettes, something I picked up in 1960 while a student at North Carolina A&T. I didn't see the light until 1977, when I finally quit that nasty habit.

There was a highly skilled surgeon in Korea, let's call him

Capt. Yardley, who used to blow off steam in spectacular fashion. Every three months, he'd say, "Now listen, I'm about to have a boys' night out." Meaning that Capt. Yardley was on the verge of getting rip-roaring drunk, and would be out of commission from Friday night until Monday morning.

Then he'd return to being a helluva surgeon for another three months, until his next 'boys night out.' One time we found him prancing on top of his hootch, naked as a jaybird and belting out "How Dry I Am!" I never saw Hawkeye and those other characters on "M*A*S*H" show pull that one off!

*   *   *   *   *   *   *   *

All told, I spent twelve months away from the United States during my Korean tour of duty. Not all of the time was spent in country, though. In 1964 I managed to slip away for two weeks of rest and relaxation in Japan. I had a wonderful time playing tourist, including visits to Hiroshima and Nagasaki, cities where the United States dropped atomic bombs less than twenty years earlier. I went with three other lieutenants from my unit.

We were in civilian clothes when we went to Hiroshima and Nagasaki, though it wasn't hard to pick us out as American tourists. I was surprised at how consistently kind and courteous the Japanese were to us. Had the shoe been on the other foot, I still may have harbored residual ill will toward the conquerors who dropped the ultimate weapon on my homeland.

On second thought, we didn't all look like Americans. Herbie Nishikawa, who was also on the trip, looked like a young Japanese gentleman dressed in casual Western clothing. People kept approaching him and firing off rapid-fire Japanese phrases. However, Herbie, who was from Hawaii, couldn't speak a word of Japanese and just stared back blankly. I probably knew more Japanese than Herbie. We went traipsing around Japan like some mini-United Nations, with African-American, Asian and Caucasian all represented.

The four of us took in all the sights, including majestic Mt. Fuji and an awe-inspiring, massive statue of Buddha, before we departed the Land of the Rising Sun.

Funny thing about vacations is that it takes a couple of days for you to decompress, but only a couple of seconds to get wound up tight once you come back to a high-stress job like surgical intensive care.

A few months after I'd returned to Korea and the 121st, a reconnaissance team of U.S. soldiers encountered some North Korean soldiers on the wrong side of the demilitarized zone. Bullets started flying, resulting in wounded G.I.s being transported into my surgical intensive care unit. There were a couple of mobile army surgical hospitals up north, but the 121st was the largest and best-equipped military hospital in Korea.

One of the guys shipped to the 121st was a black reservist from Baltimore. He was a postal worker, and whenever he and his wife had a bad argument, he would slip into the Army on active duty for six months, then go back home. Well, this time they shipped him to Korea and he got his right hand pretty badly shot up. As I was talking to him, a civilian reporter approached and asked if he could take some pictures.

I told that newsman to hold his horses, because I wasn't sure where the pictures were going to be seen. I couldn't risk having my mother flip on the evening news and get the wrong impression. Well, that little reporter assured me his work would be displayed in military newspapers, but definitely not on television or anywhere else back in the States.

So I allowed him to take snapshots of me talking to the sergeant from Baltimore, whose right hand was covered with bulky dressing and was held straight up in the air by a piece of hospital apparatus.

Don't you know that Mother saw that picture! She was in the kitchen making dinner and had pushed the television to the family room door in order to see the six o'clock news.

And there I was, in all my glory, helping a poor soldier who'd been ambushed by North Koreans. Nobody told my mom that her child was going to a place where shooting was taking place, so Mother immediately set about getting Clara Mae out of the Army and safely back home. She made Daddy take her to a Red Cross office and fired off a letter to my commanding officer, a colonel in the Medical Corps.

The colonel called me into his office and directed me to the Red Cross so that I could call home. I assured Mother everything was fine, and she was okay after that. I could have killed that reporter, though.

Three months before my tour of duty in Korea ended, I got a 'Dear Lieutenant' letter from the surgeon general's office of the Army Nurse Corps. Basically, the letter wanted to know if I had any interest in becoming a nurse recruiter when I got back to the States.

Well, recruiting nurses was the furthest thing from my mind, but I didn't share that with anyone. It was suggested that I chat with Major Ann. B. Cost, who was a nurse with some recruiting experience.

She turned out to be a very wise woman.

"Lieutenant Leach, do you want to go on recruiting duty?" she asked me point-blank.

"No ma'am."

"And why is that?"

"Because what I'd really like to do is teach. I'd like to go down to Fort Sam Houston and teach in the medical training center."

Maj. Cost smiled, impressed that I'd already mapped out my post-Korea career.

"Let me give you a little piece of advice, Lieutenant. When you turn down something the Army offers you, always come up with a counter offer. What else would you like to do?"

"I'd like to go back to school to get my master's degree."

"Well, put that in your letter, too. Might as well get two assignments here and tell them what your future is. If you look like you want to stay in the Army, it's more likely that they'll want to keep you and give you what you want."

Maj. Cost didn't know me from Adam's house cat when I wandered down to her hootch that day. But she gladly extended herself to me, and her read of the situation was on the money.

I dashed off a letter to Washington and got one back saying that I'd been selected to attend the career course at Ft. Sam Houston, to be followed by a teaching assignment there. I would then be under consideration to attend graduate school afterward.

That letter represented a turning point of sorts. It was a tacit agreement on my part that the Army was going to be my career.

When I finally boarded a civilian jetliner to leave the Republic of Korea in the winter of 1965, I was filled with regret, yet thrilled about seeing family members I hadn't seen for over a year.

I really liked Korea, I liked the people and I felt like the work I had been doing made a difference in people's lives. Those were twelve months well spent.

My flight back to the States landed in San Francisco. From there, I caught a jet to JFK in New York and then a bus to Newark. I spent about three days with Bettie and Moses, and had a helluva time getting my biorhythms off Korean time and back to U.S. time.

I made it back to Willow Springs bearing gifts, including a fifth of Old GranD-Dad that I gave to my father. That same bottle of bourbon was in the house 12 years later when Daddy died, because he wasn't much of a drinker.

After not seeing me for seventeen months, Daddy still refused to hug me, even though he was tickled to death to see me. Ignoring him, as usual, I wrapped him up in a big hug and dropped one on Mother, too.

No matter how old you get, it always feels good to return home to Mom and Dad.

Daddy had a new car by then, a Ford, and I asked to drive it. I was zooming along one of Willow Springs' country roads in it and, right after Daddy admonished me to slow down, blue lights appeared in the rearview mirror!

I admitted to the cop that I may have been going a little fast, and told him that I had just gotten back from Korea, so I wasn't quite used to driving.

"Welcome home, Lieutenant," he said cheerfully. But you need to slow down a little bit now!" I escaped with a warning on that deal.

That cop gave me some good advice as far as driving was concerned. However, from a career standpoint, I was itching to head down to Ft. Sam Houston and jam the pedal to the metal.

Chapter XII

Just Zip Your Lip!

I was one of only three lieutenants in the Army Nurse Corps advanced course, held at Ft. Sam Houston in San Antonio, Texas. Slightly more than forty officers were in that class, and most of them were senior captains and majors. I'm not sure why I was selected but whatever the reason, I was overjoyed to be there.

The advanced course was for officers who'd indicated they were going to make the Army their career, and the course director was a lieutenant colonel named Lillian Dunlap. She would become my guardian angel and mentor of mentors.

Even though I was on active duty, I was still officially as a member of the U.S. Army Reserve. In those days, an officer had to apply to join the Regular Army.

Lt. Col. Dunlap told me that I needed to march myself over to Ft. Sam's personnel office and immediately apply to join the regular Army. It was imperative that I send a signal I was serious about making the military my home, she said.

"I'm not saying you've got to go over there and say, 'All right, I'm going to do twenty years,'" Dunlap said to me in her office. "But you have to look like you're going to do it." This savvy career Army nurse took an interest in me almost as soon as we met.

I followed her recommendation and signed up for the regular Army. Doing so meant I had to go through a three-year probationary period. I also had to raise my hand and swear to "support and defend" all over again.

After living in harmony with black and white soldiers in Korea, it was disgusting to encounter Jim Crow once again back home in San Antonio. It was 1964 and the Army and the Air Force–which had six installations in the area–were putting pressure on San Antonio's city government to end housing discrimination.

Both branches of the military had a lot of single members

who needed housing. The Army and the Air Force basically told San Antonio that if things didn't change, then all off-post housing would be deemed off-limits to all military personnel.

Given that those two branches of the military dumped so much money into San Antonio's economy, the city really had no choice but to knuckle under and do away with housing discrimination. The episode represented another example, and I can't stress this enough, of the military being ahead of the rest of the country in the fight for equality.

Aside from the historical ramifications of the military's showdown with San Antonio, I was monitoring that situation closely because I had living quarters on Ft. Sam Houston, and would soon have to move off base.

Ft. Sam was listed as my temporary duty assignment and on-post housing was for soldiers who were permanent-party.

Someone informed me that another nurse who was in my course, and who claimed we had worked together at Ft. Dix, had a two-bedroom apartment on base and was looking for a roommate.

Naturally I was curious and asked what her name was. Turned out she was a sister who had worked in the newborn nursery at Walson Army Hospital. I knew who she was, but I didn't know her well because she worked a permanent nights schedule. But I figured, what the heck–I should be able to live with her.

So I moved in with Robbie, and it was evident after a week that we had very different ways of dealing with the world. For one thing, we had been warned that the six-month advanced course was intense and that we both needed to do quite a bit of studying to pass.

Well, I took that warning seriously and started cramming as soon as I got in the door of our apartment. Robbie, on the other hand, would come in and immediately hit the bottle, which left her in no shape for hitting any books.

It's one thing if you want to get well lubricated and fall into an abyss by yourself, but Robbie seemed to want to pull me down with her. She usually got home before I did and by the time I got there, Nat King Cole or Miles Davis would be playing on the box LOUD! Plus, Robbie was a mean drunk, so when I'd ask her to lower the volume to reasonable levels, that invariably started a fight.

The upshot of all this was, I would usually get home and

change into civilian clothes, then leave my apartment to study with Scottie, a captain who took the advanced course seriously like I did.

We got our first test results three weeks into the course. I got a very good grade, but I gathered that Robbie didn't do real well. My class had a busybody in it, a captain who was a self-identified leader. He determined that since I lived with Robbie, I should make it my mission to help improve her grades.

I was aloof to this suggestion, because Robbie and I were both grown women capable of setting priorities. Why did I have to assume responsibility for her education? I had also offered her the opportunity to study with me and she had declined. I meditated on the subject and it continued to trouble me, so I made an appointment to see Lt. Col. Dunlap.

I felt at ease in her presence despite the silver lieutenant colonel's oak leaf on her collar, and told her I understood that my roommate wasn't doing real well in the course.

"No, actually she isn't at present."

I related that a classmate who outranked me said it was my duty to help Robbie to get better grades. "I think we have very different study habits," I told Lt. Col. Dunlap. "I get together with another classmate and we go over our material every night."

"On the other hand, your roommate comes in from her full day and decides that she needs to have two or three drinks before getting down to studying?"

"Ma'am, how did you know that?"

"Lieutenant, I've lived a couple of days," she said drolly. "Let me tell you something right here and now. If you flunk out of this course because you are trying to help Robbie pass, I will see to it that you never get any place in the Army. The only person you are responsible for in this course is you."

This was relayed firmly but kindly.

"I'll tell you now," Lt. Col. Dunlap continued, "you just zip your lip and get your job done. And your job right now is to pass this course successfully. And I'll get you where you think your talent can carry you."

Like that, I had become Lt. Col. Dunlap's protégé. I often hear African-American officers and business executives speak of how difficult it is to encounter individuals who'll mentor them during their careers.

I was extraordinarily fortunate in that regard. I didn't even know enough to be looking for a mentor at Ft. Sam Houston and Lt. Col. Lillian Dunlap just fell into my lap.

Along with Lt. Col. Dunlap's capacity for nurturing, she had a hard-nosed side. That came to the fore when she released Robbie from the course, along with several other officers who weren't performing well academically. Poor, tormented Robbie was caught in a downhill spiral she couldn't reverse and was killed in a brawl a few years afterward.

I never did get close enough to understand the source of her demons, and I was sorry to see her leave the program. She was a nice person until she started hitting the juice. But like life, advancing in the military is about survival of the fittest. It was hardly as though I prevented Robbie from studying.

Humiliated by her release from the program, she quickly vacated the apartment we shared. I returned from class one day and her jazz records and other stuff had just disappeared. One part of me was relieved, because I could now concentrate on keeping my head above water without simultaneously acting as Robbie's savior.

On the other hand, sometimes I felt kind of sad knocking around that quiet San Antonio two-bedroom apartment by myself. Even though it wasn't my fault, I couldn't help wonder if I could have done more to help Robbie battle her monsters.

Not too long after she left, I received a message that I needed to go down to the medical training center during one of my class breaks to have a talk with a major, who was the assistant chief of the nursing science branch. Baffled, I entered her office, saluted and was told to have a seat. The major turned out to be one tough cookie.

She wanted to know why a first lieutenant who hadn't been in the military that long should teach medical trainees at Ft. Sam Houston. Her demeanor indicated that if my response wasn't compelling, I wasn't getting to teach.

Apparently it wasn't, because she informed me that once the advanced course was over, I wasn't going to be an instructor.

You know, it wasn't as though I was devastated by her decision. I was young, hadn't been in the Army all that long and being able to teach had been a long shot, anyway. I was thrilled to be one of a handful of lieutenants in the advanced course, so I looked at myself as being ahead of the curve.

Unknown to me, I was entering the Divine Intervention phase of my career, because a few days after my tête-à-tête with

My mother, Caretha Sapp Leach, with four of her 13 grandchildren. Mother was confined to a wheelchair in her latter years with rheumatoid arthritis and poor circulation in her legs. —**Photo from Personal Collection.**

My father, Otha Leach, is shown here in a photo from his driver's license. Daddy was never fond of taking pictures.—**Photo from Personal Collection.**

My siblings and me after Daddy's funeral in 1976. Front row, left to right: James William, Aaron Otha Lee, Raymond Luke, Charles Edward. Back row, left to right: Clara Mae, Doretha, Rosa Lee, Bettie Bell, Shirley Ann and Mary Elizabeth.

After our parents died, we decided to reunite each year on other occasions and we continue that practice till now.—**Photo from Personal Collection.**

Mother and me in front of our farm house when I returned from Korea in 1964.—**Photo from Personal Collection.**

Chatting with Marilyn Quayle, wife of Vice President Quayle, after she participated in rescue operations with the Fort Belvoir and Fairfax County fire departments.
—U.S. Army Photo.

The award for the high game by a female bowler in the tournament was awarded to me by the base commander.
—U.S. Army Photo.

The 1st Amry Bowling Team Champions in 1971 at Fort Knox, KY. I am third from the left. LTC Essie Wilson, another Army Nurse, is standing to my left. The other team members are enlisted women were the real bowlers and permitted us to join them.
—U.S. Army Photo.

Walking the Victory Mile as Senior Marcher for 700 U.S. Army Europe soldiers who participated in the 100-mile, four-day march in Nijmegen, Holland. The march is held each year to commemorate the liberation of the Dutch by the Allies in World War II. The quote and autograph was supplied by Major General Spencer Reid, Commander, 7th Medical Command.—**U.S. Army Photo.**

Making an impromptu speech to the troops in Bosnia in 1998. I was invited by MG Larry Ellis, Ground Commander, to motivate the troops during Women's History Month.
—**U.S. Army Photo.**

Health care personnel in a modern day hospital ward tent in Saudi Arabia in Operation Desert Shield.—**U.S. Army Photo.**

This was a hospital ward tent in the early sixties. I have just finished washing dishes after the noon meal.—**Personal Collection Photo.**

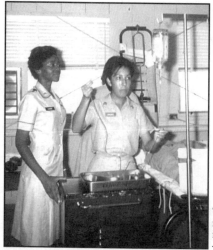

Teaching nursing procedures to Army medics was one of my assignments during the Vietnam era.
—**Personal Collection Photo.**

An Army medical evacuation helicopter in use during Operation Desert Shield. Initially used extensively in Vietnam, helicopters dramatically reduced the time required to get definitive treatment for soldiers wounded in combat and ultimately throughout the healthcare community in the United States.—**U.S. Army Photo.**

On this historical occasion I became the first woman in the Army to earn the Expert Field Medical Badge. Having been a "tomboy" early in my life, I saw it as an opportunity to play outdoors with my "brothers"–there were fifty guys and me who took the test.
—**U.S. Army Photo.**

As representative for the delegation from the United States, I am making a presentation to the Mayor of Grosbeek, Holland, for his hospitality during our march. To my right is Brigadier General Charles E. Canedy, Commander of US Troops at Nijmegen.
—**U.S. Army Photo.**

Presenting the Recruiter Ring Award to a nurse recruiting sergeant in the Recruiting Command. This was the highest award given for outstanding performance in providing the Army strength.
—**U.S. Army Photo.**

Discussing tactics and strategy with a Lebanese officer at the Command and General Staff College. He was a member of Section 17, and I was their leader.
—**Personal Collection Photo.**

Presenting a retirement certificate to Colonel John M. Hudock, the Assistant Chief of the Army Nurse Corps. John also received the Legion of Merit for outstanding service to his country and to soldiers. At the left is his wife, Gaye.
—**U.S. Army Photo.**

Two nurses at my first duty assignment, Walson Army Hospital, Fort Dix, NJ. On the right is Major Mary DeFranco, head nurse of the surgical intensive care unit. On the left is Captain Mary Frances Liberty, who taught me to trust my intuition in providing nursing care to patients.—**Personal Collection Photo.**

A visit by Brigadier General Hazel Johnson-Brown, the Chief of the Army Nurse Corps, in 1980, to the operating room staff at Frankfurt Army Regional Medical Center. General Johnson-Brown, third from the left, was the first African American woman to become a general officer. I was the vice president for nursing at the medical center and Colonel Mary F. McLean, to my right, was the chief nurse of the 7th Medical Command in Europe.—**U.S. Army Photo.**

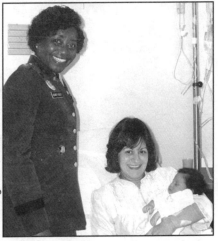

Visiting a new mother and her baby during a staff visit to the William Beaumont Army Medical Center, El Paso, TX.–**U.S. Army Photo.**

The senior nursing students at the Capping ceremony at NC Agricultural and Technical State University in 1960. The seniors are: Front row, left to right, Clara Leach Adams-Ender, Marie Martin, Pauline Brown, and Mable Mitchener. Back row, left to right, Lily Pendarvis Richardson, Sandra Montgomery Hicks, Frances Jamieson, Johnnie Bell Bunch and Betty Witherspoon Barber.—**Personal Collection Photo**

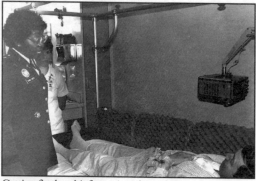

Getting firsthand information about the comfort and effectiveness of new hospital equipment from the best source–the patient who was using it.—**U.S. Army Photo.**

Greeting Senator Daniel K. Inouye, who was guest speaker at Walter Reed Army Medical Center. A World War II veteran and Medal of Honor winner, Senator Inouye was wounded in action. He is a staunch supporter of military nurses and the entire nursing profession.—**Personal Collection Photo**

To Brigadier General Clara Adams-Ender with best wishes,

Barbara Bush

Being greeted by First Lady Barbara Bush at the White House during Nurses Week in 1990.—**White House Photo.**

Taking the oath as a general officer and Chief of the Army Nurse Corps. This was truly a happy day for me because it represented the greatest triumph in my life and career.—**Rudi Williams/ American Forces Information Service.**

A gathering of the former Army Nurse Corps chiefs and the current staff in 1989. From left to right, Colonel Mildred Irene Clark, former chief, Lt. Col. Wilfredo Nieves, Army Nurse Corps Fellow, I was the chief, Major John Voetsch, my administrative assistant, Colonel Inez Haynes, former chief, Brigadier General Anna Mae Hayes, first woman general officer in the Army and former chief, Brigadier Lillian Dunlap, former chief and a great mentor, Brigadier General Connie L. Slewitzke, former chief and Colonel John M. Hudock, assistant chief. —**U.S. Army Photo.**

Presenting the Order of Military Medical Merit to Brigadier General Dorothy Pocklington. Dot was the first woman general officer in the United States Army Reserve. —**U.S. Army Photo.**

Heinz and I with General Carl Vuono, Chief of Staff of the Army. General Vuono approved my continuation on active duty and assignment as Deputy Commanding General, Military District of Washington and the Commander of Fort Belvoir, VA.—**U.S. Army Photo.**

Heinz and I with my mentor, General Max Thurman, Vice Chief of Staff of the Army. General Thurman became a mentor when I was assigned to the Recruiting Command. —**Personal Collection Photo.**

Since I had had some acting experience in my past, I volunteered to play the part of Raggedy Ann in the Christmas pageant in Korea in 1963.—**Personal Collection Photo.**

On my way to Mass on Sunday morning in Korea. The outfit was bright yellow and I made it in my spare time. In the background is the quonset hut, a tin-covered structure in which we lived.
—**Personal Collection Photo.**

Being serenaded by a German musician in Bavaria. We are both in typical Bavarian attire and the musical instrument is a zither.—**Personal Collection Photo.**

Heinz being congratulated by President Reagan for his successful fundraising efforts.—**Personal Collection Photo.**

Meeting President Reagan during his visit to Walter Reed Army Medical Center in 1985. I was vice president for nursing at the medical center at that time. To my left is Major General Lewis A. Mologne, commander of the medical center.
—**U.S. Army Photo.**

Posing in this photograph with Bishop Desmond Tutu from South Africa during one of his early visits to the United States.—**Personal Collection Photo.**

Meeting with Dr. Beverly Malone, president of the American Nurses Association, during its annual convention. A military nursing section was established in the ANA to serve the interests of military nurses.
—**Personal Collection Photo.**

Showing my appreciation to President General Wayne Blair of the National Daughters of the American Revolution in 1992. Each year, the Daughters present the Army Nurse Officer of the Year Award to an outstanding nurse officer.
—**Personal Collection Photo.**

Heinz and I at our wedding dinner in 1981. We met at a meeting of German-American health care professionals in Frankfurt, Germany. Heinz is a retired dentist and orthodontist.
—**Personal Collection Photo.**

Heinz and my best friend, Dr. Joyce G. Bowles. Joyce came to Waukegan, IL to witness our wedding vows.
—**Personal Collection Photo.**

The special couple with us is Rear Admiral Ben and Jean Hacker. Admiral Hacker was the Commander of the Military Enlisted Processing Command at Fort Sheridan, IL. He and Jean gave us a wedding reception on twelve hours' notice. They are still special to us.—**Personal Collection Photo.**

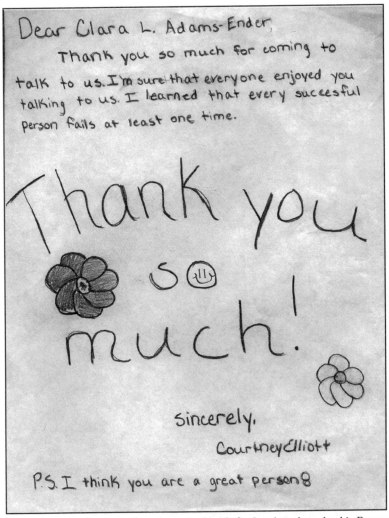

Dear Clara L. Adams-Ender,

Thank you so much for coming to talk to us. I'm sure that everyone enjoyed you talking to us. I learned that every successful person fails at least one time.

Thank you so ☺ much!

sincerely,
Courtney Elliott

P.S. I think you are a great person 😊

This message was sent to me by a nine-year old girl after I spoke at her school in Baumholder, Germany.—**Personal Collection Correspondence.**

Retirement day with Heinz at Fort Belvoir, VA, on August 31, 1993.—**U.S. Army Photo.**

the major, I was summoned to an administrative office at Ft. Sam Houston to take a phone call. The person on the line was a female lieutenant colonel from The Surgeon General's office in Washington, D.C.!

I unconsciously stiffened.

She asked if I had interviewed with the nurse major about teaching at Ft. Sam Houston. When I replied yes, I was asked how the interview went.

"Ma'am, the major was of the opinion I didn't have enough experience or education to teach at Ft. Sam Houston."

"Oh, really? Don't worry about that, we'll take care of everything."

Who were we? And how did this lieutenant colonel know what was going on in my little world? More to the point, why did she care?

The person behind all the intrigue turned out to be Colonel Mildred Irene Clark, the chief of the Army Nurse Corps. The Army's top nurse!

Like me, Col. Clark was a North Carolina native. Somehow the word had filtered back to her that I'd been denied an opportunity to teach at the medical training center. Well, Col. Clark said there was no way a fellow Tar Heel, who was an outstanding performer, was going to be blocked from doing anything.

Not long afterward, I got a call from Maj. Bailey, who simply said, "I understand you're going to be joining us." She didn't ask, but she was probably dying to know where my pull came from. That made two of us.

My good fortune continued when I got promoted to captain before the advanced course was over. I noticed that after I pinned those silver 'railroad tracks' to my collar, people's expectations of me seemed to rise immediately.

I had to switch up my way of behaving somewhat after I made captain. For one thing, I had a vaguely arrogant and cocky persona that was more likely to be accepted coming from an eager beaver lieutenant than from a captain.

An example of this occurred shortly before I was promoted. I was standing behind a podium at Ft. Sam Houston and giving a report before some of my advanced course colleagues. I had been discussing a new nursing technique some of my colleagues were skeptical of, simply because they'd never tried it themselves.

In a voice loud enough to be picked up by the microphone, I

said: "Oh, you all are kind of stuck in the way things used to be." That's precisely the kind of impertinent comment you don't hear captains making. At least not smart ones.

I immediately apologized for my off-the-cuff observation, but fortunately the instructor teaching that class happened to agree with me. When I think about some of the things I did as a lieutenant, I could just hide my face sometimes.

From the time I put on my captain bars, I made it a point to weigh my words carefully before opening my mouth. I also plunged headlong into the social responsibilities that commissioned officers have to deal with.

Officers have to learn the social graces and the traditions of the military, which is why Lt. Col. Dunlap was always prodding me to participate in tea ceremonies and things of that nature. She snapped a picture of me at one of those parties, smiling with my hair all brushed to the side as I poured tea.

Lil Dunlap must have been a blackmail artist in another life, because she was always walking around with her little camera during social affairs, popping flashbulbs in folk's faces.

When I got promoted to general, she dug out a picture of me as a lieutenant, grinning and smoking a nasty-looking cigarette. She had that shot blown up to about sixteen by twenty inches and displayed it so people could see how far I had come. Dirty dog!

My mother had warned me years ago to watch how I interacted with a man and the woman he sleeps with. Consequently, I made it perfectly clear at military functions that I didn't come looking for anybody's husband.

Of course there was never a problem when it came to the wives of officers who held the rank of major and above. Whenever I spotted some of the others, I unobtrusively made my way to the other side of the room. A few of them were naturally suspicious of single, female officers. We just had to be out on the prowl, looking to snap up unsuspecting, married officers, I guess. Give me a break!

When I wasn't attending social functions, I'd go into San Antonio for dinner. I love Mexican food, and San Antonio is a great place to indulge that appetite. There were also a lot of craft fairs in town, and I took in a fair number of those, too.

I traveled around San Antonio in a brand new, white Chevrolet Chevelle with blue interior for which I plunked down the princely sum of $3,600. That Chevy was my reward for years of disciplined, frugal living. See, from the time I entered the military, I had been putting younger siblings through college by myself.

Now that I was earning a captain's salary, I finally had an extra dollar or two to spend on Clara.

But I never lost sight of my immediate goal, which was to do well in the Army Nurse Corps advanced course. When it came to a close, I was ranked sixth out of forty students. I was a little disappointed about not finishing in the top tenth, but I had proven that I deserved to be in the course and deserved to be a nursing instructor afterward.

After graduation, I took a few weeks off and traveled home to Willow Springs before going to my new assignment at Ft. Sam Houston's medical training center.

I was twenty-six years old, a new Army captain with a new Chevelle and no romantic entanglements to speak of. And all of those things were okay with me. I was humming!

✻   ✻   ✻   ✻   ✻   ✻   ✻

Just outside Ft. Sam Houston's rear gate was a community of duplexes and single-family homes comprised mostly of African-American enlisted personnel from the Army and the Air Force.

That's where I moved to after returning from Willow Springs. I wanted a place I could reach quickly once my work day ended. Plus housing in that enclave was relatively inexpensive, because mostly enlisted folks lived there.

The residents made quite a fuss over me, a young, black Army captain who had moved into their midst.

I moved into 2010 Carson Street, a small house beside one occupied by Air Force Sergeant Bobby Scales, his wife, Fannie, and their five children. All told, the families I befriended in that community had a total of sixteen kids, and they'd all come over to my place for spaghetti dinner every Wednesday night. There were seven boys and nine girls who ranged in age from four to about nine.

Every now and then, Miss Clara, as they called me, would babysit on Saturday nights, or pack a bunch of them in my Chevelle and haul them to a movie.

Naturally the parents loved this. But I was getting something out of it too, because having all those kids around made San Antonio feel like Willow Springs Southwest.

In addition, I wasn't exempt from maternal yearnings every now and then. When you ride herd on sixteen kids once a week, that not only satisfies your motherly instinct, it stomps it into oblivion.

During times when I wanted the companionship of adults over little folks with snotty noses, I'd get together with the parents and play pinochle. My little community outside the gates of Ft. Sam Houston kept me feeling grounded, regardless of what was happening with my professional life.

As far as that realm was concerned, I had to do some practice teaching before greeting my first class of fledgling Army medics. I was to teach basic nursing procedures, which had to do with changing dressings on wounds and dealing with infectious diseases. It was basic, but important information to be grasped by soldiers who were going to be medics and take care of sick people.

I loved teaching, because in some ways it reminded me of getting onstage, which was my thing. Just like lawyers, the best teachers are showmen and showwomen.

When my first class arrived, I was eager to get going. I stood on a platform in the middle of a classroom, talking about nursing techniques and procedures. Then I'd lead a practical exercise where the medical corpsmen would do what I'd just talked about. One day I got a rude awakening from one of the trainees. I was teaching venipuncture technique, i.e., how to put a needle into a vein and draw blood. This particular trainee was very skilled, and I knew he had had some prior experience. I asked him where he had learned the technique. Surprisingly, he immediately replied that he had learned the technique by giving intravenous drugs to junkies on the streets of Chicago. I'll bet that troop survived well!

It was a tremendous experience, and we instructors threw an awful lot of knowledge at those young soldiers in the course of eight weeks. Medics assigned to infantry units had to take a second course that lasted twelve weeks and was a bit more involved.

For six months I did my part to make sure that our forces in Vietnam got a steady stream of fresh, well-trained Army medics. I often wonder how many of those boys I trained never returned home.

In the meantime, a nurse who taught in one of Ft. Sam Houston's most coveted areas, the ward training section, decided to get married and abruptly resigned from the military. I was selected to be her replacement.

Fortunately I was able to get into the flow of things fairly quickly and continued to earn outstanding performance evaluations. When I look back on Ft. Sam Houston, it was where my career really shifted into high gear.

Unfortunately, I also experienced some rather low times while stationed there.

* * * * * * * *

When it comes to making friends, the main things that draw me to people are integrity and strength of character. Sexual orientation, skin color, gender—all that stuff is secondary.

While I was a captain at Ft. Sam Houston, I tended to hang out with other captains. Obviously, we had a lot in common in terms of responsibility, career aspirations, and the like. One of my closest buddies was another nurse, Capt. Peter Fiaschi, who was also teaching at the medical training center. He was about six-foot-four, handsome, funny and a very nice person.

I've never had anything other than platonic relationships with fellow Army officers, and Peter was no exception. We used to leave the base to have lunch together in San Antonio quite a bit. Just two kindred spirits enjoying each other's company.

One day I was called into the office of the Training Center's chief nurse, a lieutenant colonel. She wanted to talk to me about my relationship with Peter.

"I don't know if you're aware of this, but I understand that you and Capt. Fiaschi hang around together an awful lot," she said. Her topic of conversation was already out of bounds, as far as I was concerned, but I sat quietly and listened. I was curious to see how big a hole her mouth would dig.

"It's probably not a great idea for the two of you to be seen together," she said, shoveling furiously. "I don't know if you can appreciate the significance of appearances in a town like San Antonio."

Just when I thought things couldn't get any stranger, they did.

"Don't tell Peter that I said any of this to you, okay? But I just think the two of you ought to act more distant in terms of how you behave, because there are people around that may not like that too much."

Yeah, there were people around all right, and I was sitting in front of one of the main ones. "Yes ma'am, thank you very much."

Shaking my head as I exited her office, I went back to the ward training section and taught another class. But as I was leaving the base that night, the devil whispered: 'How come you're not talking to Peter?'

So I drove across San Antonio to the side of town where Peter lived. I hopped from my car, rapped on his front door and he opened it with a sheepish expression. "Bet I know why you're here," he said quietly.

"What do you mean, you know why I'm here?

"They talked to you too, huh?"

The chief nurse had already contacted Peter about his relationship with that female Negro officer he was being seen around town with so much. He had been instructed not to say anything to me about the conversation.

The two of us put our heads together and came to the conclusion that others' values were being imposed upon us with which we did not agree.

Rather than avoid each other as we'd been instructed, we decided to put on a show.

"Since we don't know who's objecting to this whole situation, let's see if we can smoke them out!" Peter said defiantly. I agreed.

Not only did we keep going to lunch together, we sat a bit closer than usual. Another captain, who was clued into our rebellion, made a point of asking Peter and me things like: "What are you two lovely people going to be doing this evening?"

We never heard another word from anybody about our relationship.

After I'd been at the ward training center for about a year, the major who was the assistant chief of the branch, left to take another assignment. She was replaced by another major who soon became the bane of my existence.

Not too long afterward, the chief nurse of the branch had to take leave because of a medical problem, leaving the new major in charge. She sauntered into the ward training section one day and blithely informed me that I didn't have enough experience to work there. Mind you, I had been there dealing with this job quite well for twelve months.

"Ma'am, well, you're in charge here," I answered calmly. "You're free to do what you want to do. But I've been working here for a number of months now, and I think my performance has been satisfactory."

But the major had already made up her mind on the matter. I had to go because she wanted to replace me with one of her cronies.

So she went to the commander of the medical training center, a full colonel, and asked if she could replace me with her friend. The request was denied, because I had been doing a bang-up job.

Not to be denied, the major wrote a report saying that a sergeant and I had been stealing sheets, pillowcase, paper towels and other penny ante items from the ward training section. Taking those accusations to the colonel, she claimed they were the reasons she wanted me removed from my job.

As if that weren't bad enough, she gave me an unsatisfactory rating on my officer evaluation report. Despite the fact that two higher-ranking officers—one of them the medical center's commander—wrote glowing things about me!

A wise Army officer once told me that career Army officers typically encounter two or three crises with the potential to derail their careers. I was facing my first.

It's really instructive to see who rallies behind you when your fortunes seem to be lowest.

I stopped by the San Antonio home of Essie, a black Army major, who was also a nursing instructor at the medical training center. After looking over the report written by the hostile major, Essie advised me to keep a super-detailed paper trail.

A friend and captain was livid when I told him what had happened. "Clara, if you need a witness, I'll tell about some of the things that I've heard her say about people, including you," he said. "She's a prejudiced woman who was really angry when you weren't replaced."

Lt. Col. Lillian Dunlap, who was about to be promoted to full colonel and now worked in the Army Nurse Corps' headquarters in Washington, hinted that my situation was going to be resolved quickly. "You just sit tight," she advised me over the phone. "Don't you do a thing."

I was particularly inspired by an Air Force sergeant who didn't even work at Ft. Sam Houston. He was stationed at nearby Randolph Air Force Base, had served with my brother, Ray, and was familiar with military personnel reports. When I showed him my overall record, including the report written by that evil major, my Air Force friend had one thing to say: "Clara, you're going to be a major before the year is out!"

In the meantime, I still had to interact with the antagonistic major responsible for my predicament. She never said a word to me about the theft accusations or that ridiculous evaluation she wrote, but we both knew what was going on.

I'm usually a jovial and vivacious person, but I wasn't around that major. We had a job to do and I got on with it while keeping our interaction to an absolute minimum.

Even though I had vowed to put a lid on my flip lip after getting promoted to captain, I couldn't resist getting off a zinger regarding that major's burning desire to get promoted. She went around telling anyone who would listen that she was going to be a lieutenant colonel soon.

One day I bought a copy of the Army Times with the officer promotion list in it. And her name wasn't there. That morning, as I was picking up my mail, I saw my nemesis.

"Major, I saw the list for promotion to lieutenant colonel–did you know your name wasn't on it?"

If looks could kill, my life would have ebbed out of my body at Ft. Sam Houston, at the tender age of 28. Let me tell you something… it is always good to grow up. As my flip comment indicated, I still had a little to do. That comment was definitely uncalled-for and I regretted making it and apologized for my actions.

Ultimately, I was exonerated of the false charges that had been leveled against me, and the major's negative rating was erased from my record. She was "invited to leave the Army" as they say in military parlance. Which was fitting, because individuals like her really have no business being in the Armed Forces.

That whole business was a dreary episode in my military career. But it was a useful warning regarding how low some people would stoop to realize their petty, selfish objectives.

A highlight of my stay at Ft. Sam Houston was an achievement no female soldier had ever pulled off. I managed to earn the Expert Field Medical Badge, the non-combat equivalent of the Expert Infantry Badge.

First of all, I didn't even have to try out for the Expert Field Medical Badge, because there was a sexist assumption that women didn't have the necessary physical tools to complete the test. Female soldiers bought into that reasoning and most didn't even try, but I figured I'd rock the boat a little bit. What I really saw was an opportunity to be a tomboy again and play outside in the fields with my brothers.

For starters, I had to complete a forced march with a heavy field pack on my back. Men were required to march for twelve miles, while women only had to do eight. That struck me as patronizing weaker-sex foolishness, so I did twelve miles just like the men. My legs were on fire and my back was aching by the time I finished, but I completed that section of the test in two hours and thirty minutes, five minutes faster than the best man in the field.

Then there were tests that gauged my proficiency in areas such as physical combat, use of a compass during night and day operations and map reading. There were also written examinations that assessed technical skill in the performance of field medical operations. I had to know the correct procedures to help soldiers who were victims of chemical, nuclear or biological warfare, for example.

I didn't have some feminist agenda in mind when I volunteered to compete for the Expert Field Medical Badge. I went after the badge because the tests were challenging and because I thought I could handle them. For me, it was mostly an opportunity to play in the fields with my brothers again and be a tomboy. If people wanted to infer anything from my performance about the equality of the sexes, that was fine, too.

Before 1967 came to a close, I found myself scrutinizing another officer promotion list in the Army Times. This time, I was looking for my own name.

Most officers up for promotion fall within what's called a "primary zone," a list of officers who have spent the required amount of time in grade and in service.

Below the primary zone can often be found the names of officers who haven't spent a lot of time in grade, but are considered promotable because they have sterling records and outstanding potential for future service. When an officer appears on a promotion list "below the zone," that's the sign of an up-and-comer.

Appearing below the zone for promotion from captain to major in late 1967 was one Capt. Clara M. Leach. The gold oak leaf insignia of an Army major was pinned on my uniform in

February, 1968.

I had only been in the Army seven years and I was already a major! I kept thinking it must be a dream. I'd awaken in the morning and greet myself with a cheerful, 'Good morning, Major Leach!" Then I'd trot to the closet to make sure those gold leaves were still on my uniform.

Military folks start taking you very seriously once you become a major. Even if you happen to be one who's only 28.

I clearly began fast-tracking at Ft. Sam Houston, a place that showed me there's no substitute for hard work, integrity and an unshakable belief in God. I'm convinced that's what girded me against the biases, politics and dirty tricks my adversaries unleashed.

Wiser and tougher by the time fall of 1967 rolled around, I headed into an exciting, new phase of my military career—full-time college student working toward a master's degree.

Chapter XIII

Disillusionment, Matrimony

You haven't really experienced winter until you've felt the frigid embrace of a Minnesota gale in mid-January.

The Gopher State is where I went to study for my Master of Science degree in nursing, specifically the University of Minnesota in Minneapolis.

I drove there from Texas in 1967. In some ways, Minneapolis was every bit as alien to me as Korea was. For starters, in Minnesota, brushes with African Americans were noteworthy enough to merit a notation on the calendar!

That may be a bit of an exaggeration, but not much. Minnesota's minority population was around 3 percent when I arrived there. Trust me when I tell you the University of Minnesota, as well as Minneapolis, was almost lily-white.

That point was painfully driven home during the wedding of a woman I befriended in school. Dottie was a secretary at the University of Minnesota's School of Nursing, and we combined forces to make her an elaborate wedding dress that would have cost $6,000 if she had bought it in a store. We sewed about 1,200 seed pearls onto that thing, which was made out of beautiful peau de soie material.

I was the only black face in the church when Dottie got married. Her relatives were gracious Midwesterners, with the exception of Dottie's grandmother, who refused to shake my hand when we were introduced.

I was the first African American she had ever come face to face with, and that old woman had some unflattering ideas about who I was and what I was about, based on what she had seen on television.

"I know that people like you carry guns and shoot people," she told me warily, declining to extend her hand.

"I've never carried a gun or shot anybody," I quietly replied, letting my hand fall to my side. "But I wish you well. I will tell you, though, that this is neither the time nor place to discuss this, because it's your granddaughter's wedding day."

That old lady's snub hurt worse than an actual slap. Dottie was mortified when she found out what happened, and so was Mother when I told her. But that's what happens when people are ignorant and rely on stereotypes to form opinions about people they've never met.

The transition from Ft. Sam Houston to the University of Minnesota was memorable in a number of ways. I had traded in an environment that was pro-military twenty-four hours a day for an academic setting where the Armed Forces were generally reviled. It seemed the Vietnam War was more unpopular on Minnesota's campus with each passing day.

A week seldom went by without some sort of anti-Vietnam or anti-military demonstration taking place. That kind of hit me where I lived, because the Army was my life at that time. So I'd go to rallies at the student union and debate the protest leaders. That wasn't the only place–I argued with them in coffee shops, classrooms and anywhere else they wanted to discuss the war.

Most people didn't know I was an Army major, because I had an off-campus apartment and because I floated around campus wearing civvies. In 1967, few people would have pegged a twenty-something black female wearing colorful bellbottoms to be a high-ranking military officer.

Due to the ferocity of many college anti-war protests, the Department of Defense was telling military personnel not to wear their uniforms on college campuses during the late 1960s.

I developed a fascinating friendship with a fellow named Carl, who worked in the University's library and was one of the most vehement anti-war protesters around. Since I spent a lot of time studying in the library, Carl became my official Vietnam War debate opponent.

We argued about that conflict all the time. My favorite question to Carl was: "How can you be so anti-military, Carl, without really knowing that much about the military?"

Like a lot of civilians, Carl mistakenly thought that everybody in the Army was 100 percent behind this country's Southeast Asia policy. That simply wasn't the case. There was as much controversy and disagreement inside the Army as there was in the civilian world.

The big difference was, when it came time to do something, we saluted and did what had to be done. Everybody thinks the military is incredibly monolithic and its members unquestioningly do whatever they're told to do.

In reality, military folks are allowed to raise issues all the time. But when it's time to take action, we come together and get behind the mission, whatever it happens to be.

We may not like the mission or even agree with it, but we carry out our orders.

Carl was like many Americans, in that he had a CBS News understanding of the Vietnam conflict. That is to say, it's impossible to get your arms around a complex conflict thousands of miles away by watching five minutes of news coverage.

Carl didn't want to hear that, naturally. He argued he knew enough to sense that what we were doing in Southeast Asia was morally wrong.

I disagreed, particularly since I was writing letters to colleagues who were actually in Vietnam. Defending this country's Vietnam policy was my small way of doing something for the troops who were laying everything on the line for the folks back home.

An anesthesiologist I'd met at Ft. Sam Houston went to `Nam and we corresponded from time to time. He wrote one time to ask how graduate school was going, and I made the mistake of replying that graduate school was hell.

He replied that if I really wanted to understand hell, I should come to Vietnam. He wrote a number of long, descriptive letters about the confusion and mismanagement he observed over there.

As time went on, I began to secretly wonder if the protesters weren't right. I also began to wonder if I wanted to stay in the Army.

When I first arrived at the University of Minnesota, I badly wanted to go to Vietnam myself. What better way to test my nursing and leadership skills? That ambition turned to ashes during an edgy phone call with Lillian Dunlap, who was still in Washington and was now a full colonel.

I was adamant about going to Southeast Asia, but Lil broke the news that my next assignment would be Walter Reed Army Medical Center, in Washington, D.C. I was to be an instructor in Walter Reed's nursing school.

A damned war was raging in Asia and my colleagues were getting killed and wounded while I sat by in the States. What kind of garbage was that! What's an Army nurse supposed to do if not to help soldiers in combat?

"Ma'am, I don't mean to sound boastful here," I said, pleading my case. "But when it comes to hands-on nursing skills, I think I'm one of the best the Army has to offer. I should be in Vietnam where I can help heal combat soldiers."

Lillian was in no mood for petulance that day, regardless of how well-intentioned.

"No, Clara, actually where you're needed is in Washington. You are a fine nurse and I need you to produce equally competent nurses who can help those troops over there. That's where you're needed and that's where you're going."

And that was that. I was so angry when I set that phone receiver down that I burst into tears. That marked the third time I'd been turned down for an assignment in Vietnam! For about the next two hours or so, I ranted and raved inside my apartment, since there was no roommate to stare at me like I was crazy.

Once that was out of my system, I got with the program. Because, really, it's just a total waste of time and energy to rail against something you can't change. Like your father deciding you're going to major in nursing if he's going to foot your college bills. You either get with the program or pursue other options.

Well, I wasn't going to leave the Army, so I vented for a bit and got on with my life.

Instead of helping U.S. servicemen fight the Viet Cong, I stayed in Minnesota and battled Old Man Winter.

I'll never forget the day when the wind chill was fifty degrees below zero and I decided to walk my little skinny behind from the campus to my apartment, which was at least a mile away. When I first went outside it didn't feel too cold, so I figured my slacks, long johns and thick socks must be doing the job.

But by the time I got home, my face, hands and feet were tingling like somebody was sticking pins in them. I called a girlfriend and happened to casually mention how I was feeling.

"Get off the phone!" she shouted. "Warm up your hands and face as quickly as you can. Girl, you got frostbite!"

I ran some water over my hands and feet to warm them. I may have been a nurse, but I didn't have firsthand knowledge of what frostbite symptoms felt like.

Whenever it was bitterly cold, folks in Minnesota kept right on going as though it was seventy degrees outside. Although it may have been colder than a witch's tit, I soon learned the

University of Minnesota had no intention of postponing classes.

I had an academic experience at Minnesota's School of Nursing that mortified me–I got a 'D' in physiology, which is unacceptable on the graduate level. I passed the second time around and eventually graduated with honors, but that initial physiology grade was a blow to my ego.

On the other hand, I found anthropology to be absolutely mesmerizing and earned an 'A' there.

Within the University of Minnesota' School of Nursing, there were three master's degree paths that one could follow. They were clinical nursing, community health and nursing education. I concentrated on the last one, because in order to teach in the Army's School of Nursing, I needed a master's degree in nursing, with an emphasis on teaching.

I managed to get a little taste of what nursing education was all about by doing some student teaching one quarter.

I was pretty hard on students in the beginning. I supervised about eight of them at St. Luke's Hospital, a teaching facility in St. Paul. The students came from South Dakota State University and matriculated at St. Luke's Hospital for clinical experiences.

One of my students, Bonnie, just didn't seem to be getting it together one day, so I took her into a hallway for a chat. She related that she was fearful of screwing up, lest I start yelling or looking at her like she was an idiot. I became very sensitive to that behavior.

I learned a lot from teaching those South Dakota State University nursing students about how to talk to students without being offensive. Because I know that I can be offensive sometimes, and that's no lie.

I decided to do my master's thesis on death and dying, specifically, on student attitudes toward death and dying. I compared the attitudes of nursing students, who regularly come in contact with mortality issues, with non-nursing students.

As graduation neared, I had begun to be troubled by the Viet Cong body counts that were coming out of Vietnam. Based on what I was reading and hearing from soldiers actually there, it seemed that our politicians and military leaders were misleading the American people. Those body counts were alleged to be inflated to get public support behind the war, and that struck me as incredibly unethical.

Although I didn't talk about it, I seriously mulled over leaving the military after Walter Reed. I gave a lot of thought to getting a job as a civilian professor.

That's how much the half-truths coming out of Vietnam had disillusioned me.

* * * * * * * * *

When I came home to Willow Springs during Christmas 1968, I contacted an old flame from my high school days, Kelso Adams. We had been talking to each other and dating off and on since eighth grade.

Looking back, I'm hard-pressed to describe the state of our relationship over all those years. I guess you could say we floated along somewhere between romance and strong friendship.

However, during Christmas 1968, Kelso took a sudden interest in defining exactly where we stood. I called him when I got home and he drove by.

"You know, we really need to do something about this relationship," he said to me. I just laughed, because Kelso was so unpredictable. He was always known to have a girlfriend or two floating around, usually some light-skinned gal. Since I was far from a red bone, there was no reason to suspect he had any designs on getting serious.

"We have been messing around for a very long time," Kelso continued, seated in my family's cozy living room. Daddy, Mother and some of my siblings were puttering around us, not really paying Kelso and me much attention. "Either we need to do something with this relationship or let it be. What do you think?"

Not knowing what to think, and not sure where Kelso was taking the conversation, I didn't say anything.

"We said a long time ago that we were going to do something about our relationship and we haven't, so we've got to fix this," he pressed on.

It suddenly dawned on me that he was talking about marriage! The only thing on my mind when I left Minnesota for Christmas break was seeing my family, then finishing school.

"Let me have a little time to think about it," I said after a brief silence. "By June, I should know something."

I figured six months was enough time for Kelso's little pipe dream to disintegrate. If not, at least I would have my master's degree in nursing by then.

When graduation time rolled around in May of 1969, I sat

back and assessed my situation. I was three years ahead of the timeline I'd set for myself for getting promoted in the military, so I had a little time to kill. Why not get married?

Unfortunately, that's literally how much thought I gave to a commitment as significant as marriage. So I rolled through Willow Springs after graduating from Minnesota and told Kelso that, yes, I would be Mrs. Kelso Adams. Maybe Minnesota's frigid weather had affected my brain. Or maybe it was something they were putting in the water up there. Who knows?

Kelso seemed overjoyed, and I have to admit that I felt happy myself. I was 29, had known Kelso most of my life and had a comfort level with him that looked like it would provide a good foundation for matrimony.

And understand this—once I agreed to marriage, I was determined to honor that commitment. I may not have given it a lot of forethought, but I did not take marriage lightly, if that makes any sense.

But I also told Kelso in no uncertain terms that the Army was my career. It was a career that called for me to move about the country, and the world, and that was what I planned to do. He said that he understood and was willing to come along for the ride.

So with my impending nuptials on my mind, I drove my white Chevelle from Willow Springs, up Interstate 95 to report to Walter Reed Army Medical Center, in Washington, DC.

In some ways, being stationed there was like going from one college campus to another, because Walter Reed is a beautiful place. It has flower gardens, shrubs and grass that are always immaculate. The various buildings around the installation are closed off from the rest of the world by an impressive black, wrought iron fence.

On one side of Walter Reed runs 16th Street, a main thoroughfare that separates the base from Rock Creek Park. On the other side is Georgia Avenue, home to many black working-class neighborhoods. After Minnesota, I felt a degree of culture shock after driving along Georgia Avenue and seeing nothing but black folks on both sides of the street.

The day before I was to process into Walter Reed, I figured I'd go visit the place. That way, I'd look like I knew where I was going on my first day.

The Walter Reed Army Institute of Nursing, or WRAIN, no longer exists today, but it used to be a place where the crème de la crème of Army nurses were regularly assigned. It was an honor to be associated with the school and with Walter Reed, which routinely treats presidents and top generals and other dignitaries from all over the world.

Walter Reed is widely viewed as the flagship of healthcare facilities in the Department of Defense.

The Institute of Nursing where I was to teach was considered the West Point of nursing and was the only facility of its kind in the Armed Forces. Faculty members were hand-picked and had to have at least a master's degree, something few nurses possessed in those days. After studying at the nursing school for four years, graduates became nurses as well as commissioned Army officers.

After I processed into Walter Reed, nursing school director Col. Drusilla Poole took me around for a little tour. This was during June 1969, a time when many of the faculty members were on leave prior to the fall session.

The institute was housed in Jane Delano Hall, named after the first superintendent of the Army Nurse Corps. Delano Hall is one of the few buildings within the Armed Forces named after a woman. It was an impressive three-story structure located just off 16th Street.

The lower level housed administrative offices, while classrooms and student living quarters were on the upper floors. I had a desk in the basement in the department associated with adult health nursing, the subject I was to teach.

Most of the administrative personnel in Delano Hall were civilians. One I'll always remember was a nice man named Billy Johnson, who worked in the audiovisual department.

Even though I was an Army major, I dreaded working at Walter Reed, because I knew that generals frequently come to the place and I didn't want to encounter any.

"Lighten up, major. This is a great place to be!" Mr. Johnson would always say. He went out of his way to show me how to operate the state-of-the-art equipment WRAIN had in its possession.

I noticed that not only were a lot of people at Walter Reed, like Billy Johnson, very friendly, but so were black folks I encountered on the streets of Washington. They'd take the trouble to say hello when they ran into you. In that regard at least, Washington is a Southern city.

My sponsor at Walter Reed was Lt. Col. Audre McLoughlin.

She was responsible for showing me around the base and helping me get oriented as a nurse instructor. She also took me to the University of Maryland campus in Baltimore, with which the nursing institute had become affiliated to establish its curriculum and to award degrees.

Naturally before my first week ended, I came in touch with a general, specifically, Maj. Gen. Carl Hughes, a physician who was Walter Reed's commander. He greeted all new officers coming onto the base.

I was pretty uptight prior to seeing him. I'd never reported to a general before–what would he ask? So I mentally catalogued some of the things I thought he might want to know. He turned out to be kind of a stiff and had a full head of mixed gray hair. General Hughes seldom smiled and remained stiff and formal even after I got to know him better.

Our talk went fairly well, because Col. Poole had taken the trouble of giving him some information about my background. Drusilla Poole had taken a liking to me, because she also received her master's degree from the University of Minnesota. Its nursing curriculum was one of the best in the country, so Drusilla figured I must be okay.

She carried the conversation in Gen. Hughes' office that day, for which I gave silent thanks. Sometimes you get places in life just because of the school you attended.

I made the transition to nursing teacher fairly easily. If you can train medics headed to Vietnam at Ft. Sam Houston, you can certainly teach nursing students at Walter Reed. I loved the position and sincerely believed that this was my ultimate calling in nursing.

There were so many memorable experiences in recruiting and teaching nursing students that I can never remember them all. One that I still recall, however, involved Dian Stilwell, the daughter of a four-star general. While in her first two years of general education courses at a university in the Midwest, she kept flunking inorganic chemistry. Even with tutors, she still had problems with the course. It was my job as educational coordinator to monitor her progress so that she kept up with her classmates and transferred to WRAIN on schedule.

Dian's father, General Richard Stilwell, the 6th Army Commander at that time, often traveled to the Pentagon for meetings and briefings. Being concerned about his daughter, he often called to inquire about her progress when he was in town.

During one of his visits, his aide called me in the early morning to schedule an appointment to discuss Dian's status. I had never even met a four-star general before, so I was a bit nervous about this meeting. Nevertheless, I carefully reviewed the records and worked out a schedule for Dian that would allow her to attend summer school to repeat a chemistry course and still arrive at WRAIN with her class on time in the fall.

Because of changes happening at the Pentagon, my meeting with the general was re-scheduled several times during the day. In late afternoon, General Stilwell called me himself. I picked up the phone and there he was on the other end of the line. There wasn't even time to shake in my shoes.

"Adams," he said, "it's late now and in the rush hour traffic, it will take me one and a half hours to get to you. Why don't you go home, get comfortable, eat your dinner and meet me at your office at seven o'clock this evening?"

"Yes, Sir, I can do that," I replied.

As I returned to my office, I stepped off the curb and broke the heel of my left shoe. Finding the local shoe repair shop closed, I sought the Miss Fixit services of the residence counselor at the nurses' dormitory. She was busy at work with the repairs when General Stilwell arrived. Upon observing the situation, he smiled and quipped, "Goddammit, Adams, I didn't come here to see your shoe heels! Let's go down and discuss Dian's problem with chemistry." I led him to my office in my stocking feet! Together, we planned Dian's future of success in passing chemistry and continuing her nursing studies.

Dian cooperated in our well-laid plans, graduated and was commissioned as a lieutenant in the Army Nurse Corps. She and I kept in contact over the years and I was invited to General Stilwell's retirement. When I was promoted to general many years later, a neatly wrapped box with bright red ribbon was delivered to me at Walter Reed. Inside was a black patent leather shoe heel with a single silver star attached. The four-star note read: "Clara, now that you are a general, I hope you can keep your heels on!" Richard Stilwell. He never forgot the event, and I think he sent me the heel to express his gratitude.

*   *   *   *   *   *   *

Kelso and I jumped the broom in Glenarden, Maryland, at the home of Kay and Dan Lanier. Kay was a former Army nurse with whom I had been stationed in Korea. A local minister handled our nuptials, which took place July 12, 1969, the day after my thirtieth birthday. It was a beautiful day with plenty of sunshine, blue skies and a temperature in the 90s.

My parents and about one hundred guests saw me shake so badly that the bouquet I was holding was probably doing the bob and weave. I wore a hot pink chiffon dress with lace. Why pink? Because white is for virginity and I had been through a whole bunch of changes by that time.

My new husband and I got a seventh-floor, three-bedroom apartment in Silver Spring, Maryland, which adjoins the border of Washington. I was into sewing and being domesticated at that point and did up one bedroom in a patriotic red, white and blue theme. The carpet in that apartment was off-white, the curtains were red with white stars, and the bedspread had red, white and blue stars.

Later we moved to another three-bedroom apartment in Takoma Park, Maryland, which is also a suburb of Washington and put Kelso and me closer to our jobs. Our new place was only ten minutes away from Walter Reed, making for a very nice commute.

For about a year and a half, Kelso and I had a nice union, one where we had mutual respect, shared moments of intimacy, passion and fun and worshipped God together on Sundays.

But by January 1971, our relationship was starting to fray around the edges. A lot of the friction stemmed from the fact that my husband had never been in the military and wasn't really at ease around military people.

Like folks in most professions, individuals in the Armed Forces speak in a lingo unique to their profession. That holds particularly true of folks who are in healthcare. You could have listened to some of my Army buddies discuss work and easily missed half of what they were talking about.

That happened around Kelso a lot, and it made him feel like an outsider. I tried to help him understand some of the terminology, but he was convinced it was being done just to exclude him.

A second sensitive area was employment. Kelso was a bricklayer in North Carolina, but couldn't get similar work in the Washington area because he didn't belong to a union. He tried to join, but unions can be cliquish and exclusionary.

I reminded Kelso that he always loved working on cars and

suggested he might want to find work as an auto mechanic. So he attended a local technical school, then got a job working on cars in suburban Washington. That eased our tension somewhat, because a man needs to feel self-sufficient. Plus I figured an auto mechanic could find work wherever I happened to be stationed next.

Some of Kelso's mechanic friends weren't the best of influences on him, however. There was one in particular who didn't respect the sanctity of marriage and was adamant about women having their place, which basically was barefoot, pregnant and shuffling six paces behind their man.

Unfortunately that guy, and some of Kelso's other buddies, started a whispering campaign: 'Man, don't you know a real man doesn't follow a woman around from job to job? You're less than a man if you do that!'

Kelso would relate these conversations to me in a half-joking fashion, but I could tell the underlying message was no joke to him. I reminded him that I intended to move to my next duty station when the time came in a couple of years.

"Are you sure that's what you want to be about?" he wanted to know.

"Yes Honey, that's what I want to be about. That's what I do for a living."

I noticed a dramatic change in his behavior after that. He started coming home from work late, or else calling with lame excuses about why he'd been detained. Sometimes, the smell of beer would be on his breath when he finally got home.

I may not have known much about the auto business, but I knew it frowns upon people drinking while fixing machinery that can easily maim and injure. I did know that much.

The first time my husband floated in around three o'clock in the morning, I was sitting on the living room couch playing the role of worried wife, wondering if he'd been in an auto wreck or something. I was informed he'd been hanging out with the boys at a joint that didn't have a phone. But when the same thing happened a second and third time, it was clear something was up.

I may have been a doting wife, but I never claimed to be a damn fool.

Sometimes I would be up early in the morning meditating when he would come sauntering in. It's a good thing he never tried that while I was in the kitchen, because I had a big ol' iron skillet and would have been sorely tempted to raise a knot on his head.

Whenever I confronted Kelso about the change in our relationship, all I got were angry denials that a problem existed. That was right before he started going back to North Carolina by himself for short visits. The way I found out about these visits was that Kelso didn't come home at all.

I'd know he was back in Washington when he simply popped back up again. This was surprisingly passive/aggressive behavior, and no way for a married couple to live. I tried again and again to reach some kind of common ground with my husband, without success.

Counseling was out of the question–if I wanted to go to a counselor, I could go by myself, I was told. Meanwhile, the unexplained trips to North Carolina and late nights out continued. I put up with that disrespectful behavior for about a year.

In regards to marriage, society had clearly conveyed to me that divorce was considered failure, so it was to be avoided at all costs. I didn't want to be considered a failure when it came to the marriage game.

The other reason I stuck around was because I was feeling somewhat guilty. I didn't feel I'd done everything I could have to make sure my marriage started on solid ground, because I really didn't put much forethought into the thing.

The third reason, and this will sound absolutely crass, was because I was really busy.

One way to skirt problems in your personal life is to dive into your professional life. I was definitely a workaholic back in those days, thanks to the example set by my father.

So when things got stressful at home, I just loaded more stuff on my plate at work.

As for Kelso's suggestion that I see a counselor by myself, that's precisely what I started doing. That was a break from tradition for me. Because in the past, if I couldn't solve something on my own, I considered it a failure to seek the answer from someone else.

Naturally, the friction I was experiencing at home impacted my work, because if you're a married officer, folks automatically look for your spouse to be with you at social activities. Kelso had tons of excuses why he could no longer go to events with me. I felt dumb when people asked where he was and I'd have to offer some lame excuse for his absence.

I started seeing Sherman Ragland, a brother and lieutenant

colonel, who was the Deputy Director of Social Work Service. One of his duties was to engage in marriage and family counseling. The first time I went to his office, I mentioned in an offhanded way that I was having problems in my marriage. However, I didn't want to talk about it at the moment, because I was headed off on vacation.

Sherman comically looked me up and down and said quietly: "I am not the Lord. You do not bring your burdens and leave them here!" I could have punched Sherm sometimes.

I allotted a certain amount of time every week for sessions with Sherm, and learned an awful lot about myself in the process, particularly about how and why I made certain decisions regarding men.

During one pleading conversation with Kelso, he made a statement that was the beginning of the end of our marriage, as far as I was concerned.

We had been lying on the living room floor of our apartment, watching TV when I unexpectedly turned it off.

"Listen, we've got to talk," I said to my husband. His light, playful mood vanished as soon as I brought up our marital difficulties.

"If you think there's a problem with our marriage, it must be *your* problem," he said flippantly. "Because I'm all right."

Oh, really?

Those words may seem innocuous in print, but Kelso's tone set my teeth on edge. I had tried really hard to bridge the chasm growing between us. I was always home from Walter Reed in time to cook Kelso's dinner. I bent over backward to accommodate my husband when it came to washing and cleaning and even lovemaking.

But after being told that our marital discord was my problem, I stopped trying. Those were the wrong words to use with me.

The ball was clearly in my court and I had every intention of dealing with my problem.

Kelso's way of dealing with the situation was to return to North Carolina for good, until I "came to my senses."

I needed to get away, too, so I took three weeks of vacation and headed out to California with Capt. Joyce Bowles, who was a psychiatric nurse instructor at WRAIN, and is one of my dearest friends to this day.

We had fun going to clubs and sightseeing and that kind of stuff. I wasn't on the make or anything, because I believed in the sanctity of marriage. Even though my husband was in North Carolina doing Lord knows what, I was still married and carried myself accordingly.

When we returned to Washington, one of the first things I did was change the locks to the apartment Kelso and I had shared. I was ready to delve into the wreckage of my marriage, and do what had to be done from a legal standpoint.

But fortunately another crisis arose that allowed me to take my mind off that mess. This time my problem was work-related, and I cherished having an opportunity to spend every waking hour thinking about it..

Chapter XIV

Adding More Color To The Institute

When I claimed to be a workaholic during my time at Walter Reed, I wasn't kidding. The day Joyce Bowles and I flew to California, I stopped by my desk in Delano Hall, even though I was off. Force of habit.

Lying on my desk was a plain white envelope with my name written on it in longhand. Since I was rushing to catch my flight I didn't even look inside the envelope, but stuck it in my purse and dashed out the door.

I was 33,000 feet over America's heartland when I finally peeked at the contents of that envelope. It contained a note from an organization at Walter Reed known as U-BAD, short for United Blacks Against Discrimination.

No one knew who its members were, but they had an underground newspaper that always managed to find its way to the hands of Walter Reed's African-American employees. The paper kept a vigilant eye on the commander, heads of offices and managers in terms of what they were—and weren't—doing to achieve racial equality.

You have to remember this was during the days of Black Power and not long after Dr. Martin Luther King Jr's assassination and the urban riots that followed. So U-BAD's tone was quasi militant. I never did figure out how its members managed to circulate that paper around Walter Reed, though. It just mysteriously appeared like clockwork.

The unnamed author of my note said U-BAD planned to demand that the Department of Defense have at least ten black cadets at Walter Reed's Institute of Nursing when the fall class entered.

The note added that I might be called upon to help achieve that goal.

If at least ten black students weren't in the upcoming nursing class, buses filled with incoming students would be turned over. This in turn would generate tons of negative publicity for the

Department of Defense at a time when it was becoming increasingly sensitive to the need for improved race relations.

I put the note back in my pocketbook and didn't think about it during the rest of my vacation. Frankly, the last thing I needed was to fill my head with even more weighty thoughts. My marriage was giving me all I could deal with at the moment, and I was flying to the West to escape that.

But I wasn't surprised that U-BAD had turned its gaze to the composition of the nursing school's student body.

Of the two hundred students or so who came in every year, practically every one was white and most were the daughters of high-ranking military officers or enlisted personnel with many years of service. Why pay for a college education if your offspring could go to the four-year Institute of Nursing free, if their grades warranted it?

It was definitely a good deal and something of a well-kept secret within the military. I was part of the Institute of Nursing's administration, and had asked the school's deputy director a number of times why we had only one or two minority students? I never got a satisfactory response to that question and could see it was starting to grate, so I stopped asking.

However, I had a feeling things would change once I returned from California. Boy, did they ever.

My first day back at work from vacation I was sitting in a curriculum meeting when the top sergeant beckoned me to the door. She had a news flash: "General Dunlap wants to see you."

By then, General Lil was the chief of the Army Nurse Corps, and the second nurse to be promoted to brigadier general after Anna Mae Hays pulled off the feat in 1970. For her to make a trip from the Pentagon to the nursing school meant something big was going on.

She was in the director's mammoth office on the ground floor of Delano Hall, seated at a round wooden table with several other officers when I caught up with her. Col. Hazel Johnson Brown, who would later head the Army Nurse Corps and become the Army's first black female general was with her. So was Maggie Bailey, a black retired Army colonel. She was the first female of color promoted to that rank.

It dawned on me that this little get-together probably had to do with U-BAD.

"Clara Leach, come on in here," Lillian said cheerfully, continuing to ignore the Adams clearly printed on my nameplate.

"Listen, I have a job that needs to get taken care of and I can't go out there and do it. Have a seat."

She pushed a stack of papers across the table and started talking.

"We've had an anonymous request made to the Department of the Army, Clara," she said briskly. "Since that time, someone has also contacted officials at the Department of the Army. Basically, a demand has been made that there be some black students when the fall nursing class comes in. If not, buses will be turned over."

I sat there with a straight face, acting surprised, which came easily after Lillian informed me I was to put my teaching responsibilities aside for the next ten weeks. I would also stop my work with Walter Reed's equal opportunity office and other committees, because I was going into the recruiting business.

Maggie Bailey and I were going to hit the road and find ten qualified black nursing students for the Institute of Nursing! It was July when we were given our mission, and we had to be finished in time for the incoming fall class in early September.

For the next two hours the four of us brainstormed about ways to locate these students, and about the obstacles we could expect. At one point, Lillian looked me in the eye and said, "You do this for me and I'll make it worth your while."

That was all I needed to hear. As a result of our session, Maggie was brought back on active duty on invitational orders and the two of us set out for Detroit, to recruit black nursing prospects at Wayne State University. Maggie and I stayed at a Howard Johnson on Grand Boulevard. Fortunately she knew the city, because she had two sisters and a brother who lived there.

We didn't get an enthusiastic reception from some of the black students we approached. The main objection we kept hearing over and over was a reluctance to have anyone give them orders. Left unspoken was that those orders would likely be from a white supervisor.

My usual rejoinder was, 'Did you ever think that people who learn to take orders will also get a chance to give them?'

Maggie and I got a few Wayne State students to agree to come on board, though. Free healthcare, food, room and board, no tuition worries and a regular paycheck can be powerful incentives.

Our recruits had all finished two years of nursing studies at

Wayne State and agreed to take their final two at the Institute of Nursing. We had to bend the rules a little, because ordinarily you incurred a three-year commitment of military service for two years of nursing education. We got the commitment lowered to two years, which prompted grumbling from some quarters.

One anal-retentive Army major who was an administrator on Gen. Dunlap's staff slowed things up by insisting that the recruiting project be done in strict adherence to regulations. After a call from Gen. Dunlap, that major quickly adopted a more flexible approach.

Of the ten weeks when I was pressed into emergency recruiting duty, about four were spent in Detroit. Some of the other schools I traveled to were Virginia Commonwealth University, the University of South Carolina, the University of Wisconsin and a school out west. Naturally, I went to Howard University, a black school located in Washington.

I spent a whirlwind two and a half months flying all over the place, stopping in my apartment long enough to wash clothes, then hitting the road again. But we got the ten black nursing students we had been tasked to find. Mission accomplished.

Once that was over, I quickly reentered the grueling routine I had left behind at Walter Reed. I assumed new duties as educational coordinator, returned to keeping ridiculously long hours, partially because I was trying to forget about the implosion of my marriage to Kelso.

Along those lines, I had a lawyer draw up a separation agreement in 1972.

But another reason I was working so hard was because I was a workaholic, plain and simple.

Fortunately, someone was about to enter my life who would help me unlearn some of that behavior.

The Sick and Dying Taught Me How to Live

I chuckled under my breath the first time I saw Air Force Col. Red Stephenson, not his real name, because he was so ramrod straight in his blue uniform that I wondered if a steel rod had been implanted in his spine—or some other part of his anatomy. Basically, he was one of those stiff, handsome military warriors you'd expect from central casting.

Radiating authority by the megawatt, Stephenson stood by the nurse's station looking imperious and impatient. He had places to go and promotions to win, thanks to a sterling career that included a tour as a jet jockey during the Korean War. He'd come to Walter Reed from a desk job at the Pentagon, where ambitious Red had made a ticket-punching stop.

He looked puzzled to be at Walter Reed Army Medical Center, as he nervously waded through a numbing stream of pre-operative forms and documents.

Ol' rigid Red taught me some critical lessons about life and living. A prickly man who put little silver stars ahead of practically everything else in life, he helped me tap into my humanity in a big way–something I had not done very often.

Spiritual guides sometimes materialize in the most unexpected times and places.

A tall drink of water topped off by a rust-colored crew cut, Red was 45 and had been in the Air Force at least half his life. Beneath his glistening silver flight wings was an acre of medals and ribbons. Truth be told, that middle-aged warhorse was easy on the eyes. But my interest in him was strictly professional.

It was a typically muggy Washington summer afternoon and I was in the process of making my rounds in one of Walter Reed's surgical nursing units. From what I'd overheard about Stephenson's case, it sounded as though he was there for cancer pre-op work.

As I eavesdropped, the old fighter pilot's dark, hard eyes rose abruptly from a consent form to scan my face, then my nameplate.

His face betrayed the slightest hint of a smile. Despite Stephenson's self-important, serious mien, I picked up on something else he was trying desperately to mask–his fear.

"Good evening, Adams," Stephenson nodded, speaking in a voice devoid of warmth.

Adams? Nobody called me that! Major Adams, maybe, but not just Adams.

"Listen, I'm a major, too. Major Adams would be fine."

"Okay . . . Adams!" The set of Red's mouth and the way he arched his eyebrows was decidedly mischievous.

We remained mock adversaries the rest of his time at Walter Reed. Point, counterpoint, tit for tat. I'd thrust, and he'd parry.

"Fine, then. If you insist on addressing me as Adams, I'm gonna call you Stephenson."

The lanky Air Force colonel had already returned his attention to his admitting paperwork. Most surgery patients are preoccupied before going under the knife and Stephens was no exception.

A major operation is life-altering for anyone, but that can hold especially true for combat personnel.

I've always had a theory that infantrymen, tank commanders and fighter pilots are able to charge into battle and deal with bombs and bullets and heat-seeking missiles because they erect little fences of invincibility around themselves. Really it's a kind of a denial thing, a sense that 'it's never going to happen to me.'

Frankly, I'm glad those guys and gals are able to do that. If they didn't, you'd have a whole bunch of people on the battlefield talking about, "I'm not going out there and risk getting my tail shot off!" So invincibility definitely has its place.

Major surgery has a way of undermining that invincibility, making warriors appreciate they're as mortal as the next guy. I'm pretty sure that was weighing on Stephens' military mind.

"Hey, Clara, could you look at this for a second, please?"

A request from another nurse instantly knocked Red from my radar screen. It was time to finish my evening rounds, then make patient assignments for my students for the following morning. Evenings are busy times at Walter Reed. But I like it when problems and questions and crises seem to come flying at you non-stop.

After checking in on a few patients, I walked to the records room and pulled about 20 medical charts. I had to make patient care assignments for six Institute of Nursing students I had to teach the following day, and the charts would allow me to match the students with patients in varying stages of pre-operative and post-operative care.

When that task was finished, I drove home, cooked dinner and crashed, totally exhausted. Before I drifted to sleep, I wondered about Red and his future.

The next time I encountered him, he'd been stripped of his authoritarian togs. In place of his Air Force blues, he had on a humbling hospital gown exposing his backside to the world. Generals and privates wear the same demeaning gown around that place. Stephens was just another faceless patient who'd grudgingly ceded control of his life to me and Walter Reed's staff. Accordingly, his regal façade had nearly evaporated. Not totally, though.

A worry furrow was creasing his forehead when he looked up and spied me entering his two-bed hospital room. He hadn't been assigned a roommate yet, and I pitied the unsuspecting soul who got that dubious honor. Sitting on the side of his bed, Stephenson was focused on something a million miles away.

"How are you this morning, Colonel?" I asked, casually lifting the clipboard with his medical record on it.

"I'm doing okay, Adams. Thanks."

Still going to persist in that Adams stuff I see.

"So, what are you in here for?"

Instead of answering immediately, Stephenson rubbed a hairy right hand across his face.

"Well, I'm just here to have some tests done," he replied eventually. "I've been having some problems with the left side of my face."

Stephenson stopped talking and continued to look at me. And I made no effort to fill the silence or avoid his gaze. Thanks to years of working with patients, I'd grown comfortable with conversational lulls.

"My eyesight has been affected and I've been having problems with muscle twitches in my face," he finally said.

A young white doctor who looked to be nineteen stuck his head through the doorway. "Morning, Colonel Stephenson. Please come this way." Red Stephenson was off to be poked and prodded by Walter Reed's crack medical staff and would have his sinuses X-rayed, along with tests involving his eye, muscles, urine and blood before the day was out.

Because of my schedule, I didn't see Stephenson again until the following week. My man had done a Jekyll and Hyde in that short period of time.

"Good evening, Stephens, how are you doing?" I called out cheerfully as I entered his room.

"What's so good about this evening," he snapped, glaring evilly.

Excuse me! I laughed involuntarily, startled by his rudeness. "Do you mind if I sit down a moment?"

"No! If that's what you want to do."

Easing into a chair, I wondered what Stephenson's problem was. Meanwhile, two mean-looking eyes quietly bored into me. Like I said, I'd done enough silence to be comfortable with it. So I just waited while he quietly fumed, practically aglow with hostility.

It took a minute or so before Stephenson finally spoke. When his deep voice exploded through the silence, the words were distinct and very, very angry. Stephens was a man consumed with rage.

He'd gotten his test results back, discovered what his illness was and how the doctors planned to treat it.

Not to put too fine a point on it, Stephenson had cancer growing inside his left sinus and was going to have the left side of his handsome face taken apart and his left eye removed to get at it. And even after that radical procedure, the odds were that his cancer would just reappear anyway.

The news had just been dropped on Red, and he was trying to come to grips with the disfigurement and physical loss to be brought on by his operation, a radical mastoidectomy. But more than that, he was livid about the timing of his disease.

Here he was on the verge of being promoted to brigadier general, damn it, and just like that!—all of his dreams and plans had been destroyed. Without using a single curse word or epithet, Stephenson cussed the gods, fate and anything else conspiring to keep those precious silver stars off his shoulders.

Supporting his weight on his hands, he swung from his bed and began pacing back and forth from the window to the door in his white Walter Reed slippers. He'd survived aerial combat, carried out missions with aplomb, earned superior evaluations and now a stupid bunch of cells in his head were throwing nearly three decades of work out the window. "Where's the justice?" he wanted to know in a self-pitying tone.

I quietly took in his tirade, a little Army major without a dream of one day becoming a general. Another decade would pass before Hazel Johnson-Brown became the first black woman to achieve that milestone. So frankly, I couldn't relate to what Stephenson was going through—not the career part of it, anyway.

"Everything that I've worked for in my lifetime is gone," Stephenson sputtered, his red face glistening with perspiration in the air-conditioned room. "What was it all for if I'm going to end up with half my face?"

I didn't have the foggiest idea, nor did Red really expect an answer, so I just kept quiet. You don't offer trite platitudes to someone who, as Stephenson bluntly puts it, is about to lose half his face and an eye. So I just sat silently, nodding occasionally and looking as sympathetic as possible. Stephens wasn't really talking to me anyway—he just had to vent the anger and indignation detonating inside him.

I endured about five more minutes of Stephens' outraged soliloquy. Then I excused myself and hurriedly lost myself in my work, because the bewilderment and raw emotion cascading from Stephens had affected me. I wouldn't be human if it hadn't. You try to limit your emotional interaction with patients, but it's impossible not to have any.

Some patients you take care of simply because you're a professional and that's what you're supposed to do. Then there are some patients who affect you in a deeply personal way and Stephens was one of them. Something about the guy resonated with me, although I can't say exactly why.

When I entered Walter Reed the following morning, one of the nurses told me Red wasn't feeling well and was acting kind of uptight and tense.

When I dropped by his first-floor room, he was lying in his bed, staring at a little paper cup in his right hand. It was one of those tiny, pleated cups like they give you at the dentist's office. Two white sedative pills were inside it.

"They just don't understand me!" Red said slowly. The rage from the previous day was gone, replaced with resignation and dejection.

Who was 'they' and what didn't 'they' understand?

"I told the nurse that I needed to talk to somebody and she gave me two pills. I don't need any pills–I need to talk to somebody!" In one day he'd gone from ferocious lion to resigned lamb.

I asked Red what he wanted to do with the pills. His answer was immediate: He wanted to flush the damn things down the toilet! That ambitious colonel, who probably hadn't broken a rule since entering the military a quarter-century ago, was actually fomenting rebellion.

And you know what? I was with him one hundred percent. So we went and flushed those pills–held our own Boston Tea Party in a first-floor hospital room at Walter Reed.

I stood guard at the door while Red performed his last bombing mission as an active-duty Air Force pilot. Ploop, ploop! The pills didn't hit the bottom of the commode before Red pushed the toilet handle, sending the sedatives coursing through Washington's sewer system.

It was probably the most therapeutic act he'd performed during his stay at Walter Reed. The glee he derived from flushing those sedatives was infectious. He giggled like a mischievous 10-

year-old as he watched those pills do laps inside the white porcelain toilet bowl.

And I'm not gonna lie—I laughed too. It was genuinely funny watching that strait-laced career officer carry on like Dennis the Menace. The suffocating, hostile atmosphere that choked the room when I entered had dissipated.

Still chuckling over our secret rebellion, Stephens and I walked from the bathroom and into his hospital room.

"Adams, lemme tell you something," Stephens said, laying his lanky frame onto his bed. "I just want to tell somebody what it feels like to lose half your face. It hasn't even happened to me yet, but I just have to tell you what I'm thinking."

I nodded, interested in what he had to say.

Stephenson launched into a discussion about the loss of dreams. Specifically, what it felt like to work half your life for something, then suddenly realize you are never, ever going to get it. Through no fault of your own.

A realist, Stephenson discussed the end of his military career in matter-of-fact terms. I could see that it hurt him, but that he was coming to grips with the reality of it. He was already talking about being promoted to general in the past tense. Basically, he was beginning to grieve over his scuttled career.

Suddenly a huge wave of empathy and admiration overwhelmed me, because I don't know if I could have been calm and philosophical had the shoe been on the other foot.

It had taken illness to get Stephenson to finally transcend rank and station. We were no longer a colonel and a major talking. We were just two people who had transcended rank and were talking about our shared humanity.

Stephenson unexpectedly rose from his bed, pulled a chair in front of me and lightly placed his hands on my shoulders. His words forever changed my outlook on work.

"Adams," he said slowly, "take a lesson. I ought to be your lesson from here on in. I invested everything that I had toward getting promoted to general. I've missed out on a lot of living, because I was so determined to get those stars. And now, it's not even going to happen. Don't ever let this happen to you."

I felt goose bumps on my arms. I don't think anything in life happens by accident and I knew at that instant that Stephenson was a divine messenger.

Because I was on the wrong path, I was doing exactly what Stephenson warned me against. Even though I wasn't trying to become a general, my military career was my end all and be all. I'd placed my career above practically everything, including my marriage to Kelso, to a degree. It's not that I didn't love Kelso, I just loved the military more.

I found the military more fulfilling than marriage and never really made a secret of that.

I was routinely working long hours as a matter of course, and I was taking my military career way too seriously. Being a workaholic came honestly to me—it was passed down directly from my father. He thought that being a workaholic was how you got ahead in life.

"Idle hands get into mischief, and you need to stay out of mischief," he used to repeat over and over like a mantra. Daddy made sure my hands never stopped moving when I was a little girl, and the grownup Clara took that lesson to heart.

So running into Stephenson was a wake-up call. It really was. His words continued to resonate in my head long after I'd left his hospital room. And before the week was out, I made a pledge to act on his advice.

For one thing, I started making sure that I took time out for me. And I started taking control of my crazy schedule and setting aside a few minutes each day for Clara. I solidified a routine of getting up every morning at three a.m. and using that time for self-reflection, something I still do today.

Why three a.m.? Because it's a time when I know I won't be disturbed. It's a time when husbands and significant others tend to let you be. My quiet time usually runs an hour, hour and a half, and in a section of my home where no one will disturb me.

Sometimes I just kind of sit and let ideas and thoughts turn over in my head. And I give myself what, I guess, you could call a pep talk. I got that idea from a book called "The Magic of Thinking Big," by David Schwartz. It's a great book.

But Schwartz isn't the main reason I do that. Red Stephenson is. If I hadn't met Red, I think I would have had a good career, but I don't think I would have made general. And I shudder to think of the friends and family whose company I would have been deprived of, because I probably would have stroked out or had a heart attack.

Instead, Red—and the other sick and dying people I've encountered over the years—taught me how to live. And they taught me how to be more reflective and how to put things in perspective. I'm thankful that I met Red and even more thankful that I was receptive to his message.

As advertised, he had his surgery at Walter Reed. It took about 14 hours for a team of surgeons to finish the operation that cost Stephenson his left eye. Left a big scar on his face, too. The doctors told Stephenson there was a 70 percent chance his cancer would come back, so he had a pretty good idea the surgery merely bought him some time.

Even so, he stayed in pretty good spirits, and was putting away food like a horse within a few days after his operation. He had an active mind and loved to engage in mental jousting. I think he liked the fact I would debate him at the drop of a hat and give him new perspectives to consider.

On the day he was discharged, we hugged each other, which was something he wasn't too good at, with his stiff self! He was an independent person, and didn't want anybody putting hands on him.

"I'm gonna miss you, Adams," he said, looking debonair with his black eye patch.

"I'm gonna miss you too, Stephenson."

"Keep in touch." With that, Stephenson simply turned and walked into the hallway, where his pretty, petite wife awaited. I felt a tinge of sadness, because we had a special bond. I did stay in touch with him for about a year, but then I lost track. After a while, he ceased to respond.

That's one of my few regrets in life, because I do think he sincerely wanted to remain in contact. But it had gotten to be too much for me from an emotional standpoint. His cancer was coming back without question, and I just didn't want to have to deal with that. Stephenson had gone beyond being a patient to being a friend.

His influence continues on, though. It manifests itself every day at three a.m., when I climb out of bed to recharge my spiritual and intellectual batteries.

Chapter XV

The Affair

Throughout most of my career in the Army, I prided myself on being a prime physical specimen. Unlike most of my contemporaries, I was a runner who religiously logged three miles a day, rain or shine.

Since my health had always been excellent, I was alarmed by the onset of heavy menstrual bleeding and cramps around the spring of 1974. I also experienced spotting between periods. Initially I didn't mention my health problem to anyone, but the discomfort got to the point where I had to have some medical tests.

The gynecologist, whom I had known since he was an intern, checked me over and determined that my pain stemmed from fibroids that had grown in my uterus. He gingerly added that it looked as though a hysterectomy would be necessary to deal with my malady. However, he wanted to get a second opinion.

He was very solicitous and looked pained himself as he let that bit of news slowly sink in. With pity in his eyes, he asked if a hysterectomy was an option I'd be willing to consider?

He was surprised when I told him yes. I'd never wanted children, so a hysterectomy wouldn't affect me like it would most childless women who are thirty-five years old.

Nor was my self-image pegged to my reproductive tract, or so I'd convinced myself. Over time, I'd find out that I was wrong on both counts.

Before I underwent my operation, there was a legal matter that had to be dealt with. Rather than take the risk of dying on the operating table with my marital status in limbo, I drove down to a courthouse in North Carolina and obtained my divorce from Kelso. It was a loose end I had to tie down before going under the knife.

You know, my father never thought Kelso and I would make our marriage work. He said our backgrounds were just too different, and that I had gone further in life than Kelso had. Daddy said all this before I married Kelso, whom he never did particularly care for.

That was probably one more reason I tried to make my union work long after it was clear that it wouldn't.

I don't want to leave the impression that Kelso was a bad or evil man, because he certainly wasn't. To this day, I still place most of the blame for that ill-fated relationship on myself.

There's no way I should have entered into something like marriage as cavalierly as I did. Neither of us was truly prepared for that kind of commitment at that point in our lives.

I was still attending my counseling sessions with Lt. Col. Sherman Ragland, because the disintegration of a marriage is something that corrodes your self-esteem like acid, and robs you of peace of mind. But Sherman correctly pointed out that relationships, especially marriages, are never all bad.

Kelso and I had a lot of good times, and I found it healthy to keep that in perspective.

Officially single once again, I had my hysterectomy performed at Walter Reed.

My post-operative pain didn't fully kick in until after I'd left the hospital, because I think that anesthesia kind of keeps you numb for a while. But once I got home, there was no doubt about the fact that I'd undergone a major surgical procedure. The nerve endings in and around my incision reminded me of the operation at every waking moment.

My stamina and physical conditioning took a major hit, too. When I walked merely from my bedroom to the dining room, I'd have to sit down at the dining room table for a moment just to catch my breath.

To complicate matters, I had to take potent painkillers that really dazed and blinded me.

Fortunately a friend named Phyllis Hamparian, who was also an Army nurse, lived in my apartment building. She was a mothering kind of person and saw to it that I got my meals, medications and daily exercise.

But during those times when I was alone with my pain and my thoughts, I pondered my hysterectomy and its repercussions on my life. It's one thing to say you don't want kids, but another to know you can never be a mother under any circumstances. I won't deny the realization gave me a sense of emptiness and longing at times.

Another change wrought by my surgery was a new insight

into what post-operative patients went through. After my operation, a lot of their concerns and fears were no longer mere abstractions. I was able to sit down with people and say, "Listen, I've been where you are and I understand that it hurts." Being more empathetic definitely makes one a better nurse.

I took four weeks of convalescent, leave and toward the beginning of my final week received a call from Gen. Dunlap.

"Clara, I'm going to send you to Ft. Meade."

"Really, ma'am? When?"

"Next month."

The game plan was to send me to Ft. Meade's hospital in May 1974 to be the assistant chief nurse. That wasn't something I was necessarily dying to do, but I realized having that on my resume would make me a stronger candidate to get promoted to lieutenant colonel. So I had no problem with it.

Now comfortable with my ability to carry out her little special assignments, General Lil had one other thing she wanted me to do before I reported to Ft. Meade: I was to fly up to Boston and talk to officials at Northeastern University to find out about the possibility of recruiting some of that school's black students into Walter Reed's nursing program.

I had no problem with that request, because I had a slight case of cabin fever after all the time I'd spent convalescing in my apartment. So I caught a flight to Boston and booked myself into a hotel at Copley Square.

The night before I was to meet with the folks at Northeastern, I decided to head to a little indoor shopping center that wasn't too far from my hotel. I was in one of the shops, browsing, minding my own business when I happened to run into tall, fair-skinned brother who was about six-foot-two and had a huge Afro.

Let me tell you right now, the brother was definitely fiiiine!

He looked me up and down in my civilian clothes and said in a sexy voice: "Hello!" I have no doubt that Satan was also in that little Boston store that night, working overtime.

The fine brother's name turned out to be Gene. He asked me where I was from, along with the usual conversational icebreakers, before making a tempting offer. Namely, he was willing to show me a little of Boston if I had the time.

To my surprise, I heard a little voice reply, "Sure, that sounds like it would be nice." Oddly, the voice belonged to me. That was some real shaky and risky behavior, because had I turned up missing that night, no one would have known where to start looking.

Plus it was very uncharacteristic behavior on my part.

But away we went, zooming off in his car to take in a couple of Boston jazz joints. I had a great time listening to music and talking to Gene, who dropped me off at my hotel around two a.m. I thanked him for the evening, we exchanged phone numbers and went our separate ways.

The next morning, I proceeded to my meeting and got my goals accomplished.

After I returned home to Washington, he called me up and a long-distance courtship began to blossom. It turned out that he was recently separated from his wife, and was probably just as vulnerable as I was. After about three months of continual phone calls, Gene came down to Washington for a visit.

Know how men are sometimes accused of not thinking with their heads? I'm not gonna lie and tell you I didn't feel frisky when I opened the door to my apartment to find Gene standing in the hallway in all his handsome glory. Hallelujah!

The man was attractive, intelligent and turned out to be a passionate and attentive lover. In that last regard, I had never felt freer in my life, because the specter of 'What if I get pregnant?' was no longer there, thanks to my hysterectomy.

When he came to see me, Gene had just been released from his job in Boston. So we talked and decided he should get a position with a company in the Washington area and move in with me.

I had taken up with a man who was recently separated and on the prowl. Looking back, I'm not sure if I was in love or in lust. It may have been a little of both. I'm not proud of the way things went down with that relationship, but it happened and I can't undo any of it.

God looks out for babies and fools, it's been said. Well, I wasn't a baby, but I was surely a damn fool.

In retrospect, I had a burning need to be validated as a woman, because I think my womanhood had been questioned to a great degree and I didn't feel too good about that at all. Throughout my life, I had not placed much value on developing my femininity. On the one hand, the manner in which my marriage died had filled me with feelings of rejection and self-doubt. Then there was the matter of my hysterectomy, which triggered more nagging questions about my femininity. Did I really understand what it meant to be a woman? Was I capable of developing the feminine side of me?

I definitely could have been a little more careful in choosing someone to validate me, because shacking up with a married man was not the way to go. But let me tell you, Gene was a nice guy and he fulfilled my needs during the time we were together.

On some level, I realized my deal with Gene was not kosher. Which is probably why I waited six months before uttering a word about it to Sherman Ragland. He nearly popped a gasket when he found out about my affair, and claimed my self-esteem had sunk to the point where I'd become "an unpaid prostitute!"

Sherm had a way of taking the gloves off to get my attention, and when he did he could be absolutely brutal. But brutal or not, I was at a low point in my life where I desperately needed a man's approval to make me feel desirable and feminine.

Ultimately I was going to have to work that one out, not Sherman. Regardless of how scornful or disapproving he became, Gene was making me feel good about myself. And as long as that was the case, I had no intention of casting him off merely to please Sherman or anyone else.

In time, the damaged self-esteem that had driven me into Gene's arms in the first place began to mend. I stayed in counseling with Sherm on a weekly basis and kept looking inward at my behavior and myself. I was even getting back into meditating, something I had stopped doing shortly before I met Gene.

Our relationship was comfortable, but it didn't seem to me to have the potential to turn into something lasting. Gene confirmed that one night over dinner.

"Listen Clara," he blurted. "I've reached a point where I think it's probably best for us to go our separate ways. Because if I stick around any longer, I think I may have to submit to being Mr. Adams."

His announcement knocked me for a loop. I wrestled with a gut reaction to try and convince him to stay. Because I knew exactly what he was saying, and I really had no comeback for that.

With the same swiftness with which he'd entered into my life, Gene was gone. Prompting an amen chorus from Sherman Ragland and Mother, whom I had told about Gene. Ditto Joyce Bowles, my best friend.

But I wasn't so crazy about the development. In my book, it

basically represented another rejection, since I'd met Gene while on the rebound from Kelso. I cried a lot, but fortunately, I was much stronger and not nearly as vulnerable as when we first met.

I had gotten what I needed out of our relationship, which was to feel whole again in terms of being a woman. Maybe, eventually, I would run into a man who wouldn't feel intimidated by my career, because I had no plans to give it up anytime soon.

* * * * * * * * *

It's kind of hard to go wrong when you have a brilliant mentor like Brig. Gen Lillian Dunlap, molding and shaping your career, scything away potential obstacles. As usual, she knew precisely what she was doing when she sent me to Ft. George Meade, in Maryland, for a growth experience in nursing service administration.

I went there in May 1974 to be the assistant chief nurse at Meade's little, 150-bed hospital. Ft. Meade is about twenty miles north of Washington, so it wasn't necessary to move out of the apartment I was sharing with Gene.

The chief nurse at Meade was Lt. Col. Katherine Galloway, an Irish gal who would become another influential mentor. Not initially though, because instead of being her usual garrulous, quick-witted self, Katy Galloway was angry during our first meeting. Angry at me, angry at the Army, angry at the world.

She'd received orders to come to Meade after having worked in the Army Surgeon General's office at the Pentagon. Katy had tons of clinical nursing experience, and felt she should have been running a facility much larger than Ft. Meade's. She wasn't pleased to be there, but saluted the flag and came on out.

Then Katy received word that some one-year wonder named Maj. Clara Adams, clearly someone's fair-haired child, was to come breezing through her hospital for twelve months as her assistant. This meant that Katy would have to break in another new assistant a year later.

What she really wanted was someone who could roll up their sleeves and stay awhile.

So although I didn't know it, Katy was somewhat resentful when I reported for duty at Ft. Meade. Right off the bat, it was obvious she possessed a commanding presence. We talked for a bit in her corner office and I tried to impress her with a barrage of questions about my new job. Katy listened politely, then it was her turn to speak.

"Now here's what I'm about," she said bluntly. "I can run this hospital with my little finger, okay? But you can't. So here's what I'm gonna do. In the next year, I'm going to give you all the opportunity you want, okay?"

I nodded, wondering what I had done to trigger this proposition.

"I am going to sit back here in this office and send you out to run the place," Katy continued. "If you need me, you'll know where to find me. But if not, keep on going and do your thing.

"Oh yes, there's one other thing. When I turned forty, I said I wasn't going to do anything in the Army that I didn't want to do. I am not a social butterfly, okay? So whenever they call for the chief nurse to attend a social function, you're my designee."

And that was how I made the metamorphosis from nursing professor to being responsible for a staff of 150 nurses at an Army hospital. Katy was expert at handling people and at dealing with administrative matters, and she was a skilled teacher. So Ft. Meade's hospital became a leadership lab for me.

Where Katy fell a little short, however, was in dealing with social issues. One day she made the mistake of saying within my earshot that slavery in America was more a financial issue than anything. That statement kicked off a series of very long and interesting conversations between the two of us.

When she got really mad, Katy's face would get florid and a little tear would form on her lower eyelids, behind her glasses. I got adept at looking for the warning signs. Katy would never scream and rant when her Irish temper erupted, but instead would slice people to shreds with her sardonic wit.

In time, I became closer to Katy than any white person with whom I had ever worked. She eventually came to understand that slavery wasn't just about economics, but was an institution that stripped African Americans of their dignity and their culture.

We learned a lot from each other, and the primary lesson I learned was how to be an effective manager.

I recall an occasion when the hospital commander, during the morning report, casually dashed off a major policy change that impacted the hospital's nursing department. I was totally blindsided by this development, because Katy and I hadn't been contacted for any input before the decision was made.

From that experience, I learned the importance of talking to people and keeping one's ear to the ground, because if people don't want your input on something they'll work around you and keep things hush-hush. Managers in organizations have to gather intelligence regularly, and do some snooping around if they want to stay on top of things.

Another thing I found out at Meade is that crucial decisions are sometimes made after hours, when most people have gone home for the day. So I began keeping late hours and hanging around after most of the administrators had gone home.

Katy and I were six months into our association when the chief nurse at Walter Reed, Col. Madelyn Parks, got selected to be the next chief of the Army Nurse Corps. Col. Parks needed someone to take her old spot at Walter Reed, and she chose an old buddy she had worked with before, Katy Galloway.

I was thrilled to be with Katy and to see the joyous expression that spread across her face once she realized she was Walter Reed's next chief nurse. I would no longer be able to tap into her experience and wisdom on a daily basis, but she deserved that posting. The woman was truly a brilliant manager and an outstanding leader and nurse. She taught me that "nursing, when it's done right is hard work. A nurse must decide about the willingness to do difficult work and get on with it." Katy made it look easy, but it was clear that delivering top-caliber nursing entailed a lot of hard work.

Having learned at the knee of the expert, I felt like I was ready to serve as the chief nurse at Ft. Meade, if need be.

In a nutshell, the chief nurse manages personnel assigned to a number of areas, including clinics and nursing units. These nurses work with physicians, administrators, occupational therapists, physical therapists, dietitians, and these personnel all have varied opinions of what nursing personnel should be doing. But ultimately, it's the responsibility of the chief nurse to make that call, as well as let the commander know what resources are needed for nurses to get their work done.

I admit to having been on the cocky side, because I was willing to take on those responsibilities. But a decision was made to wait for Katy's replacement, whose identity tickled me to no end.

It was Peter Fiaschi, whom I had served with at Ft. Sam Houston, in San Antonio. You may recall that Peter was the officer I was advised to stop spending so much time with, due to concerns we might be perceived as an interracial couple.

He was glad to have me already in place at Ft. Meade,

because Peter knew that I was a team player and that he could count on me to help him get the department of nursing in tip-top shape.

Even though Peter was a lieutenant colonel by then, he had never been a chief nurse. So he basically depended on me to walk him through his responsibilities, which was no problem after almost one year of shadowing Katy. Peter stepped out front as the public face of the nursing department; then, we'd huddle in his office afterward and I would tutor him.

Toward the end of 1974, my career continued to rise. I had already been selected below the zone for lieutenant colonel and was anticipating my next challenge.

It's interesting to note that around the same time Gen. Lillian Dunlap told me Ft. Meade was my next stop, she also mentioned I might attend the U.S. Army Command & General Staff College, a facility for up-and-coming young officers located at Ft. Leavenworth, Kansas.

Instead of saying, "Thank you, ma'am, I'm flattered," or words to that effect, what did I do? I told General Lil that I was seriously contemplating attending law school and might leave the service if I was accepted.

After tartly reminding me that she ran an Army Nurse Corps and wasn't really into the law school business, Lillian said to keep her apprised of how my law school quest went. I'm sure I exasperated her to no end sometimes.

To make a long story short, I interviewed at the George Washington University School of Law, in Washington. I spoke with an assistant dean who had been an Army officer during World War II. When he learned of my fast-moving military career, and that I was being pushed to attend the Command & General Staff College, he took the law school application I had painstakingly filled out and shredded it right in front of my eyes. Riiip!

"Major," I was told, "you've got a bright future ahead of you. And it's a whole lot brighter, I think, than it would be in the legal profession. So go on back to Walter Reed, tell that general you'll do what she said and let's see what happens. You can always come back to this place if things don't work out."

Sage, sage words indeed. When the torn pieces of my law school application went into that dean's trash can, my final bid to pursue a legal career fluttered into the trash, too. In retrospect, things worked out just right.

And after I'd returned to my senses, Lillian confirmed that I, indeed, would be going to Ft. Leavenworth the following year.

✻ ✻ ✻ ✻ ✻ ✻ ✻ ✻ ✻ ✻ ✻

"Clara Mae, your father has not been feeling well for some time now. He's having health problems and he didn't want me to say anything to you about it. But I've got to tell you these things."

The anxious voice coming across the telephone line belonged to Mother, who was phoning from the farm. A chill buzzed through me, because I knew whatever was going on was serious for Mother to call. I also felt annoyed with Daddy for being so proud and secretive.

Mother let the cat out of the bag–Daddy had prostate cancer and refused to have a surgical procedure that might slow the cancer down. Mother wanted to know if I would come home and try to talk to Daddy.

So in the spring of 1975 I headed south down Interstate 95, wondering if my father had taken leave of his senses. I had been home a few months earlier for Christmas and he'd looked fine, if somewhat thinner than usual. Why are so many men so pig-headed when it comes to taking care of their health?

He was not ready to be swayed when I finally got home and started to talk to him. Daddy was not going to have surgery, he told me, but was going to put his fate in God's hands.

While I don't deny that God can certainly take care of you, I pointed out to my father that physicians can sometimes help, too.

It turned out that the reason he was in such a dither was because his doctors wanted to remove his testicles, shutting down the production of testosterone in Daddy's body. Testosterone fuels the growth of prostate cancer cells.

"If I can't be the man I always was, I really don't want to live," Daddy said.

I let that comment slide, but the line of reasoning behind it wasn't making any sense to me. As I looked at my father, I was thinking, "Doesn't fathering ten children leave an indelible stamp as far as your manhood is concerned?" But I didn't get into it with Daddy. I did understand where he was coming from. I had encountered similar responses from countless male patients over the years in nursing.

I made a point of speaking with his doctor, who confirmed that Daddy's reaction was not that unusual. The physical discomfort would probably get worse, he warned, which would likely force Daddy's hand.

About a month later, Daddy agreed to have the operation. I drove down from Washington again and stayed with him during the surgery. Afterward, he was resigned and depressed. Even worse, the cancer had spread to his brain.

I was angry with my father as I battled traffic on my way back to Washington. I believed the brain lesions might have been prevented had he jettisoned his macho hangups sooner. He told me once that I just didn't understand and I had to admit that I truly didn't.

Chapter XVI

Fighting To Fete Women

Ask most G.I.s if they would like to go to Ft. Leavenworth, and they'll look at you like you're crazy. That's because the sprawling Kansas installation is best-known for housing the U.S. Disciplinary Barracks, a maximum-security, 500-inmate facility that's the biggest prison in the military.

Established in 1827, Fort Leavenworth also happens to be where the Army formed its first all-black Regular Army regiments–the Buffalo Soldiers–in 1866. Those valiant warriors made it possible for me to stand on their shoulders more than a century later, an ambitious lieutenant colonel entering Ft. Leavenworth to attend the Command & General Staff College (CGSC).

All the students attending CGSC are officers, mostly captains and majors. Attendance at the college is considered an indispensable steppingstone for eventually becoming a member of the Army's leadership in positions of significant responsibility.

The one-year school was set up to teach infantry, artillery and armor officers basic military management skills, so a combat arms mentality dominates. Being a nurse and having to deal with a heavy diet of battlefield scenarios was definitely alien to me.

I was about the business of keeping folks in one piece, not developing strategies for blowing them apart. But those war games are a good way to teach basic concepts and principles of leadership. When you peel away the onion, being an Army officer is all about leading, and managing and serving people, regardless of what kind of work you do.

Cognizant of that, each year the CGSC folks admit a percentage of non-combat officers. Those recommended for the school are viewed as officers moving up and moving out. When I began taking classes in the fall of 1975, the Army had only one slot for a nurse to attend Command & General Staff College. And I was the first African-American nurse to earn that honor.

I'd have a few more firsts under my belt by the time I left that place.

Most officers sent to the Command & General Staff College were in the Army, with a sprinkling of Air Force, Navy, Marine and international officers thrown in.

Because I was a lieutenant colonel, it was decided that I would serve as a section leader in charge of sixty officers.

The place had never had a female section leader before. As soon as this was announced, a scheme was hatched to move me out of that prestigious position. One of the senior officers at the school called me to point out that past section leaders have traditionally had their wives organize activities for the wives of other officers. But I didn't have a wife, he noted, displaying keen powers of observation.

"No, and I'm not likely to get one, either," I replied, getting an ice-breaking laugh. "But my assistant section leader does, so we can probably involve her in those duties."

Boy, it kills me the way men can be prisoners to linear thinking. Over the years, I've helped plenty of men understand that my gender is not an obstacle, because there's always an alternative way of operating, when getting the job done is the most important thing.

The first time we had a reception at Command & General Staff College, the Army general who ran the place made a beeline to me, eager to chat with the female section leader. That was cool, because I had a bug to put in his ear, anyway.

Smiling broadly, I told him: "Sir, you all don't treat nurses too well here, I understand."

Thoroughly mystified, he asked me to please elaborate.

"Well Sir, if you look at the international officers who attend this course, there are at least two from each country. On the other hand, only one Army nurse is invited every year. If there were two, at least we'd be able to talk to and understand each other!"

He laughed and acknowledged that the shortcoming could easily be addressed.

That general was a man of his word, because every year subsequent to my appearance, CGSC has always invited at least two nurses. That episode was typical of my style when operating as an advocate for women and minorities in the Army. Being low-key and humorous, as opposed to shrill and strident, was a pretty effective way to go.

After classes started, a form was circulated notifying all CGSC students about a physical fitness exam we had to take. Everybody, that is, except the eight women in a class of 1,100. A little note at the bottom of the form stated that female officers were exempt.

I bristled at the underlying notion behind the waiver–that the 'fairer sex' couldn't cut it. That was paternalistic nonsense, and I dropped by the office of the course director, a colonel, to find out what was up. He claimed the idea was the commandant's, not his.

"Are you saying we're not officers, then?" I challenged. "Are you saying we don't have to be physically fit?"

"I'm not saying that, Clara. If you want to take the men's PT test, you can take it."

"Okay, then, I'm going to."

Hoping my mouth hadn't written a check my body couldn't cash, later that day I told the other female members of the Command & General Staff College what had happened, and tried to get them to go with me. But all seven begged off.

I knew I could ace the test with no problem, except for a section that called for me to grab a bar over my head and do eight pull-ups. I'll admit that men have an advantage in upper-body strength–but that's all I'll concede.

Word got around that Clara was taking the 'men's' PT test. I have no doubt that some people were quietly hoping I would fall flat on my face. But that definitely wasn't the case for at least one young captain in my section. He quietly let me know that if I was willing to meet him on the PT field at six in the morning, he could prepare me to do eight pull ups on the parallel bars. That was the minimum number needed to pass that portion of the PT test.

A score of 250 points was necessary to pass, with 300 being the maximum. When I took it, I scored 290 points. The other women were astounded, but it wasn't really that big a deal. All they had to do was get off their duffs and try. Before we graduated, my CGSC class gave me the 'Female Jock of the Year' award.

By Christmas 1975, I was ready for a break from CGSC. Plus I needed to check on my sick father, so I booked a flight from Kansas to North Carolina. Daddy was being treated at Wake Memorial Hospital, in Raleigh. When I made it to his bedside, it was clear that the cancer ravaging his body was starting to get the upper hand.

* * * * * * * * * *

The Daddy of my childhood was a rotund, high-energy individual who was always on the go. But the man hospitalized at Wake Memorial was alarmingly thin and lethargic, and his breathing was slightly labored. Regardless of how old you get to be, the demise of a parent makes you ache.

Seeing the concern on my face, Daddy's heart went out to little Clara Mae.

"Don't worry, you're going to be all right," he said in a raspy voice, his slim, weathered hand squeezing mine. "But I tell you, I may not make it too much longer."

The words were finally out there, meaning there'd be no more dancing around the obvious. The father and daughter who'd always shared a special, if sometimes peculiar, bond were saying goodbye.

"Well, Daddy, before you check out you let me know, because I want to come back and see you. Okay?"

Daddy gazed up at me with dry, unsmiling eyes. "Okay, Clara Mae." Never having been particularly sentimental or touchy-feely his entire life, I guess he saw no reason to start now.

I did tell him during that conversation that I loved him and I appreciated all the things he'd done for me over the years. And he said something that let me know I was kind of high on his list, too.

"Just remember to keep on doing the things that you're doing," Daddy said. "Because there's still something that you've got to do for the world that you ain't done yet."

* * * * * * * * * *

Women have a maddening way of bending over backward to placate men, of going to ridiculous extremes to gain their approval. That was never clearer to me than when I returned to Command & General Staff College in 1976, to finish the remainder of my year there.

Not only was 1976 the year of this country's bicentennial celebration, it also happened to be the International Year of Women. Given that Command & General Staff College was such a male-dominated, chauvinistic environment, I thought it would be good to acknowledge the International Year of Women at the College in some way.

The guys in my section asked me what it all meant and why

we needed to celebrate it. My comeback was that if women came from Adam's rib, it was the prime rib, and not one of the lesser cuts! The line got quite a laugh from the fellows.

Out of the eight female officers in my class, Claudia was an Army lieutenant colonel who had slightly less time in rank than I did. We arranged a time and place to gather with the other six female officers, so that we could plan an assembly highlighting the contributions of women to the military.

Well, a half hour after the meeting was to begin, the only people present were Claudia and me. Eventually two other women drifted in, but only to let us know they disagreed with having women-only meetings, because the men might find that displeasing.

I was startled and dismayed by that revelation. I honestly believed that the celebration would be a source of pride for the women in the college, not something they'd try to run from. Some members of the sisterhood had an awfully long way to go.

Claudia and I decided to go forward regardless of what the other women did. When we floated the idea past the course director, he agreed that it had merit. So our next stop was the office of the deputy commandant, a one-star general. Well, he thought a special program to talk about the achievements of women in the military was just a bad idea.

And he made no effort to disguise his distaste for the concept. He relented somewhat when we showed him a Department of Defense memo announcing the International Year of Women and encouraging ceremonies to acknowledge women's contributions to defense. So his solution was to schedule our assembly on the heels of the three-day weekend. And he scheduled it early in the morning, during a time when Command & General Staff College students weren't required to be present.

Claudia was absolutely livid, and justifiably so. But we managed to get 600 students out of 1,100 to attend, and the assembly was a huge success. The commandant, who hadn't known about it until that morning, praised it lavishly.

After graduation, Claudia and I learned that the deputy commandant had taken credit for sponsoring our tribute to military women. That enraged Claudia to no end, but frankly I didn't care. To me, the important thing was that we pulled it off, and hopefully enlightened some folks along the way.

In the meantime, I was making good grades at CGSC and

looking forward to graduation. Unfortunately, things took a turn for the worse back home in North Carolina.

On March 30, 1976, I got a phone call at six–thirty in the morning that I had been expecting, but dreaded nonetheless. The director of nursing from Wake Memorial Hospital in Raleigh, North Carolina, was on the other end of the line and informed me that my father was nearing the end of his fight against cancer.

I took emergency leave from the Command & General Staff College and flew home immediately.

Daddy died on April 2, and all of my nine brothers and sisters returned home to memorialize our father and bury him. The bottle of Old GranD-DaD I brought my father from Korea was still on top of the kitchen cabinet in our Willow Springs home. It still had a little whiskey in it, because my father only took a nip on special occasions.

My brother Aaron fetched that Old GranD-DaD and took about thirty seconds to kill a bottle my father hadn't finished in eleven years.

Even though I was back home for the saddest imaginable reason, it was good to see all of my brothers and sisters. Daddy's death marked the first time we'd flocked together in years.

We chided ourselves about not doing a better job of staying in touch and pledged to improve in the future. We also put our heads together over the issue of what to do with Mother, now that Daddy was gone. She was starting to have difficulty getting around because of arthritis, a malady that would eventually confine her to a wheelchair.

In our infinite wisdom, the Leach children decided that Mother should move in with me, since I was single and doing reasonably well. Only thing was, nobody had bothered to seek Mother's opinion first.

"Who made such a decision?" she snapped, leveling a glare at us. "I really don't know what Clara does or where she goes. I do know that she travels a lot and I don't want to be left alone in a strange place. I've got all my friends here and I've got my house here. Why should I go anywhere?"

Not surprisingly, none of her ten children stepped forward to take credit for the brilliant idea. With Mother having unequivocally declared her independence, there wasn't too much more for me to do at home. I had already bought the family farm in 1974 and had deeded the house and one acre of land to Mother and Daddy, so Mother had her home.

I was easily out of sorts for half a year after Daddy's death. But life demands that you keep putting one foot in front of the other and that's what I did immediately upon returning to CGSC.

In addition to leadership courses I was taking there, I was trying to use my time at CGSC to earn another college degree. If you wrote an approved thesis, you could get a master of military art and science degree recognized and accredited by the Central Association of Colleges and Universities.

My thesis was on the topic of death and dying, and how it affects combat officers. Not surprisingly, I encountered some reluctance and resistance on that one, but I got the necessary people to sign off and came out of CGSC with a second master's degree.

Looking back on my year at Ft. Leavenworth, it helped me to see that as far as the military was concerned, I was clearly operating in a man's world.

I guess that hadn't been evident till then, because I had been primarily in the company of female nurses. But man's world or not, I had no intention of being deterred from career objectives by something as trivial as gender.

I owed that much to myself. Plus Daddy wouldn't have expected anything less.

* * * * * * * * * *

Whenever I received orders for a new duty station, usually I cheerfully saluted the flag and moved on to wherever the Army wanted me to go. However, I balked after getting orders for my assignment after Command & General Staff College.

I was told to pack my belongings and ship them to Ft. Sam Houston, where I would become part of the Inspector General's team for the health services command. My job would be to fly around the world and inspect nursing departments in Army hospitals and medical centers.

Well, I could appreciate that IG inspectors did important work, but that didn't necessarily mean I wanted to do it. By the time June 1976 rolled around, my goal was to be an assistant chief nurse, or chief nurse, in an Army hospital somewhere in, or around, Washington, D.C. So I called up a colonel who was the career activities officer for the Chief of the Army Nurse

Corps in Washington, and told her what I wanted to do.

I was informed, politely, that my orders were cut with the needs of the Army in mind, not necessarily those of Lt. Col. Clara Adams. However, my reluctance to join the IG team at Ft. Sam Houston had been duly noted.

The Army's chief nurse at the time, Gen. Madelyn Parks, was a good friend of Katy Galloway, who was Walter Reed's chief nurse. When Parks heard that I was digging in my heels a little bit, she had Katy give me a call.

I was surprised to hear from her, speaking in her usual quiet tone.

"You're needed in that assignment and I think you'll do well," Katy said. "Now I was never an IG, but I think an IG has an opportunity to do a lot of teaching while they're seeing how well the regulations and policies of the military are being followed. I would suggest you go ahead and take the assignment."

Crafty Katy knew that teaching was one of my hot buttons. The notion of being able to instruct while inspecting was exciting and intriguing. Still, I called up Lillian Dunlap to get her read on the situation. By this time, she had retired from the Army and was living in San Antonio.

General Lil also suggested that I get my butt on down to Ft. Sam Houston. She pointed out that the last nurse to graduate from the Command & General Staff College had also been sent to Ft. Sam Houston for IG duties. In fact, she was still there, which probably explains why I subconsciously didn't want to go myself.

Sue Ann, not her real name, and I had carried on a friendly rivalry in the military. Also a protégé of Lillian Dunlap, Sue Ann's career seemed to progress in lockstep with mine. Whenever I got promoted below the zone, Sue Ann got promoted below the zone. After she had been selected to attend the Command & General Staff College, I was sent the following year.

Mind you, there was no personal animosity between us. I was just very conscious of wanting to outperform Sue Ann and vice versa. The last thing I wanted to do was follow her footsteps by joining the IG team at Ft. Sam Houston.

But after General Lil gave me another sermon about "the needs of the Army" and laughingly suggested that I could come visit her in San Antonio, I accepted orders to move to Texas for the third time.

I used a VA loan to buy a roomy townhouse in an upscale section of San Antonio for $36,000, then bought some gorgeous furniture, including an Italian modern bedroom set. You see, I had gotten into the habit of doing nice things for Clara, of buying myself little rewards periodically.

When I was at the Command & General Staff College, I actually bought myself a mink coat around Christmas time. I truly felt that I deserved it, having been able to pass tactics and strategy.

I saw no reason to stop pampering myself in San Antonio! Hence the nice furnishings. I didn't have much time to arrange things, though, because I had to fly to Washington for a two-week IG course at the Pentagon. Basically, IG inspectors are a commander's eyes and ears regarding the operational readiness of his or her unit. Every base has an IG office.

The instructors at the Pentagon made it clear that honesty and integrity were critical attributes for doing my job well. They told my classmates and me to always conduct thorough investigations, then unerringly report what we had observed.

The deputy IG of the Army, Maj. Gen. James F. Hamlet, was particularly eloquent and emphatic about how important it was to operate with integrity. His words would continue to ring in my ears once I was in the field actually conducting inspections.

At the completion of that course, I flew back to Ft. Sam Houston to learn the ins and outs of how the IG business operated in the Health Services Command. Once I actually started doing inspections, I found it to be a high-pressure job that was very gratifying.

I'd often find myself coughing after I got to work, the result of the True Blue cigarettes I'd smoked the night before. This was not making much sense to me—smoke at night, get up first thing in the morning and run three miles, then cough for half an hour.

One evening I took my remaining half pack of True Blues and tossed those suckers in the trash. That was October 17, 1977, and I haven't taken a drag since. I'm not going to tell you I wasn't out there the following day, however, desperately pawing through the garbage bin in search of those True Blues.

One of the beautiful things about being an IG is that it really did give me a great opportunity to teach. It also presented me with a fantastic opportunity to learn, and I capitalized on that, too.

When a member of an Army IG team asks questions, people scramble to get answers. Sometimes the questions I asked were related to my report, sometimes they weren't.

I'm basically a nosy person, so I learned a lot about how organizations run and how people cope with problems. I also learned that people have as many excuses for not following rules and regulations as Carter has liver pills.

Doing IG work called for traveling two weeks out of the month, three weeks if the nursing department I was inspecting was at an Army medical center. I really loved all that travel. Seems like I went to an Army installation in practically every state, including Hawaii and Alaska, as well as bases in Panama and Puerto Rico.

I was part of an inspection team that also included a dentist, a physician, a veterinarian, several administrators and any other medical specialists needed to look into special programs. There were two sergeants who were experts in personnel management and who taught me a lot.

IG teams are supposed to be guided solely by military regulations, but don't think politics doesn't occasionally come into play. One time a whistle blower alerted me to a medical center where doctors and nurses were making heroic efforts to treat patients, despite woefully inadequate resources.

It turned out to be a facility very close to our headquarters at Ft. Sam Houston. Well, my inspection team went through there, and we wanted to flunk the hospital, give it an unsatisfactory rating.

That would have been a bombshell if the medical center at the Health Services Command headquarters received a failing grade on an IG inspection. Some high-ranking heads would definitely have rolled.

Well, the old boy network started buzzing overtime and we basically had a two-star general tell us there was no way that facility would receive an unsatisfactory rating. I thought that was wrong, because any other medical facility without a two-star running interference would have gotten nailed big time.

There's a joke that says the two biggest lies ever told occur when an IG shows up at a unit. The first is when the IG says, "We're here to help you." The second is when the unit commander says, "And We're glad to have you."

Army units dread IG inspections and members of the inspection team usually get the kinds of greetings reserved for runaway lepers. I've seen a bar in an officer's club actually clear out after a visiting IG team wandered in.

People don't like being graded, particularly by officers they perceive to be very similar to themselves. When I was inspecting nursing departments, I was tough but fair. But I never lost sight of the fact that I wouldn't be an IG forever, and might eventually find myself working with the people I was inspecting.

There was no reason to act crazy with people just because I happened to have the sword and whip.

During my previous postings in San Antonio, I hadn't made a big effort to learn about the Latino culture that's prevalent there. However, during my stint as an IG, I joined a committee that plans a pre-Easter fiesta in San Antonio every year. I also began taking Spanish classes and was starting to become fairly proficient.

I didn't have a romantic interest, which was okay given that I spent so much time living out of a suitcase. Basically, I had settled into a comfortable groove, serving out what I had been told would be a three-year stint at Ft. Sam Houston, when I received an unexpected request in February 1978 to fold up my tent and move to a new duty station.

Seems that the assistant chief nurse at the Army Regional Medical Center in Frankfurt, West Germany, had made a surprise decision to retire. That was to take place in June, and I was told to scurry on over to Europe and take this woman's place.

My initial reaction to this was "Oh, no, I can't go overseas!" You see, I had gotten used to being promoted ahead of schedule and figured it was about time for me to start wearing the silver eagles of a full colonel.

In order to plant that seed in people's heads and do the politicking to support that ambition, I needed to be in the United States, preferably in Washington, D.C.

Furthermore, I had decided that I was going to build Mother a new house, and had been talking to an architect about getting that project underway.

As I had done when I left Command & General Staff College, I made a long-distance call to Washington, to the office of the Chief of the Army Nurse Corps. And I used the phone in my house, so that no one could eavesdrop on my conversation.

When the colonel in charge of career assignments came on the line, I lobbied hard to stay at Ft. Sam Houston. I noted that my assignment was supposed to be for three years, not two, and that I was doing well at my IG work.

She agreed with me, but said the resignation of the assistant chief nurse in Frankfurt was an extenuating circumstance. I had the option, I was told, of going to Frankfurt or resigning. But I could not turn down that assignment.

Well, I sure as hell wasn't going to resign after seventeen years of service. I was only three years from the twenty years necessary to receive a pension. It was pretty much a no-brainer that I had to go to Europe.

Before I gave my answer, however, I called Mother and told her what was happening. She told me to go ahead and take care of my business—we could take care of the house after I returned to the United States. My brother Raymond, who had recently retired from the Air Force the year before Daddy died, lived nearby. He said he'd visit Mother often and let me know if she needed anything. I shall always be grateful to him for his help.

Now that I had Mother's blessing, I called Washington back and told them that, yes, I'd go to West Germany to replace that assistant chief nurse in three months. Whenever you go across the ocean, you always run the risk of being out of sight, out of mind when it comes to the powers that be in Washington. There was no way I could allow that to happen.

So before I went to Germany, I took a little trip from San Antonio to Washington. A face-to-face with the assignment officer for the Chief of the Army Nurse Corps was in order.

Her name was Col. Pat Miller and we had been assigned together before. So I could dispense with formalities and just cut to the chase. She was tickled to see me when I walked through the door of her Pentagon office. Over the years I had developed a reputation for being highly competent, a hard worker and a character to boot.

Pat offered me some coffee, which I never drink because I can't stand the taste and because I'm already wired to begin with. We exchanged pleasantries, reminisced about old times, then yours truly got to work.

"Now, Pat Miller, I want to tell you something," I said smiling. "I realize that I'm going to be out of the country and away from the flagpole, but you need to understand that this is my year to get promoted to full colonel!"

Pat threw back her head and laughed at my audacity, my naked ambition. But it wasn't a situation that called for subtlety or for being namby-pamby, in my estimation. Sometimes, you've just gotta lay your cards on the table and I did.

"Get out of here, Clara," Pat said, rolling her eyes. "You know I don't have anything to do with that stuff. All that is up to the promotion board."

I knew that, of course. But I also knew that word of my encounter with Pat would get around to people who did have some say in whether I got promoted. Gossiping is a secret strategy that top leaders utilize all time. If you want something to happen, put it on the net. If you're worthy, it'll happen. If not, then you may get fired!

"Well, I just wanted to make sure you know that my name is Clara L. Adams," I told Pat.

"Clara, believe me, I know what your name is. Everybody in this office does."

Having heard that, I segued into the other reason for my visit, which was to gather intelligence about my next duty station in Germany.

When my little politicking visit was over, I flew back to San Antonio to begin the arduous task of corralling all my personal belongings and shipping them to West Germany.

I was again embarking on what was supposed to be a three-year tour of duty. I figured the odds of being wined and dined by a dashing romantic interest while in Germany were nil. Among nursing lieutenants, the running joke is that men never make passes at the chief nurse or the assistant chief, and now that fate was about to befall me.

But by June 1978, three years after my affair with Gene, I had gotten comfortable being by myself. I didn't need to be validated by a man anymore. I was okay because I believed that I was okay. What a wonderful feeling!

Besides, there would be plenty of work to occupy me once I got to Frankfurt.

* * * * * * * * * * *

When I was at Walter Reed, I purchased a red Audi Fox that I fell in love with. Rather than sell it, I drove my sweet chariot from Texas to Charleston, South Carolina, where it was placed on a ship headed across the Atlantic. My brother Ray traveled to Charleston to give me a sendoff.

From the port of Charleston I traveled to that city's airport and boarded a civilian airliner that the military had chartered to fly me and about two hundred other souls to Germany. I smiled as that jet moved down the runway, thinking about how Mother nearly had a cow the first time little Clara Mae got on a plane.

Two children, one eight, one nine, were traveling by themselves on my flight, so I was pressed into babysitter duty. Fortunately they were well behaved, so I emerged from that flight relatively rested and eager to meet with the officer, whom I'll call Col. Ann Grable, who was chief nurse at the Army medical center at Frankfurt.

It was odd to walk through a modern-looking airport like one might see in the States and hear German being spoken over the intercom system. And the signs and advertisements were as foreign to the eye as spoken German was to the ear.

Ann was waiting for me as soon as I cleared customs at Frankfurt's airport. "Good to see you, Clara, good to see you," she said, shaking my hand enthusiastically like we were long-lost buddies.

We'd briefly been assigned to the Walter Reed Institute of Nursing together, but I didn't really know her well. I soon found out that Ann was thrilled to see me because she hadn't had a vacation for some time.

She helped me with my bags and we made small talk as we walked to her car. It was hard to maintain eye contact, because I had never set foot in Europe in my life. People were dashing past us babbling in German and other languages, dressed quite different from the style that was popular in the States in 1978.

I wanted badly to stop and gawk, and felt that tingly, electric feeling I get whenever I start poking around in new surroundings. I love to travel, and West Germany would provide me with plenty of opportunities.

As we loaded my bags into Ann's car, I recall thinking that she seemed to be a stodgy, conservative, career officer—definitely not a risk-taker. Even her car, a big American sedan that was an Oldsmobile or Buick, reinforced that impression.

However, that snap judgment went down the drain the moment Ann drove from the airport and entered the Autobahn. She immediately floored the accelerator and was wheeling that big car around faster than I'd ever motored in the States. Funny thing was, all the traffic around us was moving just as fast, if not faster.

"What is this, Ann?" I asked, hunkering down in my seat as the skyline of Frankfurt whizzed past.

"Listen, if you don't drive fast around here, you'll get run over," Ann replied, looking unconcerned.

My thoughts drifted to my red Audi Fox, which probably hadn't left the port of Charleston. Maybe it wasn't such a good idea to have it shipped over.

Not only did traffic flow quickly, there was an awful lot of it. Sixty-five million people were packed into West Germany, which had an area roughly the size of Oregon.

Dealing with the cut and thrust of German traffic had become so second-nature to Ann that as she drove, she began quizzing me regarding my qualifications to be an assistant chief nurse at a large Army medical center.

Apparently my answers satisfied her, because the impromptu interrogation ended before we arrived at the Army medical center in Frankfurt. More accurately, it was located on the outskirts of Frankfurt, away from much of the congestion and traffic of that huge city.

One thing I liked about Germany right off the bat was my living quarters, which Ann had gotten for me in the U.S. Consulate General housing area. It was in a civilian neighborhood and housed personnel assigned to the U.S. Consulate and Embassy. When vacancies materialized, single military officers who were lieutenant colonel and above could move in. My accommodations were on the luxurious side, so I definitely appreciated that.

Ann was going to be vacationing in Ireland in three weeks, so she wanted to get a sense of what I knew before she left. After the first week, she was convinced the medical center's nursing department would be in good hands during her absence.

On the other hand, I wasn't feeling quite so comfortable around Ann. It didn't take long to see she had developed a hostile attitude toward the Army and was very, very bitter. Before being assigned to Germany, she had informed the Army Nurse Corps that she planned to retire in a few years.

She'd wanted her last assignment to be in the United States, but was given West Germany instead, because of her experience and seniority. Ann was furious about that, and her anger used to crop up in conversation all the time. She would pop off during staff meetings, making disparaging remarks about the Army Nurse Corps and the officers who ran it.

I was so uncomfortable with her remarks that by the end of the second week, I knew I would have to address the situation. "Clara, you're just going to have to figure out a way to deal with this civilly and get it done," I told myself, steeling my nerves.

Col. Grable's attitude concerned me because the outlook and morale of a military unit flows from the top. If a colonel is the top person and he or she is negative, those bad vibes go down-hill to lieutenant colonels, majors, captains, first lieutenants and second lieutenants. It just keeps going and poisons the atmosphere for everybody.

Her smoldering resentment notwithstanding, Ann was otherwise a superb administrator who ran a well-organized department.

The last thing I needed was for Ann to go on vacation in a week and leave behind a bunch of bad attitudes for me to deal with. Plus, it just struck me as disloyal to talk negatively about the Army Nurse Corps leadership.

Early one Friday morning I asked God for guidance and to bless my actions. Then I took a deep breath and rose from my desk, intent on confronting my new supervisor. I strode into Ann's office and gently pulled the door shut. I don't think it made a sound, I closed it so carefully. I was definitely not feeling too courageous.

Ann was working at her desk and stopped to look at me quizzically. No turning back now.

"Ma'am, I need to have a little talk with you."

Ann nodded.

"Let me tell you something, Chief. I can do anything that you want done and I can handle anything you want handled. But I have never, ever been in a situation where I was disloyal to the chief of the Corps. I'm feeling that I'm in that situation now."

I paused to take a breath. So far so good–keep going, Clara.

"I've always felt that if I had something I wanted to say to the chief, it was best to go to the chief directly."

My boss continued to look at me blankly, showing neither surprise nor displeasure.

"I think you need to give everyone here the idea that we're going to be loyal to the Corps," I said, pressing forward. "Because if not, I can't support you."

A few moments of silence followed, during which I was sure she heard my heart thumping.

"I'm sorry," Ann said mildly. "I didn't realize it was so noticeable. Please accept my apology for having left that impression.

I'll speak to the staff to make sure everybody is straight on this subject."

She held up her end of the bargain, apologizing to the staff for speaking out of school and informing them that I was to have their full support during her absence. Ann knew I was right. She was big enough to admit her mistake and I admired her for that.

A week later Ann went off to Ireland for three weeks and caught a nasty inner ear infection. After she returned, Ann spent a week hospitalized at Frankfurt's medical center and wound up being away for a total of six weeks.

So in essence, for a month and a half, I was the chief nurse for the 500 military and civilian nursing personnel at Frankfurt. I was reveling in the challenge and responsibility. There were many, many opportunities to excel.

My days began at five-thirty in the morning with a three-to five-mile run through a beautiful park near my apartment. Then I would get dressed and be at the medical center by seven.

By the time Ann returned, she had about eight months left before her retirement. That inner ear problem continued to torment her, causing headaches and messing with her equilibrium. She fought it like a trooper, however, and thought I was the greatest thing since sliced bread, because I could slip into the chief nurse's role without missing a beat. I was not afraid of hard work and typically toiled from seven in the morning until seven in the evening.

Observing the extent to which work was my primary activity in West Germany, Ann suggested I join something called the Taunus Medical Society, a group of German and American health care professionals that gathered once a month to discuss topics of mutual interest.

I thought, why not? My life revolved around the medical center, so associating with those Taunus folks would help round out my existence a bit. They used to gather at German restaurants, as well as the Army officer's club at Frankfurt. I went to that latter location for my first meeting.

That evening I was standing in the club nursing a drink, minding my own business, when a male, German-accented voice purred behind me, "Good evening, how are you?" I turned to face a little, silver-haired German gentleman with impish-looking blue eyes. He appeared to be in his late fifties to early sixties, was sure of himself and was clearly something of a charmer.

"My name is Heinz Ender . . . and who are you?" I heard him say.

"My name is Clara Adams," I replied, thinking that he was a bit on the pushy side.

"I'm a dentist with my practice here in Frankfurt." Herr Docktor Ender proceeded to tell me in halting English that he had been to Africa and spent some good years of his life there. In the middle of his tale, a little bell rang, signifying it was dinnertime.

Afterward, that persistent little Ender fellow ambled by again to strike up another conversation.

"You know," he said, "you seem like a real nice person. I would like to show you Europe in style."

I thought about the words of an old tune, "If you got the money, Honey, I got the time."

"But first," Herr Ender continued, "I have a little ranch in Italy, and I need to go there to harvest my grapes."

That sounded like such a show-off line that I had to laugh. My little pursuer seemed harmless enough, safe . . . it might not hurt to go out with him from time to time for a drink or dinner or both.

In time we were dating, and I'll never forget the time he took me to Hof, Austria, near Salzburg. We had to travel on the Autobahn to get there and like most Germans, Heinz drove like a damn fool. Whenever I got into a car with him, my ritual was to fall asleep immediately.

That way, I could just perish without witnessing the horrendous, high-speed crash that pried my soul from my body. I would just go to sleep and not have to feel it. I tried to get Heinz to slow down, but you don't tell Germans to slow down. Mind you, by this time, my red Audi had arrived and I had also learned to speed on the Autobahn. I couldn't hold a candle to Heinz's speed-demon antics.

When we reached Hof, Heinz took me to this wonderful restaurant overlooking a little blue lake that was ringed by magnificent snow-capped mountains. He ordered schnapps, which I had been warned not to drink with German citizens.

"Oh, that's foolish," Heinz scoffed, then turned to the other diners around us. "This little lady has never had schnapps before, so everybody get ready to watch this!"

Well, this American had something to prove, because I've got to show these Europeans that Americans can handle their liquor. The schnapps was served ice cold in little shot glasses and tasted fruity. I downed the first one as the folks around me laughed and clapped. But after two or three of those things, I really couldn't tell you if anyone else was there, or if I had been drinking by myself. I was tipsy and there wasn't too much I could say about that state of affairs, because I definitely had been forewarned.

Herr Ender didn't turn out to be harmless at all. A sly, silver-haired fox is more like it. We started dating seriously and he deftly managed to snag Mother's heart the first time they met. She came to see me in Germany and was confined to a wheel-chair due to arthritis and vascular disease. Heinz met her at the airport with a bouquet of red roses and that was all she wrote. Those two were fast friends from that point on. She very rarely received flowers, except from her children on Mother's Day and birthdays.

After wining and dining yours truly and showing me Europe "in style," Heinz sold his oral surgery practice and followed me to the United States to become my second husband.

I had to overcome two mental hurdles first, though. The first was a 26-year difference in our ages. The second, and I have to be honest, was that Heinz was white. And while we had fun, I had no intention of getting super serious about him.

Mother, thank her wise soul, counseled me to let my heart be my guide, not Heinz's skin color.

There were little cultural things to overcome, too. Don't ask me why, but in Germany you never cut potatoes with a fork and knife while dining. You only use your fork and it used to drive Heinz to distraction whenever I took a knife to my potato. If that sounds funny, it's not humorous when you're hungry as heck and your significant other is sitting across the table from you, gnashing his teeth over your eating habits.

Sometimes when I'm cooking I'll dab at my dish with a finger, then lick it to see what it tastes like. This also drives Heinz ballistic–he insists that I immediately wash my hands before proceeding any further. Respectable German housewives would never do such a thing, Herr Ender will grumble.

Something I love about Heinz is that he's never had a problem subjugating his ego and his needs to the demands of my career. Instead of being threatened, he was my No. 1 fan and booster, for which I will always be grateful. When we met in

1978, he used to say, "Ja, Clara, you vill be a full colonel before the year is out. And you vill become a general one of these days!"

That first prediction was borne out in July, 1979 when I was promoted–below the zone–to full colonel. I had just turned 40, making me the youngest nurse in Army history to pull that off.

Before I was promoted, Ann left, and I became the acting chief nurse. The chief nurse slot at Frankfurt was an honor usually reserved for senior colonels, but I was named Ann's replacement. One of the people who had to sign off on that decision was the commander of the medical center, also a colonel and physician.

As a formality, I had to drop by his office for an interview after he okayed me for chief nurse. Inside his office, amongst the mementos he'd gathered during his stay in Europe, we had one of the most startling conversations of my 32-year military career.

I was genuinely curious why he approved my promotion to chief nurse, when he easily could have requested a colonel with more experience.

"Why me, Sir, when you could have had a colonel with more time in grade?" Even though we held the same rank, I had to call him 'Sir' because he had been a colonel longer.

"A couple of reasons," he said, folding his arms behind his head and leaning back in his chair. "One, you got picked below the zone for colonel and that doesn't happen too often for nurses, so you must be good at what you do. Plus, I've been watching you, and I think you'll do quite well. Basically, you've been the chief nurse here since Ann came down with that ear infection several months ago."

I nodded, savoring the hard-earned praise.

Unfolding his arms, that colonel from Tennessee slid forward in his chair and leaned toward me.

"I'll tell you, there are two things you ought to know in order to deal with me here, Clara. The first thing is, no matter how good you are, because you're black you'll never be as good as a white person. The second thing is, you need to understand that in any difference of opinion between nurses and physicians, the physician is always right."

For a second, I didn't say anything, thinking that I was hearing hallucinatory voices! A little island of tightness surfaced in my belly, brought on by a gush of adrenaline.

"You know, sir, I . . ." *Don't say that, Clara. Just shut up for a moment.* I inhaled deeply, twice.

"Sir, in terms of your first comment, I'm going to give you an opportunity to demonstrate your point whenever you see fit. And I will call upon you as our commander to support the department of nursing. But if you ever stumble, and let anyone else know that's the way you feel about me, I'll slap a class-action suit on you so fast it'll make your head swim. And as for that thing about physicians always being right, I won't even grace that with a comment."

Breathing fast, I stood and quickly walked out of that colonel's office before my lips went into gear again. The colonel was dumb enough to make such derogatory remarks, but smart enough to make sure he never said it around anyone else. I was wondering if I would be faced with an opportunity to nail him.

Over the next few months we established a good working relationship. I don't know if his attitude changed about me as a person, but he never behaved otherwise. That's all I really cared about.

Remembering how Katy Galloway taught me how to be a chief nurse at Ft. Meade, Maryland, I began something in Frankfurt I dubbed the Chief Nurse of the Week program. It was a formal mentoring deal that actually lasted anywhere from six months to a year and was primarily designed to help some of the nurses hone their leadership skills.

I closely monitored these nurses as they handled all the responsibilities of a chief nurse, including making decisions and meeting department heads. Not only did the nurses benefit, but I benefited as well, because the program basically gave me another pair of eyes, hands and ears around Frankfurt. The leader of a nursing department in a large medical facility needs that kind of help. As I learned from General Lil Dunlap, mentoring is vital to becoming a top-notch leader. During my career, I mentored as many as forty to fifty officers and civilians at a time.

In the early eighties, I joined an organization that was all about mentoring. It is known as THE ROCKS, Incorporated. It began in the mid-60s on an informal basis at the Command and General Staff College, when a group of black officers met together to become acquainted. It is named in honor of Brigadier General Roscoe C. Cartwright, an enlisted soldier who became an officer via Officer Candidate School, who encouraged establishment of a formal networking organization for officers assigned to the Pentagon to network. He and his wife met an untimely death in a plane crash in 1974. They were returning to Washington, DC, where the ROCKS, Inc. was being organized that evening.

The ROCKS' main purpose is to mentor and prepare officers for leadership in the military and the civilian world. It has grown from the single DC chapter to 15 chapters and five interest groups in the States and in Europe. Membership is open to active duty, retired, reserve and former officers of all the uniformed services. Serving as ROCKS president from 1990 to 1994, I now serve as Vice-President for Mentoring on the National Board of Directors. I have been proud of the contributions the ROCKS have made in mentoring junior officers in a spirit of concern, dedication and professionalism, community service and of promoting scholarship. I have welcomed the opportunity to share my experiences with mentoring officers which I began with the Chief Nurse of the Week program in Frankfurt.

Back in Washington, Col. Hazel Johnson-Brown became the first African American chief of the Army Nurse Corps and was promoted to general. In her new role as boss of bosses, she paid a visit to West Germany in 1980. Eager to support the first sister to run the Corps, I asked what she needed me to do rather than tell her my desire for a new assignment.

Hazel asked me to roll up my sleeves and breathe some life into the moribund Army Recruiting Command's nurse recruiting program, which was based in Ft. Sheridan, Illinois. That particular job wasn't even on my radar screen, but if that's what she needed to succeed, then I'd light a bonfire under the joint. Plus, I knew General Hazel would eventually make it worth my while, to paraphrase Lillian Dunlap.

I tell you, that assignment turned out to be the most memorable of my career in more ways than one.

Chapter XVII

Talk It To Life

Its martial-sounding name notwithstanding, the U.S. Army War College in Carlisle, Pennsylvania, isn't devoted exclusively to the art of war, but is geared toward graduate-level leadership and management training. The War College stresses conflict avoidance, an objective I was in sync with. Strategy rules the day at that place, with a strong emphasis on the short-and long-range decisions that precede tactical decisions. Unlike the Command & General Staff College, the War College is for senior-level officers and civilians. Having a War College diploma is a significant feather in the cap of an officer trying to earn stars, an ambition that was starting to seem less far-fetched after my promotion to full colonel.

I was selected for the Army War College Correspondence Studies course while I was in Germany. I had a year remaining in the course when I returned to the United States in 1981 to delve into the wonderful world of recruiting. For two weeks out of the year, I went to Carlisle as an in-residence student. It was a revelation to discover that most of the colonels in my class of 247 people were no more eager to fight than I was. The majority of them had seen the carnage of war firsthand and were reluctant to send young soldiers into harm's way.

Carlisle was my first stop when I came back home in July 1981. Then I moved on to Ft. Benjamin Harrison, Indiana, for a two-week course for recruiting commanders. From there, my next stop was Ft. Sheridan, Illinois, situated beside alluring, emerald-green Lake Michigan. The Army Recruiting Command Headquarters, Ft. Sheridan, was a beautiful place to be in July, when those lake breezes wafted in and cooled the summer air nicely.

Heinz was jetting back and forth between Europe and the United States, shutting down his dental practice and tending to real estate matters. We'd decided we were going to tie the knot and live on my side of the pond. So it was a busy, frenetic time for both of us.

Prior to Ft. Sheridan, I had always arrived at duty stations where things were running smoothly and I was expected to maintain the status quo. This time, I had to be a turnaround artist.

As Chief Army Nurse Recruiter, my basic job was to establish policy for recruiting nurses within the Recruiting Command. But more than that, I was expected to turbocharge the nurse recruiting numbers coming out of Ft. Sheridan. Unfortunately, the Army Nurse Corps had a long-standing reputation for falling short of its recruiting projections.

The Recruiting Command was run by Maj. Gen Maxwell R. Thurman, an artillery officer who looked deceptively professorial with his high forehead, black horn-rimmed glasses and benign visage. "Mad Max, as he was affectionately called, took over the Recruiting Command in 1979 and revitalized the place, coming up with the famous Army "Be All That You Can Be" campaign, among other innovations.

General Thurman became a four-star general and went on to lead Operation Just Cause, the invasion in Panama in 1989. Before that, he was the Deputy Chief of Staff for Personnel and Vice Chief of Staff of the Army. General Max would become a powerful ally in my rise to the stars. But first, I had to earn my stars in his eyes and in the eyes of Brig. Gen. Hazel Johnson-Brown, back in Washington.

General Max did not waste time with sugary words and was blunt to a fault. He never left any doubts regarding his expectations, which I could deal with. "The nurse recruiting program is broken," he brusquely informed me during our first meeting. "Fix it!"

I had moved into the upper two floors of a massive Ft. Sheridan house that was two doors down from where he lived, a setup that had its advantages and disadvantages. General Max was a bachelor and an insomniac who thought nothing of calling meetings at his home on a moment's notice.

However, on July 22, 1981, I had something to do that superseded my War College homework, Max and everything else. Heinz and I were to get married in a little chapel in Waukegan, Illinois.

Heinz, who's always looking for an excuse to dress up anyway, looked quite debonair in his spiffy beige suit, purple shirt and matching tie. I wore a mint green suit and ruffled blouse that I had purchased in Germany. Unlike my first marriage, when my hands shook like I had palsy, I was serene and tranquil the second time around. I was confident that I was involved with a man who loved and respected me for who I was and was willing to accept me as I was. And I felt the same way about him.

I also made myself a promise that I was not going to let this marriage, which represented Heinz's fourth trip to the altar, disintegrate into divorce. Heinz and I didn't go on a honeymoon, because the next day I had to return to the incredible crush of work that came with my new position. Plus, Heinz had to fly back to Europe a few days after our wedding. The two of us did travel to Hawaii six months later for something of a delayed honeymoon, though.

Once Heinz came to the States for good, my workaholic leanings were the main source of friction in our marriage. I was putting in eighteen- and twenty-hour days getting that nurse recruiting program back on track. It was an absolute pressure cooker for three years. In many ways it was tougher than being chief of the Army Nurse Corps and tougher than being a general.

However, in terms of resource and personnel management, I never learned more about how the Army runs than when I was assigned to Recruiting Command. I am eternally grateful for having had that opportunity.

Looking back on my first half year there, I'm at a loss to explain how I made it. I was a newlywed, traveling 75 percent of the time and poring over thousands of pages of reading material for my War College correspondence course!

I had five recruiters assigned directly to me at the headquarters, then another thirty nurse recruiting counselors who were attached to various battalions and brigades around the country. They all had to work with me so that our recruiting efforts would be coordinated.

Each of those thirty nurse recruiting counselors managed four or five nurse recruiters each, all of whom were sergeants that did the actual work of going to colleges and universities to find nurses. We did a profile and you know who our most successful nurse recruiters were? They were male soldiers who had been in artillery units!

Women respond to men in uniform, no question about it.

The bad feelings generated by the Vietnam War were still evident during my three years in recruiting. On one occasion, I had to fly to UCLA in uniform to convince the dean of the nursing school to allow Army nurse recruiters in her facility.

I did an awful lot of crisis management in the Recruiting Command—it consumed about 50 percent of my time.

On April 14, 1982, I was sitting in my Recruiting Command office as usual before 8 a.m., coordinating my activities for the day. I had already run four miles and meditated earlier that morning, was starting to get the hang of the nurse recruiting business and generally felt positive. I was looking forward to burning up another 18-hour day.

Instead of pausing at the door as she usually did, my secretary breezed directly into my office and came to a halt in front of my desk, looking troubled. "Ma'am, your brother Ray is on the telephone," she said quietly.

Curious as to why he was calling so early, I picked up the phone on my desk and punched the button with the blinking light. No one was on the line.

"This is Colonel Adams-Ender."

"Um, are you sitting down, Clara?" Raymond sounded shocked, prompting hope he wanted to discuss a marital problem, a fist fight, something relatively trivial.

"Yeah, Ray, I am. What's going on?"

"Mother died this morning. She had a heart attack." My shoulders slumped and my pen clattered to the floor. Ray had to be mistaken on this one. He'd meant to say something else . . .

"Wait a minute, hold on a minute here, Ray. Just wait a minute now—run that by me again?"

"She was having trouble breathing last night and I took her to the hospital," my enraged brother explained. Anger was the defense mechanism his pained mind was clutching at for solace. "They kept her for about four or five hours, but they couldn't find anything wrong with her, so they released her ."

"Oh, Ray, oh God no, Ray. Oh please, nooooo." Tears rained down my cheeks as I sat immobile with the phone receiver stuck to my ear. My secretary and a sergeant stood in the doorway staring, but I barely noticed them. "Are you sure about this, Ray?"

"They should have kept her, Clara. They should have kept her."

I took ten days of emergency leave and flew down to North Carolina along with Heinz. We had been home just three weeks earlier to finalize plans to build her a new house.

Like I did after Daddy's death, I went on autopilot after returning to Ft. Sheridan. I graduated from the War College in July and I continued fighting to get more nurses for the active duty Army, Reserve units and the National Guard.

But the need to mourn always catches up with you, because the mind sort of demands that catharsis. You can tamp it down and tuck it away all you want to, but it'll bob to the surface eventually.

One morning six months after Mother's death, at about 2 a.m., the reality that I was never, ever going to see my dear mother on earth again came crashing down on me. I sobbed so hard that I rocked back and forth on my bed as Heinz gently held me.

'I remember you fondly, I'll always remember you fondly, Mother,' I thought. 'But I'm setting you free.' Actually, it was I who was being set free. I truly felt a deep and profound sense of loss when Mother died that I have never felt since that event.

*　*　*　*　*　*　*　*　*

Thankfully, the long, long hours I put in to energize the recruitment of Army nurses did yield dividends. There was a nursing shortage during my time with Recruiting Command, yet my staff and I managed to attract more than 5,000 bright young folks into the world of Army nursing.

My staff and I pumped out more than 100 brochures, award-winning ads, presentation items and leaflets during my tenure. I routinely traveled more than 100,000 miles a year in order to give about 400 speeches to professional organizations. The Army got its pound of flesh out of Col. Clara Adams-Ender while I was at Ft. Sheridan.

What made my success particularly gratifying was that I was hardly an expert on recruiting when I took that assignment.

However, by this time, I was confident in my ability to lead and manage the troops, so I went to work doing just that.

No matter how much a leader works to keep things going smoothly, conflict will still arise. You must keep in mind that you gotta have conflict to have progress, but fighting is a choice. The key is to resolve conflict without fighting with others in the process.

There were many possible conflicts in the recruiting business, and I got a good workout in conflict resolution. One that I remember started with solving a problem of fraternization between an officer and the enlisted nurse recruiting sergeants. It ended with lessons on how to overcome obstacles and to keep one's eyes on the ultimate goal.

In this case, there was a lieutenant colonel who worked in the nurse recruiting office in Washington who came out periodically to the recruiting course to present the newest policies to the recruiters. I got word that she was also partying with the sergeants the night before, which probably accounted for their less than respectful behavior during her class the next day.

Well, I confronted her about her behavior, and she admitted that it was true that she and the sergeants always got together for a few drinks and some dancing so she could get to "know them better." I told her that such behavior could not be tolerated, so I called the Army Nurse Corps Chief, told her what was happening and asked that the lieutenant colonel be kept in Washington.

Not to be outdone and to vent her anger, the lieutenant colonel started a whispering campaign to the effect that I was uncooperative and doing things contrary to Nurse Corps policies. I went on about the business of putting nurses in combat boots.

I had to make a trip to Washington to sit on a board for nurses being promoted from major to lieutenant colonel. Aware of that, the angered lieutenant colonel I'd had the run-in with planned a little surprise for me.

Fortunately, I received a call from another officer who tipped me off about the plan. I was to be summoned to a meeting with a bunch of officers from the nurse recruiting policy office. They would all present allegations designed to make me spout off and be insubordinate to the ANC chief, who would chair the meeting. Armed with that information, I had time to plan my actions and responses.

Sure enough, when I traveled to Washington for the promotion board, I was asked to attend such a meeting. When I arrived at the Pentagon conference room, fifteen officers and the Chief were already there, seated around a table and each of their eyes was locked on yours truly. Some allegations and vague accusations were made that I hadn't been following ANC policies to the letter. Since I had been forewarned, I was able to take their inquisition in stride.

The Chief, who chaired the meeting, made some statements about my need to seek policy guidance before making decisions. She expected that I would do so in the future without question. She wrapped up her remarks and asked if I had any comment.

"No, Ma'am," I said, rising from my hot seat. "Now, if you will excuse me, I must return to my promotion board, because we are adjourning this afternoon." I looked around at the shocked faces, smiled and left the room.

I will not lie and tell you that I was not angry. Matter of fact, I was livid. I had a whole plane ride back to Chicago to decide my next move. It had to be made with the main goal in mind— to recruit nurses to serve soldiers and their families in peace and war. That goal transcended any pettiness or humiliation that I would encounter.

Two days later, I called the Army Nurse Corps Chief and scheduled a meeting with her and her key policy staff. This time, we sat down and had an exchange of ideas and resolved the conflicting issues. I even managed to gain some policy concessions that I had been seeking for some time.

The lessons learned were to be courageous, strong in your convictions and never lose sight of the main goal. Obstacles may also come and are not necessarily there to stop you. They are there to be overcome and to decide if one will go over, under, around or through them to reach one's goal. As I reflected, overcoming obstacles had been the story of my personal life and my career. Obstacles had really been opportunities to excel.

When the new Chief of the Army Nurse Corps was selected in 1983, I was soon due for reassignment. I decided to call her personally and make my desires known to be chief nurse at Walter Reed Army Medical Center. By this time, I was a senior colonel and believed that I could be successful in such a position of great responsibility.

The new chief, Brigadier General Connie L. Slewitzke, agreed with me and sent me to that assignment in June, 1984. I had done a super job in Recruiting Command, and was eager to return to nursing administration in a hospital setting. I was absolutely ecstatic about getting back to Walter Reed, the ultimate plum. I thanked her and told her that she'd never regret her decision.

Heinz was tickled to be moving to Washington and threw himself headlong into the task of finding us a new nest, a 3,600-square foot, four-bedroom Tudor in Silver Spring, Maryland, about five miles from Walter Reed.

Before I left Ft. Sheridan, I received a touching telephone call from a sister we had recruited into the Army Nurse Corps at the age of forty-five, which was my age. Cynthia Houston-

Brickey had tons of nursing experience and once worked at Walter Reed as a civilian nurse.

"I've been assigned at Reed before and I know you've got a huge job ahead, but you can do it," Cynthia said breezily. "I want you to do two things: One, no matter what it takes, put a flower on your desk every day. And the second thing is, keep a little mirror in the top, right drawer of your desk. Any time you have trouble with someone who doesn't feel the same way about you that you feel about yourself, pull that mirror out and say: 'I don't care what they say about me. I'm okay!'

Until today I carry that mirror with me. And you'd be surprised how having a flower on your desk changes your disposition.

Walter Reed's commander, Maj. Gen. Lewis A. Mologne, welcomed me to the command. He commented that although he had not worked with me before, he was impressed with my reputation. I assured him that I was a team player who came to help. Despite a three-year hiatus, it didn't take me long to get back into the swing of leading a nursing staff in providing top-notch patient care.

I was happy as a lark to be running Walter Reed's nursing department and was not mulling any career opportunities beyond that one. Being in charge of 1,300 nursing personnel inside a 1,000-bed facility was heady enough for me.

Opened in 1909 in honor of Army Maj. Walter Reed, who did pioneering work against typhoid and yellow fever, Walter Reed Army Medical Center is the Rolls Royce among Department of Defense medical facilities. Foreign dignitaries and presidents regularly come there for medical treatment, along with military personnel from every branch. I honestly could have retired from there and been quite fulfilled.

My huge second-floor office had a bathroom, plenty of bookshelves and a conference area where I could seat people around a table and chat with them. Outside my office was a porch-like structure that ringed the entire building and was often used by runners during inclement weather. Sunlight streamed in through large picture windows, which provided a view of Fern Street, a residential neighborhood so named because a lot of ferns were sprinkled through it.

During my first day I closed the door to my office and propped my feet on my desk, admiring my cavernous new work area. 'Chief Nurse at Walter Reed! I have arrived! This is the big time!'

At the same time, I had a flash. The need to get organized

was greater than ever. I had to decide what I needed to do to be successful in managing my myriad of duties as Walter Reed's chief nurse. During an early morning meditation session, I concluded that there must first be a plan of self-management. I also reasoned that it included five entities: philosophy, values, knowledge, relationships and endurance. Over the next four weeks, I defined those entities for myself and wrote the rest of my self-management plan. I drew a model that demonstrated how the leader integrates these entities and establishes a plan of action of daily self-management. I worked the plan and it reaped huge successes as I worked with my staff, other department heads, colleagues and General Mologne.

The nursing department was already in good shape, because only crackerjack nurses got to be chief at Walter Reed. So I pushed to move beyond merely good to flawless. Gen. Mologne never had a moment's trouble out of nursing, no brush fires demanding his immediate attention.

That was the wrong way to proceed, as I discovered while talking to his aide, a young brother who was a Medical Service Corps captain. "Brick,' as everyone called him, lived around the corner from me in Silver Spring, Maryland, and I'd occasionally give him rides home.

We were tooling up Georgia Avenue one evening after work and Brick seemed to be in a pensive mood. "Ma'am, would you mind if I tell you something? You know, Colonel Adams-Ender, you're coming off as too perfect. General Mologne doesn't like people that are too perfect. He likes to make sure he can help solve problems for other people. You gotta bring him some problems."

Well, I made it a point to go see him every Wednesday after that, armed with a list of issues he could assist me with. That heads-up from Brick was excellent, because my relationship with Gen. Mologne became a lot warmer and less formal as a result. He was a most astute leader and administrator and I learned much from him. He surely knew how to solve problems.

As I entered my second year at Walter Reed, I found myself confronting a crisis where I genuinely needed his help. I was getting further and further behind in the number of nurse replacements doled out to me by the Army Nurse Corps' career activities office. I tried to tackle the problem by talking to the colonel in charge of the office, but to no avail.

Not only did the situation fail to improve, but it deteriorated to the point where I was sixty nurses below my authorization. I had no recourse but to draw up a detailed report showing how many nurses I was supposed to have, as opposed to how many I actually had. My report was forwarded to the Army Surgeon General, and a copy was sent to the chief of my Corps.

General Mologne and I had several meetings with the Army Surgeon General and the Chief of the Army Nurse Corps. We devised a plan to fill those nurse vacancies that was satisfactory to all. The nurses at Walter Reed were so pleased that they had armed me well with the nurse workload data that saved the day for them.

Riding herd on Walter Reed's nursing department kept me plenty busy. Plus around the early to mid 1980s, the healthcare community was in an uproar over a mysterious, fatal disease that seemed to affect homosexual men disproportionately.

Like every other major health care facility in the country, Walter Reed was battling the AIDS epidemic. From the fall of 1984 on, increased numbers of airmen, marines, sailors and soldiers were referred to us with vague symptoms–fatigue, weight loss, night sweats and pneumonia. Epidemiologists were just starting to put all the pieces together.

As with the general population, most of the men hospitalized at Walter Reed with these symptoms identified themselves as being gay. This revelation caused something of a quandary, because you were forbidden to serve in the military if you were gay. 'Don't ask, don't tell' had yet to be coined.

At Walter Reed, we decided to keep patients with minimal symptoms together in a unit outside the main hospital, over in the old hospital. However, AIDS patients can experience rapid changes in their health, and there weren't enough nurses in the unit to keep close tabs on everyone.

Gen. Mologne and I had the patients moved into a 40-bed unit in the main hospital. I made it a point to visit that crowded unit daily, because some nurses and physicians were reluctant to deal with AIDS victims. Furthermore, the patients were sensitive about ostracism, and many just wanted someone to talk to. I tell you, I found out a whole lot more about human sexuality and other social issues associated with the epidemic than I ever wanted to know.

It was a taxing time, because I spent a lot of time dealing with the family members and friends of AIDS victims. They struggled with the stigma attached to the disease, and many times didn't even know their loved one was gay or was doing drugs.

The AIDS crisis made nursing more mentally and emotionally draining than it ordinarily is. I found refuge and tranquility in meditation sessions that Walter Reed began offering its health care professionals.

Around the time all that was going on, I experienced a minor health crisis of my own. It affected me while I was sitting at a conference table at Walter Reed, surrounded by other colonels. I was making a point, to be interrupted by a sensation that felt like someone had lit a fire around my neck. Sweat started pouring down my face, because I'm not one of those dainty little women who perspire–I sweat.

Someone asked if I was okay and I replied that I was, which was a lie. Well, as soon as that meeting was over, I flew into the office of Col. Tom Klein, chief of obstetrics and gynecology. He ordered some blood tests that showed that I was experiencing menopause.

Tom prescribed something called Premarin and I got into the habit of taking my little anti-hot pill every day. What usually happened if I didn't wasn't pleasant or pretty.

Prior to my arrival, some of the other chief nurses tended to cloister themselves in their office, but my management style called for managing by walking around a lot and poking my nose into things. That allowed me to be more hands-on and involved than if I'd stayed stuck in my ivory tower of an office. Anyway, when you work in a 1,000-bed facility that's usually 90 percent full, it pays to stay on top of things. Of course, I was always there during my twelve-hour days, and I added periodic evening and night rounds. I needed to see how the lieutenants were doing, and these were the hours they usually worked.

Sometimes I just needed to get as far away from Walter Reed as humanly possible. So I went to Europe several times while I was stationed at Walter Reed, as well as Thailand, the Caribbean and Panama. I had an able and willing travel partner in Heinz. Our excursions continued even after Heinz's teenage son, Ingo, came from Germany to live with us. Ingo eventually became a physician after majoring in biology at the University of Maryland and graduating with a 3.84 average. Heinz and I are so proud of Ingo, who is now a board certified physician in internal medicine and cardiology.

For the first time, my personal and professional lives were on the ascendancy at the same time!

I was feeling generally content and fulfilled when I met with Maj. Gen. Mologne after receiving another glowing officer evaluation report in 1986. He surprised me by confiding that he was mulling over a run at Army Surgeon General slot, giving him a third star. Would I be interested in being his chief nurse, which called for a promotion to general?

Coming out of the blue like that, his offer flabbergasted me. I honestly was not sitting there dying to have stars on my shoulders. Out of the 22,000 military and civilian nurses in the Army Nurse Corps system, I already felt like I had the top job. But with this intriguing proposition on the table, I would have been a fool to flatly reject it.

Telling Gen. Mologne that I needed time to think, I immediately called Sherman Ragland, who had counseled me during my first marriage and the affair that followed. He had retired as a lieutenant colonel from the Medical Service Corps by then, and was living in Maryland.

I told Sherm about Gen. Mologne's offer, and confided that I hadn't given much thought to becoming a general.

"Well, what have you been working for all this time, then?" Sherman demanded.

"Just trying to be all that I could be, Sherm," I said, slightly annoyed with his characteristic directness.

"Clara, you are in the position that probably 95 percent of the chiefs of the Army Nurse Corps have served in," Sherm shot back, sounding exasperated. "I think I mentioned this to you before."

That was true—he had on a number of occasions. Thanks to my talks with Gen. Mologne and Sherman, the dream of becoming an Army general started to take root. Why not talk it to life, as I had my previous promotions?

Getting to general would call for a lot more finesse and backroom maneuvering than moving from lieutenant colonel to colonel, however. First I would need to see which of my influential allies would be willing to throw their support behind me.

I talked with many general officers about how one gets to be a general. I talked with successful people about how one got that way. I listened at the feet of some wise old folks who just told me about having a purpose in life. They all encouraged me to keep up my high level of performance and the rest would work out. Most of them also told me what they would do to influence the situation.

It was suggested that I contact the Honorable John Shannon, a brother who was Assistant Secretary of the Army for Installation and Logistics at that time. He was a retired Army colonel who had a reputation for being frank and candid with everyone. I visited him at the Pentagon. Mr. Shannon asked if I knew any of the generals who would be likely to sit on my promotion board. I told him that I didn't.

"Let me tell you something," Mr. Shannon said wryly. "If you've got a choice between having a good record and having friends on the board, choose friends. Everybody trying to get promoted from colonel to general has a good record."

Another valuable bit of advice. And so it went, with my bending ears and cashing in chits in an effort to talk brigadier general to life. I easily talked to about thirty generals, most of whom offered to lend a hand.

I even buttonholed Republican U.S. Sen. Strom Thurmond, from South Carolina. I was no great fan, but political maneuvering in the military, or the Senate, isn't about a popularity contest. Good ol' Strom told me he had nothing to do with selecting generals, which I knew. However he promised that if my name went before Congress for approval, he'd see to it that I made it.

In the last weeks of 1986, I reviewed and prepared my personnel records to go before the selection board to pick the next chief of the Army Nurse Corps. The board, which was composed of active duty and reserve generals, convened in March, 1987. Their decision wasn't to be announced until June, though.

For the first time in my life, I found myself literally sitting on the edge of my chair, awaiting that promotion board's decision. At home, all I heard from Heinz during that period was, "Calm down, Clara, calm down! You are going to get it!"

The nurses at Walter Reed had taken to hanging little signs that said stuff like, 'The Future Chief of the Army Nurse Corps.' Friends came up to me and said, 'Oh, we're going to speak this thing into existence!'

Were it only that easy.

Two days before the board's decision was to be announced, I got a call in my office at Walter Reed from Lt. Gen. Quinn Becker, the Army Surgeon General. It was late, so most of the staff had gone home. "Clara, I'm calling to give you some information, because I want you to know how to behave whenever the board gets announced on Wednesday," he said. Oh goodness, here it comes! Closing my eyes, I squeezed the phone receiver so hard I thought it would melt. There was an unmistakable smile in his voice.

"Yes, Sir?

"You were selected to be the next Chief of the Army Nurse Corps, and it was a unanimous vote. Congratulations."

General Becker said I needed to act surprised when the official announcement came out in two days, and I told him I thought I could manage. Then I gently hung up the phone. "Yesssss!" I screamed quietly, jumping from my chair and laughing. "Yes, yes, yes!"

I don't think I have an addictive personality, but if I could bottle the euphoria I felt at that instant, I would take a hit every day. I haven't achieved anything, before or since, that's brought me that kind of joy, satisfaction and gratification.

I had worked hard, played by the rules and I clawed my way to the summit, into an incredibly elite fraternity. "Yesssss!"

As I left the building for the evening, a member of a civilian cleaning crew remarked that I seemed to be in an awfully good mood. "Yeah, I'm always in a good mood at the end of the day," I replied.

I was driving up 16th Street to my house, when it hit me that I WAS REALLY ABOUT TO BE A GENERAL! And then I started trembling uncontrollably, just like I had before my first marriage. I trembled the rest of the way home, grinning the whole time! Other motorists were probably wondering what was wrong with the crazy female colonel in the Mercedes.

Chapter XVIII

Crashing The Fraternity

I experienced some emotional peaks and valleys after my selection to head the Army Nurse Corps was officially announced. There was plenty of back-slapping and scads of friends and relatives calling and dropping by to wish me well.

But there were also moments when I longed for Mother and Daddy to be able to see their daughter become a general. I had the feeling that they were smiling and dancing around in heaven, though.

Another thing that let a little air out of my balloon involved the man who jump-started my quest to become a general, Lew Mologne. Unfortunately, he would never achieve his goal of becoming Army Surgeon General, because he was diagnosed with liver cancer, which is rarely survivable.

Before he passed away, General Lew Mologne congratulated me again and wished me well in my role as Chief of the Army Nurse Corps, which I was able to draw some solace from.

I wouldn't be reigning over the Corps from the Pentagon, as my predecessors had. The Pentagon had grown to the point where officers were practically tripping over each other, so a number of offices were moved into office space in suburban Virginia, including the office for the Chief of the Army Nurse Corps. Even though we weren't physically located in the Pentagon, we were still listed as Pentagon staff.

So my new work place was a tall office building in Falls Church, Va. My office was on the sixth floor, directly across from the elevators and with a pleasant view of the skyline at Bailey's Crossroads.

People entering the office immediately found themselves in a small main reception area that was used by a secretary and by an administrative assistant, an Army major. The quarters were fairly cramped, considering that we were directing the activities of 22,000 military and civilian nurses worldwide.

My first major task after being designated the incoming Chief of the Army Nurse Corps was finding an assistant chief. I picked Col. John Hudock, who was a whiz at dealing with nursing administration, especially personnel matters. A selection board was assembled filled with colonels who unanimously selected John. As soon as that took place, I immediately came under sniper fire.

My critics had the following complaint: How dare I put a man second in command of the Army Nurse Corps? Furious that a male nurse was going to be the second highest-ranking officer in Army Nurse Corps, a complaint was lodged with a two-star who was the Army's deputy Surgeon General. Why, I don't know, because John Hudock's selection was legitimate and aboveboard.

I was working at my temporary desk in the Chief of the Army Nurse Corps area, when I received a request to meet with the Deputy Surgeon General in his office. I was still a colonel-promotable because the Army Nurse Corps was allotted just one general star and the current chief was still wearing it. So I was a colonel going before a two-star. However, I already had a good relationship with him, so we were on good terms.

"So, I heard you picked an assistant chief today," the general said after I entered his office. I indicated that was the case.

"I understand you picked a male nurse," he continued. The two-star general was a physician and a man, so his line of questioning struck me as odd.

"No Sir, I didn't pick a male nurse," I replied, eliciting a frown.

"Well, they told me you picked John Hudock."

"That's right, Sir."

"Well, he is a male nurse." Hmm, I was starting to detect some concern or objection. "That's true, Sir, he's a male nurse," I answered warily. "But I don't look at it as picking a male nurse. What I did was pick the best nurse to be Assistant Chief of the Army Nurse Corps."

The general confirmed my suspicions—"There are those who seem to think the whole Army Nurse Corps is going to fall apart because you picked a man."

"Sir, on September 1, I'm going to be Chief of the Nurse Corps, and I can assure you that it won't go to pieces, simply because a man is the assistant chief. He was the best qualified candidate available."

The deputy Surgeon General allowed that if I was comfortable with John, that was good enough for him. That was that.

While an anti-male faction within the Corps grumbled about John, the 27 percent of the Corps that was represented by men was delighted by his selection. I felt that first and foremost, it was most important to choose an outstanding nurse, which I was confident that I had done. The gender was irrelevant.

＊　＊　＊　＊　＊　＊　＊　＊　＊　＊　＊

One officer who took me on as a protégé was Maj. Gen. Bill Lefler, who appreciated that I had a lot to accomplish before my stars were pinned on my shoulders. Bill headed the Army Dental Corps and took me under his wing regarding protocol and policy for Army generals in the health care field.

Three times a week Bill would call me over for a half-hour session where we talked about what was happening in the Army Surgeon General's office and how he saw things. Bill also sent me around to other generals in our building and even clued me in to certain activities such as joining other generals at a biweekly prayer breakfast. I appreciated that, because all new generals need to know how the fraternity operates and what do's and don'ts to observe. I still attend that prayer breakfast, which has been a wonderful fellowship for nearly fifteen years.

My office was cleared and ready for occupancy by the second week of August, allowing me to move in and get settled. My administrative assistant, Maj. Jay Voetsch, and I worked furiously to get the office up and running by August 28, because August 29 until September 1, marked three days of activities honoring the outgoing Chief of the Army Nurse Corps, as well as the incoming Chief.

The preliminary celebrations culminated in my swearing-in ceremony on Monday, September 1. It took place in a wonderful fifth-floor Pentagon auditorium whose small stage was covered with beige carpet and was ringed by red velvet curtains.

Four steps led to the stage, prompting a fervent prayer that I not trip in front of 500 people on my way to becoming an Army general. You might think my mood was totally joyous that day. For the most part it was, except when I thought about Mother and Daddy.

I know they undoubtedly saw their Clara Mae from on high, but there's nothing like a flesh and blood presence. Mrs. Thelma Estill, a kindly black woman I had met while at the Walter Reed

Army Institute of Nursing, and who had adopted me as her goddaughter, was present to represent my mother.

I'd had to buy several general officer uniforms a few weeks earlier and had taken great pains to have them pressed for the big occasion. So naturally the day I was to have my stars pinned on, my skirt had a big ugly San Andreas fault of a wrinkle coursing across the front.

Oh goodness, not now of all days! Must have happened in the back seat of my car, which was parked in one of the Pentagon's mammoth parking lots. There was no way I was going to stand in front of 500 onlookers with that hideous thing in my uniform! And I had fifteen minutes before I was to become a brigadier general.

So I'm standing in one of the Pentagon's bathrooms, looking in the mirror and trying to fight back a rising tidal wave of panic. I cracked the bathroom door and stole a glance down the hallway in search of a rescuer. God sent Capt. Millie Johnson, an Army nurse I had worked with in San Antonio.

"Psssst! Millie! Come here."

The minute she laid eyes on my skirt, she concurred there was no way I could step on stage with it looking like that. With beseeching eyes, I took off my skirt and handed it to Millie, telling her there was a dry cleaners on the lower concourse.

Millie went sprinting through the polished corridors of the Pentagon, clutching my precious skirt. When she got to the cleaners, Millie said she was informed by the establishment's nonchalant employees that no clothes were pressed during lunch hour, so she'd have to wait.

Replying that a general needed to have the skirt pressed right now, Millie bullied her way behind the counter and actually pressed my skirt herself. Then she ran back upstairs to where I stood in a women's bathroom in my slip, praying. Millie, God bless her soul, was back in less than fifteen minutes. And my skirt looked pristine.

If you don't think a general-to-be looks kindly upon a captain who comes through in the clutch like that, think again!

I don't even recall putting my skirt back on, because the next thing I remember is standing on that Pentagon stage alongside Heinz, Maj. Gen. Bill Suter, the Deputy Judge Advocate General and Lt. Gen. Quinn Becker, the Army Surgeon General.

Wouldn't you know the shakes started as soon as the ceremony got underway, the moment strains of the National

Anthem began wafting through the auditorium.

Gazing into the audience I saw beaming family members and friends, including Colin Powell, who would eventually get a fourth star and become Chairman of the Joint Chiefs of Staff. In fact, much of the crowd for my pinning ceremony looked like a who's who of the Army's top brass—past, present and future. In addition, my brothers and sisters, aunts, cousins, and dear friends had come from far and wide.

When those silver stars were finally on my shoulders, I gave Heinz a little smooch that we had choreographed the night before. Heinz is shy and hates public displays of affection! Still trembling slightly, I laid my left hand on the Bible and raised my right to take the oath that catapulted me into the general officer ranks.

"Ladies and gentlemen, I present to you the eighteenth Chief of the Army Nurse Corps, Brigadier General Clara Adams-Ender," a smiling Quinn Becker intoned.

Everyone was applauding wildly and looking at me expectantly, wondering what my first words as a new general would be. I stood behind the podium on that stage, adjusted the microphone and gave a speech I had painstakingly rewritten about eight times. There were even a few phrases of German thrown in, to acknowledge my guests from across the Atlantic.

I kept my remarks under five and a half minutes, a cardinal rule, and when I was finished the audience jumped to its feet. If I must say so myself, my speech was worthy of . . . a general.

Afterward, I stood in a receiving line shaking hands and making small talk with those who'd graced my pinning ceremony with their presence. I was one sore-armed sister by that point, having shaken thousands of hands during the festivities leading up to my pinning.

Naturally I was elated and in shock over getting my stars. But I also felt a sense of humility, because there was a side of me that said to be worthy, I had to go out and serve others well.

I basked in the glow of my promotion for exactly one day, because a ton of work awaited me. Guiding the fortunes of 19,000 nurses in the Army Reserve, 4,700 on active duty and 3,500 civilian nurses keeps you hopping.

When September 1 finally wound down, an exhausted, newly minted general collapsed into her bed and started to drift off to dreamland. A shaking mattress jarred me from semi-sleep, however. I opened my eyes to see Heinz, who had hopped into bed and was grinning.

"Darling, this is the first time," he said in his German accent.

"What are you talking about, Heinz?"

"The first time I ever slept with a general!"

Leave it to wise-cracking Heinz to come up with that one.

My first week as Chief of the Army Nurse Corps was devoted to understanding how the hierarchy of the Army Medical Department operated. It was divided into six branches, representing nurses, physicians, dentists, veterinarians, medical specialists and administrators.

Not surprisingly, all six branches pursued their own agendas. I decided immediately that some bridge-building was necessary in order to help everyone, including nursing, operate more effectively.

The Army Medical Department budget was fixed every year, so the jousting and competitiveness were all about survival. To keep close tabs on things, the generals and the colonel heading the five professional corps held a staff meeting every morning in the offices of the Army Surgeon General.

To get a better handle on my workload, and to beat the Washington area's infernal rush-hour traffic, I started leaving my home in Maryland about three-thirty in the morning, putting me at my desk in Falls Church, Va., around four o'clock.

I'd wear running clothes into the office and kick off the day by meditating at my desk. Then I'd sort through paperwork until six, then catch the elevator downstairs and jog inside a health club located in my building.

My assistant chief, Col. John Hudock, and I usually spent about an hour a day brainstorming about ways to make the Army Nurse Corps more of a force when it came to personnel. One of the main issues we had to deal with was getting nurse staffing to sufficient levels.

Before I became a general, one of my mentors used to say that real power in any organization comes from having control over personnel or finances. So even though John was designated my assistant, he was still working downstairs in the Surgeon General's personnel directorate. He had worked there for several years before becoming my number two.

John devoted himself to turning around the Army Nurse Corps' personnel situation, freeing me up to concentrate on other matters. Those matters included promoting relationships between the Army Nurse Corps and other offices, commands and agencies with whom we worked. I had been encouraged by the Surgeon General to make this matter a priority. One thing I'd learned over the years was to tackle what the boss considers important first, then pursue my own agendas.

I wasn't too proud to pick up the phone and say, "My reason for calling is to see if we can sit down and discuss how we can most effectively accomplish our mutual goals, as well as those of the Army." So many challenges awaited when I first became Chief of the Army Nurse Corps that I could hardly see the trees through the forest. But John and I leaped into the fray with shovels and bulldozers and began to set our own direction. The positive responses of cooperation were overwhelming.

* * * * * * * * * *

Contrary to what some people think, generals don't have squadrons of helicopters idly awaiting their beck and call, or squads of enlisted soldiers dutifully serving as valets.

However, if I flew into an airport on business and then had to drive another two and a half hours to reach my destination, my administrative assistant, Maj. John Voetsch, could easily arrange for an Army helicopter to meet me at the airport.

Generals once had personal cars and drivers at all times, which would have made my commute and travel around the Washington area a lot more bearable. However, that rule was changed about five or six years before I got to be a general because somebody abused it. Why do the rules always change just before I become eligible to take advantage of them?

I could have a car and a driver when I was out in the field, but not around Washington, D.C., taking care of day-to-day matters.

When generals attend social functions, our names are usually on a special list that allows us to blow past lines and go directly inside to grab a seat.

Another nice perquisite generals enjoy is being able to place telephone calls anywhere in the world. All I had to do was tell my secretary to do a priority call through the Pentagon switch-board and, voila!

Members of the fraternity also have the ability to send back-channel messages. When a general places a note or letter in an envelope marked personal, no one dares open it before it reaches its destination.

For me, one of the best perks that came with being a general was seeing how people under my command reacted to random acts of kindness on my part. I had a habit of calling nurse lieutenants during holidays like Thanksgiving or New Year's Day, just to let them know their work was appreciated. I singled out lieutenants because they're the ones who always get stuck with work on holidays. I'd been there and done that.

One time I called the home of a first lieutenant stationed in Heidelberg, West Germany, to extend Christmas greetings. Unfortunately the poor young woman was stunned into silence to find the Chief of the Army Nurse Corps on the other end of the line. Her husband had to get on the phone and finish the conversation. I met her in person after she returned to the States. She was still apologizing for being mute on the telephone.

❖ ❖ ❖ ❖ ❖ ❖ ❖ ❖ ❖ ❖ ❖

Once I took the reigns of the Army Nurse Corps, a fix for my personnel concerns came about in a most unexpected way. It started with a desire and a need to ensure that a general officer was available to assist with personnel matters for the Army Surgeon General when they were being discussed and decided in the Pentagon. The current arrangement was that the Chief of the Personnel Directorate was a colonel, who would call upon one of the general officers when needed for decision-making. That arrangement proved to be problematic, because it did not allow for continuity in dealing with personnel matters. There was a need for a general officer to assume the functions of Chief of the Personnel Directorate as an additional duty. I decided to volunteer for the position. While it would be an additional duty on my plate, the position would give me a lot of influence on personnel affairs at the decision-making level.

The more I thought about it, the more sense it made. But when I ran it past John Hudock, my assistant chief, he was adamantly opposed. He felt I had enough to deal with just running the Army Nurse Corps.

Well, there was a method to my madness. First, I really believed that the process of taking care of Army Medical Department personnel issues in the Pentagon had to be stabilized, and I knew I could do it. Second, there were 248 people working in the personnel division of the Army Surgeon

General's office. If I had some authority over them, it would be a cinch to have them concentrate on matters related to nursing. As it was, 75 percent of the personnel issues they dealt with already had to do with nursing, anyway.

Plus, if I had to write performance evaluations for them, they'd be far more predisposed to look at things from a nursing perspective. However, I didn't mention that angle to anyone, not even to John. I kept it under my hat and took the job.

So in addition to running the Army Nurse Corps, I was responsible for more than 100,000 health professional personnel with a salaried budget exceeding $1.7 billion.

Within two weeks, John had come around to my point of view. Personnel issues that had previously monopolized his time were now being worked on in the Personnel Directorate, then brought to the sixth floor for John's blessing and approval. He loved this arrangement.

Since I was the head honcho for personnel, my first deputy was Col. Tom McGibony. Tom soon retired; then, Col. John Sierra became the deputy in the directorate. John was a very capable individual who was a people person and an expert personnel manager. Plus, the employees in personnel researched and resolved nursing issues, which freed John Hudock to function more as the final authority before actions came to me for a decision.

My new responsibilities brought me in regular contact with the Army Deputy Chief of Staff for Personnel, which was headed by a three-star general I knew well from having worked with him in Recruiting Command. Lt. Gen. Allen K. Ono was a tough taskmaster who had been a superb mentor and guide over the years.

The decision to get involved with personnel turned out to be a very, very good move.

It was a tremendous challenge and an opportunity to write and disseminate sensible personnel policies helpful to soldiers around the globe.

Generals Ono and Becker had been War College classmates, and both of them implicitly trusted my judgment. I found that trust goes a long way toward promoting solid working relationships.

In an effort to expand the influence of the Army Nurse Corps, I also started making trips to Capitol Hill. We needed to authorize incentive pay for Army nurses, but Congress wasn't buying it.

One of the first people I went to see was Senator Daniel Inouye, a Democrat from Hawaii, who headed the Senate Appropriations Committee. I'd made it a point to talk to Inouye during a couple of visits he made to Walter Reed when I was chief nurse. He was a World War II veteran who had aspired to be a thoracic surgeon, but saw that dream evaporate when he lost an arm during the war. Senator Inouye had a very high regard for nurses; then saved his life after he was injured in the war.

The senator was a decent man, as was his legislative assistant, Pat DeLeon. He was in my corner on the nurse pay issue, but the problem was drumming up support from his colleagues.

I arranged to have a couple of nurses with master's degrees work in Senator Inouye's office on health care policy matters. That turned out to be a productive arrangement, too, because they were able to provide information and share the Corps' perspective before policies were made.

When I wasn't going to Capitol Hill, or handling personnel for the Army Surgeon General, or running the Army Nurse Corps, I did a great deal of public speaking where I articulated the views and perspectives of the Army, the Army Medical Department and the Army Nurse Corps.

In 1988, my first full year as Chief of the Army Nurse Corps, I gave fifty-three speeches in locales ranging from Vail, Colorado; to Vienna, Austria; to Jacksonville, Florida. In February 1988 alone, I spoke six times in five states and the District of Columbia. The nurse recruiters in Recruiting Command and Cadet Command loved to see me coming, because they were always approached by larger numbers of prospective nurses after one of my presentations.

In 1989, I picked up the pace by giving sixty-three speeches and one-upped that total by stepping up to the podium seventy-four times in 1990, my last full year as Chief.

I expounded on things such as "The Army of the 1990s: Leadership During Times of Change," "Nursing–In Step With the Future," "How Successful Are You?" "Issues Facing Women in the Federal Workforce" and "What Black Americans Have to Say to America." The venues I hit included universities, the Sierra Club, conferences and symposiums, and Black History Month observances.

I did interviews for radio, television, newspapers and magazines. How people perceive you and your organization is really, really important, and I worked hard to enhance the image of the Army Nurse Corps. Image was also why I came up with a catchy slogan for my charges: "Army Nurses are Proud to Care!"

I also found time to serve in my local community. In 1991, my efforts were rewarded by induction as an honorary member of Delta Sigma Theta Sorority. I enjoy the sisterhood because of their emphasis on community and political involvement in issues affecting the daily lives of all citizens.

I was traveling 125,000 miles a year and holding down a schedule that seems grueling in retrospect. But my stamina never wavered, thanks to my daily workouts, meditation and a calm and supportive family and home life.

The ultimate test for any Chief of the Army Nurse Corps materialized toward the end of my four-year assignment. It was clear at the end of 1990 that the United States was going to be part of a coalition force aimed at stopping Iraq's occupation of Kuwait. I was in personnel, so I knew long before the rest of the country that U.S. combat troops were headed for the Gulf.

President George H. Bush had yet to make an official declaration about the Gulf War, and I wasn't sure if he planned to mobilize the Army reserves, which could give me up to 16,000 additional nurses to work with. There was no way I could adequately support American battlefield troops using just over 4,000 active duty nurses.

Once the first soldier falls in battle, the Army Nurse Corps can pretty much get whatever it needs. But in the meantime, I had to do the usual bureaucratic wrangling regarding the personnel and equipment my organization needed to be combat-ready.

Not only did I view combat as the ultimate test of my leadership skills, it was also a scenario I had dreamed of being thrust into at some point. No question about it, the old adrenaline starts pumping when someone says you've got to get soldiers ready to fight.

The fact that somebody might get killed has never been one of my favorite ideas, but it was one I was fully prepared to deal with.

We were eventually authorized to activate more than 25,000 Army reservists who were medics, a welcome addition to augment active duty personnel. We then had sufficient personnel on hand to get the job done in the Gulf, and also to care for the families of the deployed soldiers back home as well. When all the shooting and bombing ceased, I thanked God that there were only minimal U.S. casualties.

No nurses lost their lives in the Persian Gulf, but several medics were killed in accidents not directly related to battle. Most people don't realize that two-thirds of soldiers killed during wars die in incidents not directly related to battle–vehicular accidents, disease, mines, those kinds of things.

With the Gulf War over, I had to deal with a battle raging within the ranks of my own organization. You see, I was coming under tremendous criticism from nurses agitating to get nurses into positions of command. Their feeling was, since physicians are routinely put in command of Army medical centers and hospitals, why aren't nurses?

I understood and backed that argument, but also appreciated that a sea change of that magnitude wasn't going to occur overnight. A lot of times things don't just happen, they evolve over time.

By this time my immediate boss was Maj. Gen. Alcide LaNoue, who was deputy Army Surgeon General. I ran the question of nurses being in command past him, and he had absolutely no problem with it. His belief was that a leader is a leader, regardless of gender or profession. However, when he promised to run it past his boss, I quietly groaned.

I already knew how the Army Surgeon General would react, because we had had a related conversation on the subject before. So I wasn't surprised the next time I ran into General LaNoue, and he recounted how the meeting with him had transpired.

"After he broke out all the windows in his office and threw all the books from his bookcase on the floor, I got the feeling he didn't favor nurses being in command," General Cid wryly and facetiously related.

What made that situation even more ludicrous was that the Navy was already putting nurses in command of hospital units, as opposed to using physicians who were inexperienced or clearly unprepared to be commanders.

That just gave more ammunition to Army nurses who claimed I wasn't being proactive enough. It's the easiest thing in the world to lob brickbats at the person in the top job. But sometimes she or he may be hindered by handcuffs and leg irons that others may not be able to see, I now realize.

My proudest accomplishment during my tenure as top nurse in the Army was to establish the Army Medical Department Early Commissioning Program because of its benefit to enlisted soldiers. Col. John Hudock gets credit for the extensive research required to complete the proposal and action plan for implementation. My main duty was to present the proposal to the deputy chiefs of staff of the Army and finally to the Chief of Staff, a four-star general. General Carl Vuono, "The Chief," as we called him, approved the proposal and permitted 125 school seats to be used for enlisted soldiers to enter their last two years of college in a nursing program and get a commission upon graduation as an Army nurse. The program was so popular that we had over 2,000 applicants for the 125 seats. Because of this and other successes, General Vuono was prompted to retain me on active duty after my four-year tenure as Army Nurse Corps Chief was completed.

"Listen, you need to do more for the Army before you retire. The ultimate in Army leadership is to command," Vuono said during a call to my office. "Tell you what I'm going to do. I'm going to send you to command a base, specifically Ft. Belvoir in Virginia. Don't screw it up." I was also to be the Deputy Commanding General of the Military District of Washington.

I was shocked and truly speechless, one of the few times that's ever happened in my life.

Not long afterward, General Cid LaNoue was promoted to Army Surgeon General and decreed that hospitals and medical centers would be run by whoever was best qualified, be it a nurse or doctor or administrator. Some things do change.

Those developments shut up critics who were wailing that I hadn't done much to elevate nurses into leadership positions beyond heading nursing departments. The order to head down to Ft. Belvoir also extended my military career, because I was facing mandatory retirement after stepping down from the Army Nurse Corps' top job.

One of the final things I accomplished in that position was to anoint a capable soul who could lead the Army Nurse Corps after my departure. She was Col. Nancy Adams, who later became the first nurse to become a two-star general and command a medical center.

But in the meantime, I had a little trailblazing of my own to do. I set about the business of learning to run a major military installation, lest I "screw it up" in Gen. Vuono's words. While I wasn't too worried about that happening, I wasn't leaving anything to chance.

*   *   *   *   *   *   *   *   *

U.S. Army Garrison Fort Belvoir is on an 8,656-acre tract of Virginia land that was once home to sprawling slave plantations. So there was a delicious irony to African-American Brig. Gen. Clara Adams-Ender becoming base commander more than a century later.

For seventy-six years, Fort Belvoir was home to the Army's Engineer School until 1989, when that facility relocated to Ft. Leonard Wood, Missouri. Belvoir had undergone a transformation from a traditional military installation to one providing base operations support to eighty-five units by the time I arrived in 1991.

Those units, which included a military intelligence command and an ordnance battalion, to name two, depended on Fort Belvoir for water, electricity, roads and schools—the same kinds of services cities provide. In addition to billing units every month for those services, we rented buildings and facilities to them that they needed to perform their missions.

About ten miles south of Washington's Beltway, Ft. Belvoir was home to 20,000 people during my tenure, and provided 12,000 jobs to the economy of Northern Virginia.

As Ft. Belvoir's commander, my duties were synonymous with those of a mayor, city manager and magistrate all rolled into one. The base was so closely intertwined with Fairfax County, Virginia, that in many ways it was just another Fairfax community. Military police handled its law enforcement, but the administration of Ft. Belvoir's three public schools was under Fairfax County, and the electricity and water used on post originated in Fairfax County.

So Ft. Belvoir had to get into the business of integrating into a community setting, and I had to interact with national, state and local politicians to facilitate that goal. As commander, I had a $90-million annual operating budget to oversee, along with $965 million earmarked for building construction.

My transfer to Ft. Belvoir brought instant upheaval to Heinz's settled, comfortable existence, because regulations called for me to reside on the post. Heinz was vehemently opposed to moving from our home in Silver Spring, Maryland, and had to be cajoled into taking up residence at Ft. Belvoir.

Something had to give, because I definitely was not going to retire and pass up the kind of fascinating opportunity and challenge Ft. Belvoir represented. We were assigned to a spacious three-bedroom house that was close to the officer's club and had an attic that covered the entire house, giving Heinz and me scads of storage space. There was also a large basement, a study and a formal living room and dining room. The base was also home to twenty-three other generals.

The word 'Belvoir' dates back to Norman times and means "beautiful to see," which is quite apt for the Northern Virginia Army installation bearing that name. It is without a doubt one of the most picturesque bases in the Army.

Ft. Belvoir has cliffs that offer a breathtaking view of the Potomac River below. More than 1,450 acres of shoreline, wetlands and forests have been set aside for wildlife refuge, and about 30 percent of the post has been deemed environmentally sensitive forest and wetlands. In 1991 my new installation received an Army Communities of Excellence Award for the best medium-sized post in the continental United States. That same year, Ft. Belvoir also had the Army's busiest commissary, with sales of more than $76 million.

I knew I was getting into a different kind of deal when I started getting cards and letters about Ft. Belvoir before setting foot on the place. Five letters had unflattering things to say about the base commissary, while 450 contained complaints about not being able to get tee times on the base's eighteen-hole golf course! An immediate priority of mine was to learn how to play golf, so that I could see what the fuss was about.

Prior to taking command I had to pick an aide, and selected Rene Woo, a discreet, highly efficient Medical Service Corps first lieutenant who was of Chinese descent. I picked her because we spoke the same kind of language with our health-care backgrounds, and because I sensed I could trust her implicitly. That turned out to be the case.

To support my transition from the Army Nurse Corps to Ft. Belvoir's commander, I needed to switch from the special branch Army, which is for medics, chaplains and lawyers, to the line Army, which covers everybody else. For some reason, there was a lot of foot-dragging on getting the paperwork processed, and it didn't go through until I had been at Ft. Belvoir for several weeks.

I took command of the post on August 16, 1991, and initially enjoyed a honeymoon period where everyone was quite polite and bent over backward to be accommodating. It was a novel situation all around, because the base had never been commanded by a nurse, and it was my first assignment outside the aegis of the Army Medical Department. The change of command took place in a ceremony called a Twilight Tattoo, which occurs at sundown. My fondest memory of that evening was the flyover that spontaneously occurred at the end—a formation of geese moving from one wildlife refuge to another.

My welcome in the command was somewhat less than stellar by Ft. Belvoir's top officers. While they were courteous and polite, it was evident that they believed that their new commander was "only a nurse." The officers decided they would bring me up to speed about Ft. Belvoir by talking to me as though I were a third-grader, instead of a brigadier general with two master's degrees. My staff included a deputy commander and officers and civilians representing the provost marshal; resource management; community affairs; information management; and plans, operations and training.

After three weeks, I tired of being talked down to as if I were retarded—they apparently never gave me credit for the fact that I might learn. So at one morning staff meeting, I put an end to the condescension.

"For the past three weeks, you all have been treating me like a newbie," I began. "And I want to tell you I appreciate that, because there are a lot of things I had to learn as your base commander and as the Deputy Commander for the Military District of Washington. But I want to tell you now, I think I've got it."

I paused as glances were exchanged around the conference table.

"I know part of your motivation came from believing that I wouldn't know a lot about what goes on here, due to my hospital background. But I want to tell you something about dealing with people in hospital settings, as opposed to this base. The patients in those hospitals knew they were sick."

Then I skipped to the next topic, leaving most of the people in that room oblivious to the needle they'd just received. The art of the comeback still worked for me!

It didn't take the deputy commander long to determine that he was going to run Ft. Belvoir as he saw fit, regardless of what that new commander thought. I would tell the staff what my expectations of them were, and it came to my attention he would often give other guidance to them that was diametrically opposed. Not only does that confuse staff members, but it tends to engender disloyalty.

The deputy commander had been at Ft. Belvoir three years and had even served a year as interim commander. I eventually found it necessary to bring him into my office for a come-to-Jesus meeting.

To his credit, he didn't deny countermanding my instructions to Ft. Belvoir's staff. So I informed him that if he had a problem dealing with my expectations, maybe he needed to pursue other options.

When he observed his only option was to leave, I pointed out that if we couldn't operate on the same page, maybe that would be the best option for him to exercise. He left my office understanding me a whole lot better than when he entered. I didn't have any further problems with him.

Which is good, because the new mayor of Ft. Belvoir found herself facing an immediate crisis. We had two huge elevated water tanks for storing the water we got from Fairfax County. The base engineer decided to clean sediment from one of the tanks and shut down the water supply for a few hours. The only problem was, when the water came back on, one tank was empty and the other was too low to handle the sudden demand from Ft. Belvoir's 20,000 residents. They sucked that tank dry in no time, which clogged water lines full of silt and sediment.

Bottom line, my base was without water for three weeks, and I hadn't even been there a good month. When I was the chief nurse at Walter Reed, Maj. Gen. Lew Mologne used to talk about the loneliness of command and leadership and how there are some things the people you lead will never be able to help you with.

Well, the great water tank fiasco was one of those lonely, mortifying, maddening moments. It didn't help when the *Washington Post* and the rest of the area's news media jumped on that story and methodically rode it into the ground. If you're the commander, it doesn't matter if you don't know the first thing about operating the base's water system—if the taps dry up on your watch, you're responsible.

When that crisis first began to unfold, my thoughts immediately went to the base hospital. A hospital can go without water for a short period of time, but not for long. "Lord, this foulup is a biggie, this is a big one!" I thought.

In the meantime, I knew better than to show anything remotely resembling panic, because everyone emulates what the commander does. We had to deploy water trucks to serve the hospital and the fort's residents. We also had to bring portable toilets onto the post.

While all this was going on, generals who were my friends used to approach me at parties and functions and make a show of sniffing at the air loudly. "Clara, have you had a bath today?" was the silly remark that usually followed that foolishness. I laughed right along with them. Throughout my career I took my job seriously, but never myself.

That's not to say I wasn't annoyed at the engineer who triggered that whole mess, however! I made sure that all the extra expense we incurred because of that water snafu came out of his budget. And I used a few well-chosen words to express my utter dissatisfaction and disgust with how that chain of events played out. I do believe he got the message.

I also had to deal with my responsibilities as Deputy Commanding General of the Military District of Washington (MDW) on a regular basis. The largest base belonging to the command happened to be Ft. Belvoir. Army Fort Richie, Fort Myer, Fort McNair and Vint Hill Farms also belonged to the MDW, which was commanded by Maj. Gen. Bill Streeter.

One primary mission of the command was to provide ceremonial and special event functions for the President and other dignitaries in Washington, DC. The major units included the 3rd U.S. Infantry (The Old Guard), the U.S. Army Band (Pershing's Own) and the U.S. Army Chorale.

Whenever Gen. Streeter was unable to deal with the never-ending stream of MDW activities and ceremonies taking place, he would ask me to step in and help him. Honor guards wear special uniforms and put a high value on spit and polish, so I was called upon to do that, too. We participated in events such as the Presidential Inauguration, wreathlaying at the Tomb of the Unknowns, and receptions and ceremonies on Capitol Hill.

A long-standing problem that took a lot of my time and energy had to do with three elementary schools on the installation that were falling into disrepair. Fairfax County handled administration for the schools, while Fort Belvoir had to provide infrastructure—things such as lights, water, and refuse collection. Those schools were built in the 1950s by the Department of

Education and had become maintenance nightmares by 1991. Fairfax County had no authority to build new schools at Fort Belvoir. The federal Department of Education had the authority, but said it didn't have the funds. The Department of Defense had no authority over the school and couldn't provide funding.

On the surface, this looked like an "ain't it awful" dilemma. There were some very important persons (VIPs) caught up in this dilemma–the school children. I knew them well because I visited those schools frequently and others in Fairfax and Prince William counties. I had been in the schools to read to them on Reading Day. I had cheered them on in athletic events. I had spoken at their graduations, career fairs and boy and girl scouting events. I had encouraged them to dream big and go for their dreams. Oh, I knew them very well. Finding myself caught in a bureaucratic Catch 22, I put on my politician hat and approached Virginia Democratic U.S. Representative Jim Moran, who was receptive to my problem.

He attached a rider to a congressional bill that made it possible for Ft. Belvoir to get a brand-new 900-student school. Today, it is a beautiful edifice on the grounds of Fort Belvoir.

I was successful in that quest, but most of the time I faced the budgetary challenge of not having enough money to take on every needed capital project. An awfully large part of my job as base commander had to do with setting budgetary priorities.

Military bases can raise money through what are known as morale, welfare and recreation activities. Some of the money collected from MWR activities goes into a big pot available to the entire military. A big money generator was Ft. Belvoir's 18-hole golf course. The base built another 18-hole course during my tour of duty, which brought in a lot of money from tournaments.

I even learned to play and usually got in 18 holes on Saturday until my left shoulder started hurting. That forced me to limit my excursions to nine holes. I love golf. It is a great game that teaches you about life. One day you may be in a sand trap, and the next day you are rolling down the fairway.

While leading Ft. Belvoir, I had a fairly high profile in the Washington area. Both Democrats and Republicans approached me about running for public office, and I always declined. Entering politics just wasn't something I ever gave serious thought to, although the entreaties were flattering.

Something I did look into while at Ft. Belvoir, though, was

getting my second star. I was selected to attend the Capstone Course. Capstone was designed to familiarize general officers with the commands within the Department of Defense. I was sent to Central America with 19 other general and flag officers to observe the drug-fighting efforts of the U.S. military's Southern Command for two weeks, which was an absolutely fascinating experience. W also visited other major commands at the headquarters of the Canadian armed forces in Ottawa.

However when the promotion board met in 1993, I was not picked to get a second star. Facing mandatory retirement in six months, I started tightening up my resume and made a number of queries that resulted in job offers.

MCI offered me a position, as did the Library of Congress. But the more I started thinking about doing a nine-to-five after my military career, the less appeal that concept held for me. "Clara, after all these years of working like a dog, isn't it time to chill out at the age of 54?" I asked myself.

Plus Heinz made it crystal clear that he wanted to be able to spend time with me after I left active duty.

Frankly, I wasn't sure if I was ready to go out to pasture just yet. I've always been a high-energy person who's needed a succession of new challenges to keep me occupied. Sitting around reading AARP literature didn't float my boat, but neither did the prospect of rising every morning to commute to work in Washington.

There were about 500 folks in the reviewing stands during my retirement parade at Ft. Belvoir. I thought I would experience a rush of powerful emotions and feelings during my last day in the Army, but that wasn't the case.

The day was pretty much a blur, to be truthful. One minute I was in the Army, the next minute I wasn't. When my last day finally wound down, following a reception after my retirement parade, I went home and stood in front of a mirror as I took my uniform off one last time.

A weary-looking, fifty-four-year-old black woman stared back. "You are retired," I told her. Instead of reacting visibly, she seemed almost indifferent.

Hmmpphh! I took my uniform off and hung it up, as I had done thousands of times. Then I went to bed and immediately fell asleep.

Chapter XIX

The Afterlife

I'd operated at full-throttle for thirty-four years to push the goals and objectives of the U.S. Army forward. So to wake up one morning and find my appointment calendar totally empty–no brushfires to extinguish or strategic plans to implement–was a truly jarring, discombobulating experience. Not to mention depressing.

The day after my retirement parade, I sat up in bed at four o'clock in the morning, the time I typically arose to prepare for work. Heinz was snoring, and it was still dark outside as the realization dawned that I had nowhere to go. This was it–I was retired, the active-duty phase of my career was over forever!

I started crying softly, sad that Ft. Belvoir and the rest of the Army were going to keep humming along without me on August 27, 1993, and beyond. I'd served the military with honor and distinction and felt things had gone well as a result. And I missed that.

The best analogy I can think of is to suddenly cross the finish line after running a three-decade marathon. A marathon where the competition and camaraderie have you feeling pumped about participating every day. I loved the Army, and I loved my service in defense of my country.

Consequently, the first four days after I retired I was a little weepy, as well as exhausted as hell. After waking up at four that first morning, I lounged in bed until nine o'clock the next three days. That may sound funny to some people, but to me nine o'clock was downright decadent!

I did stop sleeping late, but was a lost soul for a good month after my retirement. The void retirement had carved into my existence was almost similar to the passing of a friend or relative. I grappled with sadness and fond remembrances and even a little self-pity.

Heinz and I were still living in our three-bedroom house on Ft. Belvoir, which I was allowed to stay in for six weeks until I could find civilian housing. That was a good thing, because searching for a new house helped keep my mind off being retired. So did delving into personal affairs such as making sure powers of attorney and bank accounts were in order.

About thirty days after I left the Army, the old Clara started to reemerge. She was still energetic, ambitious and in search of challenges. Life didn't begin with the Army, nor did it end with retirement, so it was time to move on.

I began to enter a new, exciting phase of my life where I explored who I really was as a person and what I really believed. Because I had spent thirty-four years not able to fully think for myself. By that, I mean that there were many times when I harbored strong opinions that weren't suitable for a high-ranking Army officer to verbalize.

After I left the Army, it was liberating to be able to air my thoughts freely with no worries I might be assigned to some godforsaken installation as a result. I didn't have to walk on eggshells anymore, and it was a glorious feeling.

So was being able to say 'no' when someone asked me to do something I really didn't want to. Mind you, I didn't get obnoxious about these things, but it was nice to know I had a whole new set of options.

Heinz and I eventually rented a house in Virginia that afforded a great view of the Potomac. I learned how to sit on the deck of that house and leisurely watch the Potomac flow by. During my Army days, I would have felt guilty doing that, because there was always a matter somewhere that required my attention. In my retirement years, I've been giving a lot of that attention to Clara. And luxuriating in it.

I may have learned to relax more and dote on myself to a greater extent, and I'm hardly ready to pad around the house all day in slippers and a housecoat, clutching a TV remote control. I'm too curious and energetic and competitive for that.

So I've channeled those attributes into running a consulting business that I wrote a business plan for before leaving the military. Caring About People With Enthusiasm Associates, Inc., is the full name of my firm, which also goes by CAPE Associates, Inc. The corporation logo is a jazzy star and the motto is "We make stars out of people." I landed my first client, Syracuse University, about two months after leaving the service.

Syracuse was downsizing its workforce at the time, and needed me to advise severed employees about out-placement services. I'd had a little expertise in that area, because from 1988 to 1992, the Army lopped 187,000 troops from its ranks.

CAPE Associates has taken off like gangbusters, initially aided by the healthcare reform putsch of the mid-1990s. I've found it personally gratifying to discover that the same characteristics that led to success in the military—attention to detail, hard work and willingness to serve others—are the hallmarks of successful entrepreneurs.

I definitely cherish the sense of independence and control I get from working for myself. Free enterprise is a real chance for freedom.

Nowadays, I have a heightened interest in finances, investing and network marketing. Heinz has always had such interests and I managed his investments. I thought it was about time I learned what I was doing.

In 1994, I was elected to the board of directors at Andrews Federal Credit Union, whose headquarters office is across the street from Andrews Air Force Base, in Maryland. Andrews Federal Credit Union has roughly 113,000 members and assets of about $540 million. Heading its board of directors has been very satisfying experience, because I've seen how what we do can have an immediate and positive impact on people's lives. And I'm pleased to say that among member-owned financial institutions, we achieved a No. 1 ranking in terms of customer satisfaction. The philosophy of people helping people is alive and well in the credit union movement.

As a volunteer in my community, I chose to be involved in teaching money management to elementary school students. I find it astounding that the one subject that comes up in our lives every day—money, is not taught routinely in schools. Youngsters need to know about money management early so that they can take charge of their lives. I am very proud to be a volunteer in this important movement.

I continue to mentor and guide military officers and women and men in all walks of life. As Vice-President of Mentoring for the ROCKS, Inc., a formal mentoring program has been implemented that pairs young officers who need mentoring with a more senior officer who will provide the opportunities for them to learn. Secretary of State Colin Powell, a life member of the ROCKS, has participated in the program for many years.

Since my Army days, I have done a tremendous amount of traveling with Heinz, my best buddy, who is tickled to death that he no longer has to share his spouse with the Army. We have taken extended vacations and trips to Europe, Peru, Ecuador and Brazil, as well as leisurely cruises in the Carribean and Alaska. In 1999, we traveled to Africa on a safari, from Capetown, South Africa, to Cairo, Egypt. That trip was a tremendous educational and uplifting experience for me. I can and do take time to "smell the roses" these days, and it is wonderful.

Another of the joys of my military afterlife is my renewed connection and re-acquaintance with my brothers and sisters. We were always in touch through Mother, who ran the "operations center" when she was living. Everyone called in to Mother; then, she spread the information around to everyone. I called her every Sunday morning and got the "scoop" on all the others.

After Mother died, the connectedness became sporadic. When I got promoted to general, we decided that it was time to begin annual reunions and celebrations of each other. At first, we met at family reunions with other family members. Now we all get together ourselves with our spouses, children, grandchildren and great-grandchildren. What great fun it is to tell the stories of our childhood and see how far we've come.

Mother's dream of all her children getting a college education has not been realized. However, five of us daughters have baccalaureate and master's degrees. Four others have taken college and technical courses to learn specific skills. We have all been self-sufficient and contributors to society.

I am so proud of my brothers and sisters, because they have encouraged me over the years. Bettie, the oldest, retired last October from 45 years of teaching, mostly in Newark and East Orange, NJ. I guess she decided that after getting me started in reading at age four, it was a career for a lifetime. Aaron, my oldest brother, retired this year from the New York transit system where he was employed for over 35 years. After a stint in the Navy, he moved to Brooklyn and has been firmly entrenched there ever since. My brother Raymond, with whom I was always close, was a career man in the Air Force. After his retirement, he has been successful in electronic sales.

My sister Rosa is a math teacher in Newark. She and sister Doretha were the first two that I supported in college. Doretha is a registered dietitian, who has worked in marketing, sales and modeling over the past 30 years in Chicago. Sister Mary comes next and she is a health unit coordinator at Duke University Medical Center, Durham, NC. She has been employed at Duke for over 30 years and is proud of the work she is doing on the heart and lung transplant units. After completing his military obligation in the Army, brother James was employed by United Parcel Service. However, he always dreamed of owning his own business. Today, he runs a highly successful pallet business in Lumberton, NC. My youngest sister Shirley lives on the outer banks of NC and works as a rehabilitation counselor for the state. Baby brother Charles, who all of us tried to send to college, attended a technical school on the GI bill and is a steel rebar bender at a steel company in Raleigh, NC. I am so very proud of all of them and will spend as much time as possible sharing with them my love and fond memories of our lives together.

But I will always feel an unbreakable bond with soldiering and with the Armed Forces. My continued association with the military and serving troops was ensured when I was nominated to be a member of the Defense Advisory Committee on Women in the Services, commonly known as DACOWITS.

Basically, it's a watchdog group that was established in 1951 by Secretary of Defense George C. Marshall to assist and advise him on policies and matters relating to women in the military services. The DACOWITS is composed of women and men who are well respected in their fields of endeavor and communities. The members are a vital link between the civilian community and the Department of Defense regarding the need for and role of women as an integral part of the armed forces. The volunteers serve for three years without compensation and spend considerable time researching and deliberating issues affecting women in the military.

Under the auspices of the DACOWITS, I've visited bases run by the Marines, Air Force, Navy and Coast Guard, in addition to Army bases.

In 1998, I was invited by the ground commander in Bosnia to visit the troops and share information about women's history—some of which I had lived, especially in the military. As I observed the women and men doing their duties in their places of work, I smiled and thought to myself that "the military is still in good hands."

As much as I'm enjoying civilian life, I still care about the military and am eternally grateful for what it did for me.

Looking back on my 34-year Army career, you could really sum it up in two words—caring and serving. I served in defense of the country that I love, and I served people. And I learned a lot by doing both. At the end of the day, I can look back and say that I was a good soldier, a very good troop. And I am fiercely proud of that.

The Army provided me an opportunity to be all that I could be, and I think I took full advantage of that opportunity.

A famous writer and poet once said that "the purpose of life is to count, to have made a difference that you lived at all." I sincerely believe that I contributed and that I made a difference in the Army. I also believe that I am still making a difference in the lives of others by caring and serving.

At the end of the day, that's what life is really all about.

Clara's Aphorisms

1. Whatever you do, do it with enthusiasm.

2. In all relationships with people, relate to them so that they will speak kindly of you, especially when you are not present.

3. There is only one thing in life over which you have total control, and that is your attitude.

4. Always encourage others, especially youngsters.

5. Taking action will cure most fears.

6. Keep your body tuned.

7. Only to the extent that you love yourself can you ever love another person.

8. Possess high expectations of yourself. After all, it is what you expect of you that really counts.

9. You have choices in all situations—whether you like them or not.

10. To not decide is also a decision.

11. Giving service makes you feel better about yourself that you made a difference in someone's life.

12. It is not what happens to you in life that is important—it's how you react to what happens to you.

13. A good sense of humor will help you over many rough spots.

14. Take your work seriously, but never take yourself too seriously.

15. Above all else, be kind.

About The Author

General Clara L. Adams-Ender was born in Wake County, North Carolina, the fourth oldest of ten children. She received her baccalaureate degree in nursing from North Carolina Agricultural and Technical State University, Greensboro, NC; a Master of Science Degree in Nursing from the University of Minnesota, Minneapolis, MN, a Master of Military Art and Science degree from the Command and General Staff College, Fort Leavenworth, KS. She has been awarded ten honorary doctorate degrees in law, public service, humane letters and science.

General Adams-Ender rose from a staff nurse in the Army Nurse Corps to become the chief executive officer for 22,000 nurses, a brigadier general and director of personnel for the Army Surgeon General. She was vice-president for nursing at the prestigious Walter Reed Army Medical Center, the largest health care facility in the Department of Defense and was the first female in the Army to be awarded the Expert Field Medical Badge. General Adams-Ender also commanded an army base, a position equivalent to city manager, magistrate and mayor of a city. She was responsible for a $90-million budget while providing quality customer services to 85 different constituent groups. She is an educator, lecturer, consultant and leader who has given over 1000 presentations to audiences of health care professionals, community leaders, businessmen and women, lawyers, credit union managers, volunteers and staffs, veteran groups and students, both at home and abroad.

General Adams-Ender is President and Chief Executive Officer of Caring About People With Enthusiasm (CAPE) Associates, Inc., a management consulting and inspirational speaking firm. The agency specializes in health care management and health care reform, leadership issues and leader development, cultural diversity, women in the workplace and conflict management and resolution. She is a charismatic, knowledgeable and inspiring speaker and one never leaves her presence without being impressed by these qualities.

General Adams-Ender is Past Chairperson, Board of Directors of the Andrews Federal Credit Union, a Charter Member, Board of Visitors, U.S. Marine Corps University and a former member of the Defense Advisory Committee on Women in the Services (DACOWITS). She has received many awards for her community work and service, including the Roy Wilkins Meritorious Service Award of the NAACP, Gertrude E. Rush Award for Leadership from the National Bar Association, Distinguished Service Medal with Oakleaf Cluster and the Regents' Distinguished Graduate Award from the University of Minnesota. In 1996, she was named by Working Woman magazine as one of 350 women who changed the world from 1976-1996.

General Adams-Ender is married to Dr. F. Heinz Ender and resides in Lake Ridge, VA.

About The Co-Author

Blair S. Walker is a former journalist with USA Today, New York Newsday and The Associated Press,. He has written two mystery novels featuring fictional newspaper reporter Darryl Billups, as well as a bestselling biography of late financier Reginald Lewis.

Blair served a three-year Army stint as a Korean linguist and lives in Maryland with his wife and two daughters.